Prentice Hall
LITERATURE

All-in-One
Workbook

Grade Nine

PEARSON

Upper Saddle River, New Jersey
Boston, Massachusetts
Chandler, Arizona
Glenview, Illinois

BQ Tunes Credits
Keith London, Defined Mind, Inc., Executive Producer
Mike Pandolfo, Wonderful, Producer
All songs mixed and mastered by Mike Pandolfo, Wonderful
Vlad Gutkovich, Wonderful, Assistant Engineer
Recorded November 2007 – February 2008 in SoHo, New York City, at Wonderful, 594 Broadway

PEARSON

ISBN-13: 978-0-13-366814-8
ISBN-10:   0-13-366814-2

12 V039 16 15 14

CONTENTS

"I Have a Dream" and "First Inaugural Address"

"The Talk" by Gary Soto
"Talk" retold by Harold Courlander and George Herzog

UNIT 4   Poetry

The Poetry by Pat Mora

Poetry Collection: Langston Hughes, William Wordsworth, Gabriela Mistral, Jean de Sponde

Poetry Collection: Richard Brautigan, Emily Dickinson, Stanley Kunitz

Poetry Collections: Langston Hughes, William Wordsworth, Gabriela Mistral, Jean de Sponde; Richard Brautigan, Emily Dickinson, Stanley Kunitz

The Tragedy of Romeo and Juliet, *Act III*, by William Shakespeare

The Tragedy of Romeo and Juliet, *Act IV*, by William Shakespeare

The Tragedy of Romeo and Juliet, *Act V*, by William Shakespeare

"Pyramus and Thisbe" by Ovid
Scenes *from* **dramatic works** by William Shakespeare

"The Inspector-General" by Anton Chekhov

from **The Importance of Being Earnest** by Oscar Wilde
from **Big Kiss** by Henry Alford

UNIT 6 Themes in Folk Literature

"Play Hard; Play Together; Play Smart" *from* The Carolina Way by Dean Smith with John Kilgo

from the Odyssey, Part I, by Homer

from the Odyssey, Part II, by Homer

Poetry by Edna St. Vincent Millay, Margaret Atwood, Derek Walcott, and Constantine Cavafy

"Three Skeleton Key" by George Toudouze

Situation & Circumstance, performed by the Fake Gimms

Oooo . . .

I attempt to **convince**, to lead you to see,

To see things my way.

It's my **perspective**,

So, don't you agree?

I can take it out of **context**.

Twist the facts and the **evidence**.

Yea, I **distort** the **truth**.

So, won't you agree?

Now don't you agree?

I stand firm in my **belief,**

That things are exactly as I see them to be.

It's what I **perceive**.

And I'm sure you'll agree.

Now you're starting to see it my way.

You've got to question if it's **credible**.

Or if it's even capable of being believed or trusted.

No, it's not enough to make **assumptions**.

Got to check the facts, **verify,** confirm and make sure . . . Oooo . . .

The situation and the **circumstance,**

I **speculate,** I think about . . .

But can the truth be changed?

No, no it can't!

I hear the **skeptics** that say they do not believe.

They **manipulate,** shape it their own way.

But the truth cannot be changed.

Oooo . . .

Continued

I attempt to **convince,** to lead you to see,

To see things my way.

It's my perspective,

And I'm sure you agree.

Song Title: **Situation & Circumstance**
Artist / Performed by Fake Gimms
Vocals & Guitar: Joe Pfeiffer
Guitar: Greg Kuter
Bass Guitar: Jared Duncan
Drums: Tom Morra
Lyrics by the Fake Gimms
Produced by the Fake Gimms
Studio Production: Mike Pandolfo, Wonderful
Executive Producer: Keith London, Defined Mind

All-in-One Workbook
2

Name _____ Date _____

Unit 1: Fiction and Nonfiction
Big Question Vocabulary—1

The Big Question: Can truth change?

A story can differ depending on who tells it. Every person sees things in his or her own way. So, if you ask three witnesses about the same event, you may get three different versions of the truth. Each is a subjective version of the truth.

credible: believable or trusted

distort: to explain or report something that is incorrect or untrue

evidence: a fact, an object, or a sign that convinces you that something is true

manipulate: to fool people into thinking or acting a certain way

verify: to find out if something is correct or true

DIRECTIONS: *Continue the story, using each vocabulary word at least once.*

"Your bicycle came out of nowhere!" Stuart said. "I was minding my own business and—boom! There you were!"
   "Actually," Carlotta replied, "you ran into the street after your soccer ball without looking. If you had looked, you would have seen me. Now, because of you, I swerved into that fire hydrant and damaged my bicycle. You owe me money for the damage."
   Just then, Stuart's older brother came by and asked, "What happened?"

_____

_____

_____

_____

_____

_____

_____

_____

Unit 1: Fiction and Nonfiction
Big Question Vocabulary—2

The Big Question: Can truth change?

Who you are and what your experience has been greatly affect the way you view a situation. Never assume that others experience things the same way that you do.

belief: a feeling that something is true or exists

circumstance: a fact or condition that affects a situation, an action, or an event

convince: to persuade someone to believe something

perspective: point of view

skeptics: people who question what others believe to be true

DIRECTIONS: *Fill in the dialogue below using all of the vocabulary words.*

Ms. Patty was new to Canyon High School. She was excited about the art class she would teach the ninth graders. For their first project, they would spread a canvas on the floor of the art room and then take turns throwing paint at the canvas. It would be a group work of art. What a great way for the class to get to know each other.

The class got underway, and it went really well! At least that's what Ms. Patty thought. Some others at the school were not so sure. . . . What did they have to say about Ms. Patty's project?

Mr. Langston, Principal

Ms. Grace, Teacher, with classroom next door

Mr. Tompkins, Janitor

Willa Burke, Art Student

Name _____ Date _____

Unit 1: Fiction and Nonfiction
Big Question Vocabulary—3

The Big Question: Can truth change?

We often form opinions based on situations and prior experience. The danger in this is that sometimes we jump to incorrect conclusions.

assumption: something that you think is true even though you have no definite proof

context: the situation, events, or information that are related to something, and that help you understand it better

perceive: to see or recognize something

speculate: to guess about the possible causes or effects of something

truth: the actual facts about something

DIRECTIONS: *Use the vocabulary words above to help Jason tell his mother that she may have jumped to an unfair conclusion.*

"I want the facts!" Jason's mother said. "How did this lamp break? And why is there an orangutan in our living room?"

Jason looked at her. She thought it was his fault, when, really, he knew nothing about it. . . .

_____

_____

_____

_____

_____

_____

_____

Unit 1: Fiction and Nonfiction
Applying the Big Question

The Big Question: Can truth change?

DIRECTIONS: *Complete the chart below to apply what you have learned about the truth and whether or not it can change. One row has been completed for you.*

Example	A Statement of Truth or Fact	Evidence	How It Could Change or Why It Could Not	What I Learned
From Literature	In "The Cask of Amontillado," Fortunato insults Montresor.	Montresor says that Fortunato insulted him.	If Fortunato narrated the story, he might say he never insulted Montresor.	The truth can change, depending on who tells it.
From Literature				
From Science				
From Social Studies				
From Real Life				

Elizabeth McCracken
Listening and Viewing

Segment 1: Meet Elizabeth McCracken
- Where does Elizabeth McCracken get inspiration for the characters she writes about in her books?
- If you were writing a fictional story, would you base your characters on real people or invent them entirely? Why?

_____

_____

_____

_____

Segment 2: Fiction and Nonfiction
- Why does Elizabeth McCracken enjoy writing fiction?
- Why do you think it is important for a fiction writer to also read nonfiction books?

_____

_____

_____

_____

Segment 3: The Writing Process
- Why is it important for Elizabeth McCracken to develop her characters?
- Which fictional character left a lasting impression on you? Explain.

_____

_____

_____

_____

Segment 4: The Rewards of Writing
- What advice does Elizabeth McCracken offer young writers?
- What do you "get out" of reading fiction?

_____

_____

_____

_____

Learning About Fiction and Nonfiction

The following chart compares and contrasts two types of prose literature.

Characteristics	Fiction	Nonfiction
Elements	Fiction tells about **characters,** *imaginary* people or animals. They participate in a **plot,** or a series of made-up events, that contains a **conflict,** or problem, to be solved. The plot takes place in one or more **settings.** The story conveys a **theme,** or idea about life.	Nonfiction tells about *real* people, animals, places, things, experiences, and ideas. Nonfiction can contain facts, opinions, and ideas.
Sample forms	short stories, novels, novellas	articles, autobiographies, biographies, essays, journals
Author's purpose	to entertain	to explain, inform, persuade, or entertain

A. DIRECTIONS: *Write* fiction *or* nonfiction *to identify the kind of literature described.*

_____ 1. a piece of literature that features a talking tiger

_____ 2. a piece of literature about travel to Japan

_____ 3. a piece of literature about the lessons two friends learn about themselves when they go to summer camp

_____ 4. a piece of literature that explains how a runner trains for victory

B. DIRECTIONS: *Read the paragraph. Then, answer the questions that follow.*

The modem on Alicia's laptop computer had been blown apart in the lightning storm. Try as she would, she could not connect to the phone line. But Alicia refused to give up. Opening the cover on her cell phone, she held the instrument firmly and pressed a silver-colored button for precisely three seconds. Within another three seconds, she was small enough to slither through the back of the laptop. She saw the modem glinting on the motherboard. She was ready to begin the repair job.

1. Does the preceding paragraph introduce a piece of fiction or nonfiction? _____
2. Explain your answer to Question 1.

_____

_____

Name _____ Date _____

from **The Giant's House** by Elizabeth McCracken
Model Selection: Fiction

A fictional story is told by a **narrator.** The narrator may or may not be a character in the story. If the narrator is part of the story, he or she tells the plot using **first-person point of view,** with pronouns such as *I, me,* and *our.* If the narrator stands outside the story, he or she tells it in **third-person point of view,** using such pronouns as *he, she,* and *them.*

In reading fiction, you need to distinguish between plot and theme. The **plot** is what happens. The **theme** is the message carried by the plot, the characters, and the setting.

A. DIRECTIONS: *The excerpt from* The Giant's House *is a piece of fiction. Answer these questions about the narrator of* The Giant's House.

1. Is the narrator of *The Giant's House* inside or outside the story? _____

2. Does the narrator use first-person or third-person point of view? _____

B. DIRECTIONS: *Study the following example, which distinguishes between the plot of a story and its theme. Then, in your own words, state the plot of* The Giant's House *and the theme that grows out of the plot.*

Plot of story:	Maria practices her lines for the school play every day. She wants to bring her character to life, so she experiments in front of a mirror with different gestures, facial expressions, and tones of voice. On opening night, she turns in a first-rate performance, and the audience applauds warmly.
Theme of story:	Hard work leads to success.

Plot of excerpt from *The Giant's House:*

_____

_____

_____

Theme of excerpt from *The Giant's House:*

_____

_____

_____

Name _____ Date _____

The author of a piece of nonfiction has one or more purposes for writing. The purpose or purposes relate to the kind of nonfiction the author is producing.

- The purpose of **narrative** nonfiction is to tell about a real-life event. Examples of narrative nonfiction include autobiographies and memoirs. Some narrative nonfiction is **reflective writing,** which gives the writer's thoughts and feelings about a personal experience, an idea, or a concern. Examples of reflective writing include reflective essays and journals.
- The purpose of **expository** nonfiction is to inform or to explain. Examples of this type of nonfiction include analytical essays and research reports.
- The purpose of **persuasive** nonfiction is to make the reader act or think in a certain way. Examples include editorials and political speeches.
- The purpose of **descriptive** nonfiction is to create mental images for the reader. Examples include character sketches and scientific observations.

DIRECTIONS: *Authors often have more than one purpose in mind when they write a piece of nonfiction. Here is a list of purposes:*

to explain	to inform	to report a real-life event
to persuade	to entertain	to share thoughts and experiences

What two purposes do you think Elizabeth McCracken might have had in mind when she wrote "Desiderata"? Support your answer with reasons and examples from the selection.

_____

_____

_____

_____

_____

_____

_____

_____

_____

_____

_____

_____

_____

_____

"**The Washwoman**" by Isaac Bashevis Singer
Writing About the Big Question

 Can truth change?

Big Question Vocabulary

assumption	belief	circumstance	context	convince
credible	distort	evidence	manipulate	perceive
perspective	skeptics	speculate	truth	verify

A. *Use one or more words from the list above to complete each sentence.*

1. Andrew made a(n) _____ about his neighbor
   that prevented him from getting to know the truth about him.

2. The washwoman had a strong _____ that kept
   her going.

3. The _____ of the washwoman's life forced her
   to work.

4. Reading about the washwoman's life gives _____
   that everyone's truth does not have to be the same.

B. *Follow the directions in responding to each of the items below.*

1. Describe a time when something you thought was true changed. It might be something you did or that you observed.

   _____

   _____

2. What happened in the situation you described above that made you realize truth
   wasn't what you thought it was? Use at least two of the Big Question vocabulary
   words.

   _____

   _____

C. *Complete the sentence below. Then, write a short paragraph in which you connect this
   experience to the Big Question.*

   In **"The Washwoman,"** a Jewish family learns to appreciate a Gentile washwoman whose son has abandoned her. Complete this sentence:

   A mother's relationship with her son _____

   _____

   _____

"The Washwoman" by Isaac Bashevis Singer
Literary Analysis: Narrative Essay

A **narrative essay** is a short piece of nonfiction in which the author tells a story about a real person or event. In a narrative essay, the author chooses to include **significant details** that help move the story forward or that help to make his or her point about the subject. For example, if Singer were writing a narrative essay about his own childhood, he would include the significant detail that his father was a Hasidic rabbi who presided over a rabbinic court. In the same essay about his childhood, however, he would not mention the fact that Anjelica Huston starred in the 1989 movie *Enemies, a Love Story,* which is based on one of Singer's novels. That would not be a significant detail for an essay about his childhood. As you read, notice how the author's choice of significant details influences your impressions of the people and events he or she describes.

DIRECTIONS: *Follow the directions to answer each numbered item.*

1. In no more than two or three sentences, summarize the essay's narrative, or story.

   _____

   _____

2. Now, look back over the essay. Find two significant details that Singer includes about (a) the washwoman's appearance, (b) what she says, and (c) what she does. Write the details exactly as Singer expresses them, enclosing the words and phrases in quotation marks.

(a) Her appearance _____

_____

_____

(b) What she says _____

_____

_____

(c) What she does _____

_____

_____

---

3. Think about why Singer wrote this essay. What main point about the washwoman do you think he makes in this essay?

   _____

   _____

   _____

Name _____ Date _____

"The Washwoman" by Isaac Bashevis Singer
Reading: Ask Questions to Make Predictions

A **prediction** is an informed guess about what will happen later in a narrative. Predictions are based on details in the text and on your own experience. When **making and verifying predictions,** predict what will happen, and then read on to see if the prediction is correct.

- One way to make predictions is to pause periodically while reading and **ask questions** about text details and events. You can ask yourself questions such as *Why does the author mention this detail? How might it become important later on?* Then, look for the answers to those questions as you read ahead.
- As you read, use the following chart to record your predictions. Then, see how many of your predictions were correct.

DIRECTIONS: *In the left column are some of the major events in "The Washwoman." As you read, ask yourself questions about what may be the outcome or consequence of each event. Write your questions in the center column. In the right column, record your predictions. The first one has been done for you.*

Event	Question	Prediction
1. The frail old washwoman works hard to produce beautiful, clean laundry.	Will the Singer family be satisfied with her work?	The Singers will like her work and employ her for many years.
2. She has a rich son who does not see her or give her any money.		
3. The rich son gets married but does not invite her to the wedding.		
4. One very cold winter day, the washwoman staggers away under a huge bundle of laundry.		
5. Weeks pass, and she does not return.		

"The Washwoman" by Isaac Bashevis Singer
Vocabulary Builder

Word List

accumulated   atonement   forebears   obstinacy   pious   rancor

A. DIRECTIONS: *Follow the instructions to use each vocabulary word in a sentence.*

1. Use <u>rancor</u> in a sentence about unsportsmanlike conduct.

   _____

2. Use <u>obstinacy</u> in a sentence about a two-year-old.

   _____

3. Write a sentence about something a king inherited from his <u>forebears</u>.

   _____

4. Use <u>atonement</u> in a sentence about littering a public park.

   _____

5. Use <u>pious</u> in a sentence about an old family friend.

   _____

6. Write a sentence about a collection you have <u>accumulated.</u>

   _____

B. WORD STUDY The Old English prefix *fore-* means "earlier" or "in front of." Answer each of these questions using one of these words containing the prefix *fore-*: *foreshadow, forefront, foreboding.*

1. Why might you feel a sense of *foreboding* if a black cat crossed your path one gloomy night?

   _____

2. If your teacher pointed to you as an example of someone at the *forefront* of your class, how would you feel?

   _____

3. In a novel with a happy ending, what might the arrival of a rich stranger *foreshadow*?

   _____

"New Directions" by Maya Angelou
Writing About the Big Question

 Can truth change?

Big Question Vocabulary

assumption	belief	circumstance	context	convince
credible	distort	evidence	manipulate	perceive
perspective	skeptics	speculate	truth	verify

A. *Use one or more words from the list above to complete each sentence.*

1. If he could change one _____ of his school life, he thought it would change everything.

2. When we _____ that our lives are not going well, we should change them, just like Annie did.

3. For Annie, _____ is what she made it.

4. The _____ that truth cannot change is false.

B. *Describe a time when you or someone you know changed as a result of some change in life's circumstances. Write three or four sentences. Use at least two of the Big Question vocabulary words.*

_____

_____

_____

_____

C. *Complete the sentence below. Then, write a short paragraph in which you connect this experience to the Big Question.*

In "New Directions," Mrs. Annie Johnson finds herself on her own with two young children. Complete this sentence:

The truth about a person can change as a result of _____.

_____

_____

_____

_____

All-in-One Workbook
15

"New Directions" by Maya Angelou
Literary Analysis: Narrative Essay

A **narrative essay** is a short piece of nonfiction in which the author tells a story about a real person or event. In a narrative essay, the author chooses to include **significant details** that help move the story forward or that help to make his or her point about the subject. For example, if Maya Angelou were writing a narrative essay about her own childhood, she would include the significant detail that she and her brother Bailey spent much of their childhood living with their grandmother in Stamps, Arkansas. In such an essay about her childhood, however, she would not mention the fact that in 1993, at President Clinton's inauguration, she recited her poem "On the Pulse of Morning." That would not be a significant detail for an essay about her childhood. As you read, notice how the author's choice of significant details influences your impressions of the people and events he or she describes.

DIRECTIONS: *Follow the directions to answer each numbered item.*

1. In no more than two or three sentences, summarize the story that the author tells in the essay.

   _____

   _____

   _____

2. Now, look back over the essay. Find two significant details that Angelou includes about (a) Annie Johnson's appearance, (b) what she says, and (c) what she does. Write the details exactly as Angelou expresses them, enclosing the words and phrases in quotation marks.

   (a) Annie Johnson's appearance _____

   _____

   _____

   (b) What she says _____

   _____

   _____

   (c) What she does _____

   _____

   _____

   ---

3. Think about why Maya Angelou wrote this essay. What points or main ideas do you think she makes in this essay? _____

   _____

   _____

   _____

Name _____ Date _____

"New Directions" by Maya Angelou
Reading: Ask Questions to Make Predictions

A **prediction** is an informed guess about what will happen later in a narrative. Predictions are based on details in the text and on your own experience. When **making and verifying predictions,** predict what will happen, and then read on to see if the prediction is correct.

- One way to make predictions is to pause periodically while reading and **ask questions** about text details and events. You can ask yourself questions such as *Why does the author mention this detail? How might it become important later on?* Then, look for the answers to those questions as you read ahead.
- As you read, use the following chart to record your questions and the predictions you make from them. Then, see if your predictions were correct.

DIRECTIONS: *In the left column are some of the major events in "New Directions." As you read, consider what you think may be the outcome or consequence of each event. Write your questions in the center column. In the right column, record your predictions.*

Event	Question	Prediction
1. Annie Johnson's marriage ends, leaving her with two young sons.		
2. She needs to earn money to support herself and her family.		
3. She starts to sell her home-made meat pies to workers at the lumber mill and cotton gin.		
4. She is so successful selling pies that she builds a stall between the cotton gin and lumber mill.		

Name _____ Date _____

"**New Directions**" by Maya Angelou
Vocabulary Builder

Word List

amicably   balmy   conceded   meticulously   ominous   unpalatable

A. DIRECTIONS: *For each of the following items, think about the meaning of the italicized word, and then answer the question.*

1. What happens when two people settle an argument *amicably*?

   _____

2. If you were to clean a kitchen *meticulously*, what would it look like when you finish?

   _____

3. What kind of weather would you describe as *ominous*?

   _____

4. What task do you find most *unpalatable*?

   _____

5. Why might a politician have *conceded* the election?

   _____

6. What would the day be like if it were *balmy*?

   _____

B. WORD STUDY The Latin prefix *con-* means "with" or "together." Answer each of the following questions. Use one of these words containing the prefix *con-* in your new sentence: *converge, conceive, concur.*

1. Why would someone *concur* with an opinion when they don't really agree with it?

   _____

2. Why might three groups *converge* on the state capitol?

   _____

3. What method can you *conceive* of that will help you improve your writing skills?

   _____

"The Washwoman" by Isaac Bashevis Singer
"New Directions" by Maya Angelou

Integrated Language Skills: Grammar

Common and Proper Nouns

A **noun** is a word that names a person, place, or thing. Nouns name things that can be seen and touched as well as those that cannot be seen and touched. Notice in the following chart that among the things nouns can name are ideas, actions, conditions, and qualities.

People: Aunt Cele, Esteban, musicians, doctor	
Places: Sacramento, Lincoln Park Zoo, mountain, desert, park, lake	
See and touch: grass, dish, table, truck	
Ideas and actions: freedom, confusion, election, censorship	
Conditions and qualities: optimism, courage, shyness, bewilderment	

A **common noun** names any one of a class of people, places, or things—for example, *day, river,* or *woman.* A **proper noun** names a specific person, place, or thing and always begins with a capital letter—for example, *Tuesday, Cuyahoga River,* or *Harriet Tubman.*

In the following example, the common nouns are underlined and the proper nouns are in boldface.

Example from "New Directions"

He did not tell her that he knew a <u>minister</u> in **Enid** with whom he could study and who had a friendly, unmarried <u>daughter</u>. They parted amicably, **Annie** keeping the one-room <u>house</u> and **William** taking most of the <u>cash</u> to carry him to **Oklahoma.**

A. DIRECTIONS: *In each numbered item, underline the common nouns and draw a circle around the proper nouns.*

1. The only Gentile in the building was the janitor. Fridays he would come for a tip, his "Friday money."

2. She lived on Krochmalna Street too, but at the other end, near the Wola section.

3. My mother spoke a little Polish, and the old woman would talk with her about many things.

4. The son had not invited the old mother to his wedding, but she went to the church and waited at the steps to see her son lead the "young lady" to the altar.

B. DIRECTIONS: *Write a three-sentence paragraph in which you describe the town where you live. Use at least three common nouns and three proper nouns in your paragraph. Remember that proper nouns are always capitalized.*

_____

_____

_____

_____

Name _____ Date _____

Integrated Language Skills: Support for Writing an Anecdote

Use the following cluster diagram to gather information for your **anecdote**—your very brief story. In the middle circle, write the name of a person whom you admire. In the surrounding circles, write several characteristics that you like and respect about that person. (You do not have to fill in all of the circles.) Then, make some notes about a specific event that shows what the person is like.

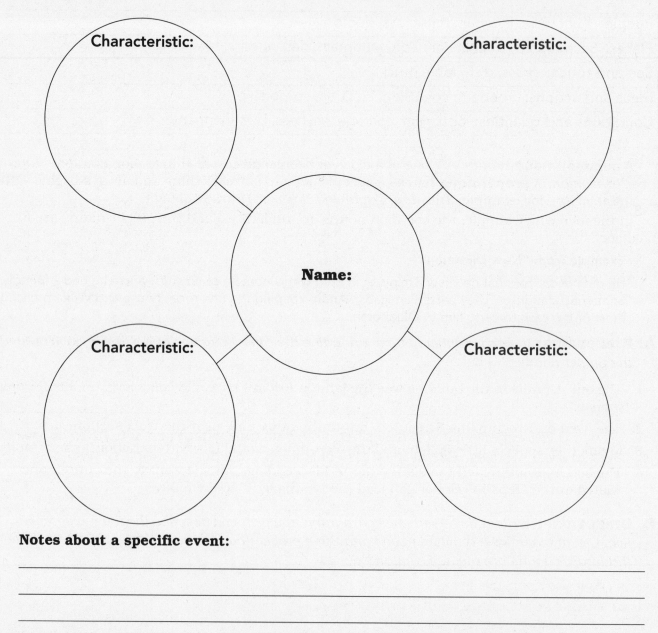

Characteristic:

Characteristic:

Name:

Characteristic:

Characteristic:

Notes about a specific event:

_____

_____

_____

_____

Now, write your anecdote. Describe in detail a specific event or action that illustrates what you admire about the person whom you have chosen. Be sure to tell what you learned from the person's actions.

Name _____   Date _____

"Sonata for Harp and Bicycle" by Joan Aiken
Writing About the Big Question

 Can truth change?

Big Question Vocabulary

assumption	belief	circumstance	context	convince
credible	distort	evidence	manipulate	perceive
perspective	skeptics	speculate	truth	verify

A. *Use one or more words from the list above to complete each sentence.*

1. Disbelief at losing the competition served to _____
Mona's perception of the truth.

2. Hearing strange noises in the empty building might _____
us that it is true that ghosts exists.

3. If we allow ourselves to _____ on whether there
are ghosts, we might have to consider the possibility of different truths.

4. Seeing a ghost in person may force even _____
to see new truths.

B. *Follow the directions in responding to each of the items below.*

1. Describe a situation when an unexpected event changed what you thought about
someone or some thing.

_____

_____

2. How did the experience you described above change what you thought to be true?
Write two sentences. Use at least two of the Big Question vocabulary words.

_____

_____

C. *Complete the sentence below. Then, write a short paragraph in which you connect this
experience to the Big Question.*

In "Sonata for Harp and Bicycle," miscommunication leads to tragedy and a curse
on a building. Complete this sentence:

You can change your own fate by _____

_____

_____

_____

Name _____ Date _____

"Sonata for Harp and Bicycle" by Joan Aiken
Literary Analysis: Plot, Foreshadowing, and Suspense

Plot is the sequence of events in a narrative. It is structured around a **conflict,** or problem, and it can be divided into the following parts:

- **Rising action**—the central conflict is introduced
- **Climax**—the high point of intensity in the conflict
- **Falling action**—the conflict's intensity lessens
- **Resolution**—the conflict concludes and loose ends are tied up

Writers use a variety of techniques to keep readers interested in the plot. One of these, **foreshadowing,** is the use of clues to hint at events that will happen later in a story. Authors use this technique to create **suspense,** a feeling of tension that keeps readers wondering what will happen next.

Read the following passage from "Sonata for Harp and Bicycle," in which Jason Ashgrove has a conversation with his secretary, Miss Golden. They are working on advertising copy for a cereal called Oat Crisps:

> "What do you want for your birthday, Miss Golden? Sherry? Fudge? Bubble bath?"
>
> "I want to go away with a clear conscience about Oat Crisps," Miss Golden retorted. It was not true; what she chiefly wanted was Mr. Jason Ashgrove, but he had not realized this yet.

What possibility does the passage foreshadow? Do you think the story will make clear whether or not Miss Golden and Mr. Ashgrove have a romance?

A. DIRECTIONS: *Read the following passage, and identify details the author uses to create suspense. Underline the words in the passage that make you curious about the outcome.*

> Jason was frustrated. "You'll be sorry," he said. "I shall do something desperate."
>
> "Oh, no, you mustn't!" Her eyes were large with fright. She ran from the room and was back within a couple of moments, still drying her hands.
>
> "If I took you out for a coffee, couldn't you give me just a tiny hint?"
>
> Side by side Miss Golden and Mr. Ashgrove ran along the green-floored passages, battled down the white marble stairs among the hundred other employees from the tenth floor, the nine hundred from the floors below.

B. DIRECTIONS: *Identify two clues the author gives that foreshadow the story's ending. Did you expect the story's ending, or were you surprised? Describe your response, and tell why you reacted that way.*

Clue 1: _____

Clue 2: _____

My response to story's ending: _____

_____

Name _____ Date _____

"Sonata for Harp and Bicycle" by Joan Aiken
Reading: Read Ahead to Verify Predictions

A **prediction** is an informed guess about what will happen later in a narrative. **Making and verifying predictions** keeps you actively involved in the story you are reading.

- Notice details that may foreshadow future events. Make predictions based on those details, and then read on to verify your predictions. If a prediction turns out to be wrong, evaluate your reasoning to determine whether you misread details or whether the author purposely created false expectations in order to surprise you later in the story.
- Use a chart like the one shown to record your predictions and evaluate their accuracy. Analyze any inaccurate predictions to determine why they were incorrect.

The key to making accurate predictions is paying close attention to the story you read. In "Sonata for Harp and Bicycle," the author provides many colorful details about what will happen.

Aiken's Original: Jason turned and stared at Grimes Buildings. Somewhere, he knew, there was a back way in, a service entrance.

Prediction: Jason is going to enter the Grimes Buildings through the back way.

DIRECTIONS: *Fill in the second and third columns of the following chart. Write your predictions based on the details in the first column. Then, read ahead to find out the outcome of your predictions, and record the outcomes.*

Details	My Prediction	Outcome
1. The bell stopped beside him, and then there was a moment when his heart tried to shake itself loose in his chest. He was looking into two eyes carved out of expressionless air; he was held by two hands knotted together out of the width of the dark.		
2. "We must remedy the matter, Berenice. We must not begrudge our new-found happiness to others."		
3. "We don't want our evening to be spoiled by the thought of a curse hanging over us," he said, "so this is the practical thing to do. Hang onto the roses."		

"Sonata for Harp and Bicycle" by Joan Aiken
Vocabulary Builder

Word List

encroaching   furtive   menacing   preposterous   reciprocate   tantalizingly

A. DIRECTIONS: *Write the letter of the word that is the best synonym for the numbered word.*

____ 1. furtive
   A. quiet
   B. stolen
   C. sneaky
   D. honest

____ 2. reciprocate
   A. refuse
   B. return
   C. respond
   D. renew

____ 3. tantalizingly
   A. with great care
   B. with a lot of noise
   C. in an angry way
   D. in a teasing way

____ 4. menacing
   A. hoping
   B. challenging
   C. threatening
   D. regretting

____ 5. preposterous
   A. ridiculous
   B. resentful
   C. pretentious
   D. angry

____ 6. encroaching
   A. despairing
   B. intruding
   C. retreating
   D. considering

B. WORD STUDY The suffix -*ate* means "to become or form." Write sentences using a word formed with the suffix -*ate*. Choose from among these words: *incorporate, activate, captivate.*

1. Use the word *captivate* to describe how you might react to a colorful sunset.

   _____

2. Use the word *incorporate* to tell what you might do with information you gathered for a report.

   _____

3. Use the word *activate* to describe what might happen if you pushed a mysterious button.

   _____

Name _____ Date _____

"The Cask of Amontillado" by Edgar Allan Poe
Writing About the Big Question

Can truth change?

Big Question Vocabulary

assumption	belief	circumstance	context	convince
credible	distort	evidence	manipulate	perceive
perspective	skeptics	speculate	truth	verify

A. *Use one or more words from the list above to complete each sentence.*

1. Ericka tried to _____ people by telling false-hoods.

2. Fortunato wanted to believe Montresor's flattery, but the _____ was that Montresor only wanted to kill him.

3. Fortunato wouldn't believe what was happening to him until he saw _____ rising before him, one stone at a time.

4. When did Montresor _____ the truth of what was happening?

B. *Follow the directions in responding to each item below.*

1. List an example of a situation when you noticed the truth was being manipulated.

_____

_____

2. Why do people sometimes manipulate the truth? Explain your answer. Use Big Question vocabulary words in your answer.

_____

_____

C. *Complete the sentence below. Then, write a short paragraph in which you connect this experience to the Big Question.*

In "The Cask of Amontillado," a wronged man seeks revenge. Complete this sentences: The truth about a person is a result of _____

_____

_____

_____

_____

_____

"The Cask of Amontillado" by Edgar Allan Poe
Literary Analysis: Plot, Foreshadowing, and Suspense

Plot is the sequence of events in a narrative. It is structured around a **conflict,** or problem, and it can be divided into the following parts:

- **Rising action**—the central conflict is introduced
- **Climax**—the high point of intensity in the conflict
- **Falling action**—the conflict's intensity lessens
- **Resolution**—the conflict concludes and loose ends are tied up

Writers use a variety of techniques to keep readers interested in the plot. One of these, **foreshadowing,** is the use of clues to hint at events that will happen later in a story. Authors use this technique to create **suspense,** a feeling of tension that keeps readers wondering what will happen next.

Read the following passage, which is the opening paragraph of "The Cask of Amontillado."

> The thousand injuries of Fortunato I had borne as I best could, but when he ventured upon insult I vowed revenge. You, who so well know the nature of my soul, will not suppose, however, that I gave utterance to a threat. At *length* I would be avenged; this was a point definitely settled—but the very definitiveness with which it was resolved precluded the idea of risk. I must not only punish but punish with impunity.

In the opening paragraph, what details does Poe include that suggest something about the narrator's personality and his plans? The paragraph arouses our curiosity: What does the narrator plan to do, and how can he possibly get away without being punished?

A. DIRECTIONS: *Read the following passage, and watch for details the author uses to create suspense. Underline the words and phrases in the passage that make you curious about the outcome.*

> The wine sparkled in his eyes and the bells jingled. My own fancy grew warm with the Médoc. We had passed through long walls of piled skeletons, with casks and puncheons intermingling, into the inmost recesses of the catacombs. I paused again, and this time I made bold to seize Fortunato by an arm above the elbow.
>
> "The niter!" I said; "see, it increases. It hangs like moss upon the vaults. We are below the river's bed. The drops of moisture trickle among the bones. Come, we will go back ere it is too late. Your cough—"
>
> "It is nothing," he said; "let us go on. But first, another draft of the Médoc."

B. DIRECTIONS: *Identify two clues the author gives that foreshadow the story's ending. Did you expect the story's ending, or were you surprised? Describe your response, and tell why you reacted that way.*

Clue 1: _____

Clue 2: _____

My response to story's ending: _____

_____

Name _____ Date _____

↗ Workbook

"The Cask of Amontillado" by Edgar Allan Poe
Reading: Read Ahead to Make and Verify Predictions

A **prediction** is an informed guess about what will happen later in a narrative. **Making and verifying predictions** keeps you actively involved in the story you are reading.

- Notice details that may foreshadow future events. Make predictions based on those details, and then read on to verify your predictions. If a prediction turns out to be wrong, evaluate your reasoning to determine whether you misread details or whether the author purposely created false expectations in order to surprise you later in the story.
- Use a chart like the one shown to record your predictions and evaluate their accuracy. Analyze any inaccurate predictions to determine why they were incorrect.

The key to making accurate predictions is paying close attention to the story's details as you read. In "The Cask of Amontillado," the author provides many colorful details that serve as hints about what will happen.

Poe's original: I took from their sconces two flambeaux, and giving one to Fortunato, bowed him through several suites of rooms to the archway that led into the vaults. I passed down a long and winding staircase, requesting him to be cautious as he followed. We came at length to the foot of the descent, and stood together upon the damp ground of the catacombs of the Montresors.

Prediction: The narrator is going to do something terrible to Fortunato in the catacombs.

DIRECTIONS: *Fill in the columns on the following chart. In the second column, write your prediction based on the details in the first column. Then, read ahead to find out the outcome. How closely did your predictions match the outcomes? Record the outcomes in the third column.*

Details	My Prediction	Outcome
1. "Thus speaking, Fortunato possessed himself of my arm; and putting on a mask of black silk and drawing a *roquelaure* closely about my person, I suffered him to hurry me to my palazzo."		
2. "There were no attendants at home; they had absconded to make merry in honor of the time."		
3. It was in vain that Fortunato, uplifting his dull torch, endeavored to pry into the depth of the recess. Its termination the feeble light did not enable us to see. "Proceed," I said: "herein is the Amontillado. . . ."		

"The Cask of Amontillado" by Edgar Allan Poe
Vocabulary Builder

Word List

afflicted   explicit   precluded   recoiling   retribution   subsided

A. DIRECTIONS: *Write the letter of the word that is most nearly* opposite *in meaning to the Word List word.*

____ 1. precluded
   A. allowed   B. prevented   C. discouraged   D. interrupted

____ 2. retribution
   A. punishment   B. reward   C. criticism   D. response

____ 3. explicit
   A. distinct   B. clear   C. complete   D. vague

____ 4. afflicted
   A. invigorated   B. confused   C. sickened   D. worried

____ 5. recoiling
   A. retreating   B. forgetting   C. lurching   D. advancing

____ 6. subsided
   A. weakened   B. relaxed   C. intensified   D. begun

B. WORD STUDY The suffix *-tion* means "the act of." Rewrite each sentence. Use the underlined word plus the suffix *-tion* in the new sentence.

1. As I walked up the mountain, the trail began to <u>elevate</u> more and more.

   _____

2. The huge male lion will <u>protect</u> the rest of the group.

   _____

3. When he could not pay his rent, the landlord threatened to <u>evict</u> him.

   _____

4. The coach sent in a <u>substitute</u> player when John was injured.

   _____

"Sonata for Harp and Bicycle" by Joan Aiken
"The Cask of Amontillado" by Edgar Allan Poe

Integrated Language Skills: Grammar

Abstract and Concrete Nouns

A **noun** is a word that names a person, place, or thing. Nouns name things that can be seen and touched as well as those that cannot be seen and touched. **Concrete nouns** refer to items that can be known by the senses—things that we can see, hear, taste, smell, or touch. **Abstract nouns** refer to ideas, qualities, states of being, and feelings—things that can be known only through the mind.

CONCRETE NOUNS
People: Sam Richman, sister, grandmother, Edgar Allan Poe, athlete, friend
Places: City Hall, Market Street, creek, school, Mount Rushmore
Things: raft, sidewalk, airplane, kittens, keyboard, water, lemons

ABSTRACT NOUNS
Ideas and actions: justice, independence, war, peace, reunion, trust
Conditions and qualities: strength, bravery, patience, optimism
Feelings and states of being: love, disappointment, friendship, fear

A. DIRECTIONS: *In the following sentences from "Sonata for Harp and Bicycle" and "The Cask of Amontillado," underline every concrete noun. Circle every abstract noun.*

1. The thousand injuries of Fortunato I had borne . . . but when he ventured upon insult I vowed revenge.

2. Jason could see two long passages coming toward him, meeting at an acute angle where he stood.

3. It must be understood that neither by word nor deed had I given Fortunato cause to doubt my good will."

4. "We must remedy the matter, Berenice. We must not begrudge our new-found happiness to others."

B. DIRECTIONS: *Write a paragraph in which you describe a person whom you know well. Use at least three concrete and three abstract nouns in your paragraph.*

_____

_____

_____

_____

"Sonata for Harp and Bicycle" by Joan Aiken
"The Cask of Amontillado" by Edgar Allan Poe

Integrated Language Skills: Support for Writing a Critique

Use the following chart to list the qualities that make a story suspenseful and that make the ending of a story satisfactory. Then, put a check mark in front of the qualities that you think apply to "Sonata for Harp and Bicycle" or "The Cask of Amontillado."

Qualities That Make a Story Suspenseful	Qualities of a Satisfactory Ending
☐ _____	☐ _____
☐ _____	☐ _____
☐ _____	☐ _____
☐ _____	☐ _____
☐ _____	☐ _____
☐ _____	☐ _____

Now, use your notes to write your critique in which you evaluate the ending of "Sonata for Harp and Bicycle" or "The Cask of Amontillado."

"**Checkouts**" by Cynthia Rylant
"**The Girl Who Can**" by Ama Ata Aidoo

Writing About the Big Question

Can truth change?

Big Question Vocabulary

assumption	belief	circumstance	context	convince
credible	distort	evidence	manipulate	perceive
perspective	skeptics	speculate	truth	verify

A. *Use one or more words from the list above to complete each sentence.*

1. Ana was so shy, she could not _____ herself to even say hello.

2. The checkout boy and the girl were _____; neither believed the other could be interested.

3. If Ned and Ana would just say "hi," they could _____ their interest in each other.

4. The girl's fear will _____ what she thinks is true as easily as a lie.

B. *Follow the directions in responding to each item below.*

1. Describe a situation in which you didn't expect much of yourself but were surprised.

   _____

   _____

2. Think about the experience you described above. How did it change what you think about yourself? Use at least two of the Big Question vocabulary words.

   _____

   _____

C. *Although the characters in the stories seem sure of certain things, when circumstances change, new possibilities—and new questions—emerge. Complete the sentences below. Then, write a short paragraph in which you connect this experience to the Big Question.*

People may have assumptions about others or themselves based on _____.

Those beliefs can be changed when _____.

_____

_____

_____

"Checkouts" by Cynthia Rylant
"The Girl Who Can" by Ama Ata Aidoo
Literary Analysis: Point of View

Point of view is the perspective from which a story is narrated, or told.

- **First-person point of view:** The narrator is a character who participates in the action of the story and uses the first-person pronouns *I* and *me*.
- **Third-person point of view:** The narrator is not a character in the story but is a voice outside the action. The narrator uses the third-person pronouns *he, she, him, her, they*, and *them* to refer to all characters. There are two kinds of third-person points of view. In the **third-person omniscient** point of view, the narrator knows everything, including the thoughts and feelings of all the characters. In the **third-person limited** point of view, the narrator sees the world through a single character's eyes and reveals that character's feelings and thoughts. The narrator can describe what other characters do or say but not what they feel or think.

A story's point of view affects what readers are told and what they must figure out. It may also affect which characters they identify or sympathize with and which characters they do not.

DIRECTIONS: *To understand point of view, readers must examine its effects on the telling of the story. It is sometimes useful to consider how a different point of view would affect the telling of the story. Answer the following questions to analyze the point of view in "Checkouts" and "The Girl Who Can."*

1. In "Checkouts," imagine that the author uses the first-person point of view with the girl as narrator. Review the description of the scene in which the bag boy drops and breaks the jar of mayonnaise. How would this scene be different if it were written from the first-person point of view?

   _____

   _____

   _____

   _____

   _____

2. Suppose that "The Girl Who Can" were told in the third-person omniscient point of view. Review the final scene in the story, in which Nana carries the trophy cup home on her back. How would this scene be different if it were told in the third-person omniscient point of view?

   _____

   _____

   _____

   _____

   _____

"Checkouts" by Cynthia Rylant
"The Girl Who Can" by Ama Ata Aidoo
Vocabulary Builder

Word List

comprehension   dishevelment   fertile   humble   perverse   reverie

A. DIRECTIONS: *Revise each sentence so that the underlined vocabulary word is used logically. Be sure not to change the vocabulary word.*

1. Sunk in <u>reverie</u>, the six-year-old twins had surprised expressions on their faces.

   _____

2. She brags endlessly about her accomplishments in a <u>humble</u> manner.

   _____

3. Hours of careful grooming resulted in Sam's state of <u>dishevelment</u> at the party.

   _____

4. May's sister took a <u>perverse</u> pleasure in making her laugh.

   _____

5. The soil is so extremely <u>fertile</u> that nothing can be grown in it.

   _____

B. DIRECTIONS: *Answer the following questions in the space provided.*

1. How would a person with a <u>humble</u> attitude behave?

   _____

   _____

2. Describe the appearance of a <u>fertile</u> piece of land.

   _____

   _____

3. How would you feel if you were sure of your <u>comprehension</u> of a complex topic?

   _____

   _____

   _____

Name _____ Date _____

Support for Writing to Compare Literary Works

Use a chart like the one below to make prewriting notes for your essay of comparison and contrast.

Points of Comparison/Contrast	"Checkouts"	"The Girl Who Can"
Who is the narrator in each story?		
What is the point of view?		
What do we learn of the thoughts and feelings of the girl and of Adjoa?		
How do other characters react to the girl and Adjoa?		

from **The White House Diary** by Lady Bird Johnson
Writing About the Big Question

 Can truth change?

Big Question Vocabulary

assumption	belief	circumstance	context	convince
credible	distort	evidence	manipulate	perceive
perspective	skeptics	speculate	truth	verify

A. *Use one or more words from the list above to complete each sentence.*

1. Lady Bird Johnson's _____ as the vice-president's wife gave her a unique _____ into events.

2. Did her personal account of the experience _____ your understanding of events or _____ it?

3. For many people, time changes what we _____ to be true.

4. The role someone like Lady Bird Johnson has in an event can make the stories more or less _____.

B. *Follow the directions in responding to each of the items below.*

1. Describe an experience in which you were surprised by a sudden, unexpected event.

   _____

   _____

2. In two sentences, tell how your reaction to this experience changed over time. Use at least two of the Big Question vocabulary words.

   _____

   _____

C. *Complete the sentence below. Then, write a short paragraph in which you connect this experience to the Big Question.*

In this passage from *A White House Diary*, Lady Bird Johnson recalls details about the day President John F. Kennedy was assassinated. Complete this sentence:

Abrupt changes in circumstances can _____

_____

_____

_____

from **A White House Diary** by Lady Bird Johnson
Literary Analysis: Autobiographical Writing and Author's Voice

Voice is the way a writer sounds on the page. For example, the writer's voice in a work can be *smooth and sophisticated, choppy and blunt,* or *breathless and full of wonder.* Voice is a result of several elements:

- *word choice:* the kinds of words the writer uses
- *attitude:* the way the writer feels about his or her subject
- *sentence length and structure:* the arrangement of words and ideas in sentences

In **autobiographical writing,** the author tells all or part of his or her own life story. The kinds of details that are included show what the writer notices, thinks, and feels about events. The voice of autobiographical writing usually reflects the writer's own personality and way of speaking.

In the following excerpt from *A White House Diary,* notice the words that seem to reveal feeling, and think about what they say about Mrs. Johnson's attitude toward her subject.

It's odd the little things that come to your mind at times of utmost stress, the flashes of deep compassion you feel for people who are really not at the center of the tragedy.

Words that reveal feelings: utmost stress, deep compassion, tragedy

Writer's attitude: All of these words help to show the depth of her very sad feelings.

DIRECTIONS: *Analyze the writer's voice in each passage. First, underline words that help reveal the writer's feelings. Then, tell what you think the writer's attitude is. Finally, tell what the syntax (sentence length and structure) reveals.*

1. We got in. Lyndon told the agents to stop the sirens. We drove along as fast as we could. I looked up at a building and there, already, was a flag at half-mast. I think that was when the enormity of what had happened first struck me.

   Words that reveal feelings: _____

   Writer's attitude: _____

   Syntax: _____

2. I looked at her. Mrs. Kennedy's dress was stained with blood. One leg was almost entirely covered with it and her right glove was caked, it was caked with blood—her husband's blood. Somehow that was one of the most poignant sights—that immaculate woman exquisitely dressed, and caked in blood.

   Words that reveal feelings: _____

   Writer's attitude: _____

   Syntax: _____

from **A White House Diary** by Lady Bird Johnson

Reading: Preview the Text to Identify an Author's Purpose

An **author's purpose** is his or her main reason for writing. An author writes for a general purpose, such as to inform, to entertain, or to persuade. He or she also writes for a specific purpose, such as to expose a particular problem in society. Before you read, **preview the text to look for an author's purpose.**

- Notice the focus of the title.
- Look for any organizing features, such as subheads.
- Identify the subject of photos, illustrations, or diagrams.
- Read the first sentences of the opening paragraphs.

Make educated guesses about the author's purpose based on your preview. Later, as you read the full text, confirm whether your ideas are correct.

DIRECTIONS: *Preview the following opening paragraphs from an article. Then, answer the questions below.*

First Ladies Hall of Fame

Of course, there is no such thing as the First Ladies Hall of Fame, nor is there ever likely to be one. But if there were, two Presidents' wives—Abigail Adams and Eleanor Roosevelt—would be among the first to be nominated.

A Legacy in Letters

Abigail Adams was the wife of the second President of the United States, John Adams. She was also the mother of the sixth President, John Quincy Adams. Fortunately, her letters to her husband and sister have been preserved. They are filled with details that provide an accurate, lively account of Colonial life during the Revolutionary period.

Her Childhood and Education

She was born Abigail Smith in Weymouth, Massachusetts, in 1744. Both her mother's family and her father's were leaders during the Colonial period. Like the girls of her time, even wealthy ones, Abigail had no formal education. Abigail was an avid reader, however, and extremely curious about everything. It was partly her intelligence that attracted the young lawyer, John Adams, whom she married in 1764.

Her Major Accomplishments

During long separations from her husband, she managed the family farm and taught her children. (You may remember how she was vividly portrayed in the musical *1776*.)

1. Identify the author's purpose in this article. _____

_____

2. Identify the main subject or subjects of the article. _____

_____

3. When the author finishes writing about Abigail Adams, what will the author discuss next?

_____

_____

4. What does the title reveal about the author's attitude toward his subject? _____

_____

from **A White House Diary** by Lady Bird Johnson
Vocabulary Builder

Word List

confines   desolate   immaculate   implications   poignant   tumultuous

A. DIRECTIONS: *Write the letter of the word or phrase that is the best synonym for the Word List word.*

____ 1. tumultuous
   A. in order
   B. in an uproar
   C. in a rage
   D. in surprise

____ 2. implications
   A. hints or suggestions
   B. signs or symbols
   C. important events
   D. indirect results

____ 3. poignant
   A. tense and exciting
   B. terrifying
   C. emotionally touching
   D. surprising

____ 4. confines
   A. expands
   B. limits
   C. restores
   D. begins

____ 5. desolate
   A. colorful
   B. appealing
   C. ideal
   D. wretched

____ 6. immaculate
   A. perfect
   B. sensible
   C. approximate
   D. dangerous

B. WORD STUDY The Latin root -*fin*- means "end." Answer each of the following questions using one of these words containing -*fin*-: *refine, infinity, definitely.*

1. Why do scientists use the word *infinity* when they describe space?

   _____

2. Why might a writer want to *refine* his writing before submitting it to a publisher?

   _____

3. When would you *definitely* want to impress your teacher?

   _____

"My English" by Julia Alvarez
Writing About the Big Question

 Can truth change?

Big Question Vocabulary

assumption   belief   circumstance   context   convince
credible   distort   evidence   manipulate   perceive
perspective   skeptics   speculate   truth   verify

A. *Use one or more words from the list above to complete each sentence.*

1. Juan thought there was one _____ in life until his experience forced him to see that everything changes.

2. To _____ the truth, Keiko began looking for more _____.

3. What _____ in Alvarez's life changed her perception of the truth?

4. From Mia's _____, life would never be the same after they moved.

B. *Follow the directions in responding to each of the items below.*

1. Everyone occasionally misunderstands what someone says. Give an example of a time when you misunderstood someone.

_____

_____

2. How did the misunderstanding you listed above change what you thought or how you acted? Use at least two of the Big Question vocabulary words.

_____

_____

C. *Complete the sentence below. Then, write a short paragraph in which you connect this experience to the Big Question.*

In "My English," Alvarez describes how her view of her place in the world changes as she learns English. Complete this sentence:

Learning a language can affect our _____

_____

_____

_____

"My English" by Julia Alvarez

Literary Analysis: Autobiographical Writing and Author's Voice

Voice is the way a writer sounds on the page. For example, the writer's voice in a work can be *smooth and sophisticated, choppy and blunt,* or *breathless and full of wonder.* Voice is a result of several elements:

- *word choice*: the kinds of words the writer uses
- *attitude*: the way the writer feels about his or her subject
- *sentence length and structure, or syntax*: the arrangement of words and ideas in sentences

In **autobiographical writing,** the author tells all or part of his or her own life story. The kinds of details that are included show what the writer notices, thinks, and feels about events. The voice of autobiographical writing usually reflects the writer's own personality and way of speaking.

As you read an autobiography, notice the words that seem to reveal feeling. Think about what they say about Julia Alvarez's attitude toward her subject.

In sixth grade, I had one of the first in a lucky line of great English teachers who began to nurture in me a love of language, a love that had been there since my childhood of listening closely to words.

Words that reveal feelings:	lucky, great, nurture, love
Writer's attitude:	All of these words have positive connotations and help to show the writer's great joy in using words.

DIRECTIONS: *Analyze the writer's voice in each passage. First, underline words that you think reveal something about the writer's voice. Then, tell what you think the writer's attitude is. Finally, tell what the syntax (sentence length and structure) reveals.*

1. Those women yakked as they cooked, they storytold, they gossiped, they sang—boleros, merengues, canciones, salves. Theirs were the voices that belonged to the rain and the wind and the teeny, teeny stars even a small child could blot out with her thumb.

   Word choice: _____

   Writer's attitude: _____

   Syntax: _____

2. *Butter, butter, butter, butter.* All day, one English word that had particularly struck me would go round and round in my mouth and weave through all the Spanish in my head until by the end of the day, the word did sound like just another Spanish word. And so I would say, "Mami, please pass la mantequilla." She would scowl and say in English, "I'm sorry, I don't understand. But would you be needing some butter on your bread?"

   Word choice: _____

   Writer's attitude: _____

   Syntax: _____

"My English" by Julia Alvarez

Reading: Preview the Text to Identify an Author's Purpose

An **author's purpose** is his or her main reason for writing. An author writes for a general purpose, such as to inform, to entertain, or to persuade. He or she also writes for a specific purpose, such as to expose a particular problem in society. Before you read, **preview the text to look for an author's purpose.**

- Notice the focus of the title.
- Look for any organizing features, like subheads.
- Identify the subject of photos, illustrations, or diagrams.
- Read the first sentences of the first few paragraphs.

Make educated guesses about the author's purpose based on your preview. Later, as you read the full text, confirm whether your ideas are correct.

DIRECTIONS: *Preview the following opening paragraphs from an article. Then, answer the questions below.*

Evolving English

The one thing you can count on with a living language (one that is still in use) is that it changes. English has been changing since it first appeared as Old English about A.D. 500. Here are four ways in which English changes: new words, old words with new meanings, out-of-fashion words, and borrowed words.

New Words

Once these words did not exist: *cell phone, laptop, DVD player.* New words enter the English language when manufacturers invent names for their new products. Some people send new words they have made up to dictionary editors and try to sell them, but that is not how words are added to a language. They enter the language by being in common use.

Old Words With New Meanings

Another way language changes is by words taking on new meanings. *Memory,* for example, added a computer meaning when computers became common. Slang is another way that old words acquire new meanings. Long ago, *cool* simply meant the opposite of *warm,* but the slang meaning of *cool* has been around for a long time.

Out-of-Fashion Words

Dictionaries label some words as archaic or obsolete, which means they are no longer in common use. *Thee, prithee, whilst,* and *ere* are some examples of words that have disappeared.

1. Identify the author's purpose in this article. _____

_____

2. Identify the main subject or subjects of the article. _____

_____

3. When the author finishes writing about out-of-fashion words, what will the author discuss next? _____

_____

"My English" by Julia Alvarez
Vocabulary Builder

Word List

accentuated   bilingual   countenance   enumerated   interminably   ponderously

A. DIRECTIONS: *Write the letter of the word or phrase that is the best synonym for the Word List word.*

____ 1. bilingual
    A. being confused
    B. having three languages
    C. using two languages
    D. learning new languages

____ 2. countenance
    A. face
    B. thoughts
    C. reaction
    D. feelings

____ 3. interminably
    A. excitedly
    B. terrifyingly
    C. emotionally
    D. endlessly

____ 4. ponderously
    A. in a hesitant manner
    B. in a dull way
    C. in a quick way
    D. in a reluctant manner

____ 5. enumerated
    A. listed
    B. created
    C. required
    D. forgot

____ 6. accentuated
    A. estimated
    B. excited
    C. emphasized
    D. abbreviated

B. WORD STUDY The Latin root -*term*- means "limit, end, boundary." Answer each of the following questions using one of these words containing -*term*-: *determined, exterminator, interminable.*

1. Why might a football player be very *determined* in the final minutes of a game?

_____

2. Why might you call an *exterminator* if your house had roaches?

_____

3. On what occasion have you felt that every minute seemed *interminable*?

_____

from **A White House Diary** by Lady Bird Johnson
"My English" by Julia Alvarez

Integrated Language Skills: Personal Pronouns

The most common pronouns are those that you use to refer to yourself and the people and things around you. These pronouns are called **personal pronouns.** Personal pronouns refer to the person speaking (first person), the person spoken to (second person), or the person, place, or thing spoken about (third person). Here is a chart of the personal pronouns.

	Singular	**Plural**
First Person	I, me, my, mine	we, us, our, ours
Second Person	you, your, yours	you, your, yours
Third Person	he, him, his; she, her, hers; it, its	they, them, their, theirs

The ending *-self* or *-selves* can be added to some personal pronouns to form reflexive pronouns. A **reflexive pronoun** indicates that someone or something performs an action to, for, or upon itself. Reflexive pronouns point back to a noun or pronoun earlier in the sentence. The eight reflexive pronouns are *myself, ourselves, yourself, yourselves, himself, herself, itself,* and *themselves.*

Reflexive Pronoun   She asked *herself* why everyone spoke English in New York.

A. DIRECTIONS: *Underline all of the personal pronouns in these passages from "My English."*

1. Why my parents didn't first educate us in our native language by enrolling us in a Dominican school, I don't know. Part of it was that Mami's family had a tradition of sending the boys to the States to boarding school and college, and she had been one of the first girls to be allowed to join her brothers. [You should find eight personal pronouns.]

2. There was also a neat little trick I wanted to try on an English-speaking adult at home. I had learned it from Elizabeth, my smart-alecky friend in fourth grade, whom I alternately worshiped and resented. [You should find five personal pronouns.]

B. DIRECTIONS: *You are planning to meet a pen pal, whom you have never seen before, in the train station. Write a short description of yourself so that your pen pal will recognize you. Use several personal pronouns and at least one example of reflexive pronouns in your description. Then, underline the pronouns.*

_____

_____

_____

_____

_____

_____

_____

Name _____ Date _____

from **A White House Diary** by Lady Bird Johnson

"My English" by Julia Alvarez

Integrated Language Skills: Support for Writing a Journal Entry

Use the chart below to gather information for your **journal entry.** Write your ideas in complete sentences.

1. My subject:
2. Why my subject is important to me:
3. Who else was affected by the event:
4. How they were affected:
5. How I felt during/about the event:
6. Specific words I associate with my subject:
7. Specific images I associate with my subject:

Now, write your journal entry about a subject that is important to you. As you describe your subject, try to use the specific words and images you thought of, but feel free to add others.

Name _____   Date _____

"The Secret Life of Walter Mitty" by James Thurber
Writing About the Big Question

Can truth change?

Big Question Vocabulary

assumption	belief	circumstance	context	convince
credible	distort	evidence	manipulate	perceive
perspective	skeptics	speculate	truth	verify

A. *Use one or more words from the list above to complete each sentence.*

1. Although a story is fiction, an author can still tell the _____.

2. A narrator's _____ determines what we know and believe.

3. Writers deliberately _____ the truth to make stories interesting.

4. The reality Mitty _____ as true differs from the one his wife sees.

B. *Follow the directions in responding to each item below.*

1. Do you sometimes daydream? Give an example.

   _____

   _____

2. How does the daydream you listed above change how you see your life? Use at least two of the Big Question vocabulary words.

   _____

   _____

C. *Complete the sentence below. Then, write a short paragraph in which you connect this experience to the Big Question.*

In "The Secret Life of Walter Mitty," Mitty lives two lives: the life dominated by his wife and the life of his imagination. Complete this sentence:

Compared to our everyday lives, the life of our imagination is _____

_____

_____

_____

"The Secret Life of Walter Mitty" by James Thurber
Literary Analysis: Character

A **character** is a person or an animal who takes part in the action of a literary work.

- A **round character** is complex, showing many different qualities—revealing faults as well as virtues. For example, a character might be honest but foolish or dishonest but intelligent. A **flat character** is one-dimensional, showing only a single trait.
- A **dynamic character** develops, changes, and learns something during the course of a story, unlike a **static character,** who remains the same.

The main character of a story is almost always a round character and is usually dynamic. The main character's development and growth are often central to a story's plot and theme. As you read, consider the traits that make characters seem round or flat, dynamic or static.

DIRECTIONS: *For each numbered item, write a sentence telling what character trait or traits the passage reveals.*

1. **Mrs. Mitty:** "We've been all through that," she said, getting out of the car. "You're not a young man any longer." He raced the engine a little. "Why don't you wear your gloves? Have you lost your gloves?"

   Character traits of Mrs. Mitty: _____

   _____

2. **Walter Mitty:** Once he had tried to take his chains off [the tires], outside New Milford, and he had got them wound around the axles. A man had had to come out in a wrecking car and unwind them, a young, grinning garageman. Since then Mrs. Mitty always made him drive to a garage to have the chains taken off. The next time, he thought, I'll wear my right arm in a sling; they won't grin at me then.

   Character traits of Walter Mitty: _____

   _____

3. **Walter Mitty:** A woman's scream rose above the bedlam and suddenly a lovely, dark-haired girl was in Walter Mitty's arms. The District Attorney struck at her savagely. Without rising from his chair, Mitty let the man have it on the point of the chin. "You miserable cur!" . . .

   Character traits of Walter Mitty: _____

   _____

4. **Mrs. Mitty and Walter Mitty:** "Did you get the what's-its-name? The puppy biscuit? What's in that box?" "Overshoes," said Mitty. "Couldn't you have put them on in the store?" "I was thinking," said Walter Mitty. "Does it ever occur to you that I am sometimes thinking?" She looked at him. "I'm going to take your temperature when I get you home," she said.

   Character traits of Mrs. Mitty and Walter Mitty: _____

   _____

Name _____ Date _____

"The Secret Life of Walter Mitty" by James Thurber
Reading: Reflect on Details and Events to Determine an Author's Purpose

An **author's purpose** is his or her main reason for writing. In fiction, the specific purpose is often to convey the story's theme, message, or insight. Pause periodically while reading and **reflect** on the story's details and events to determine the author's purpose. Ask questions such as, *What significance might this event have?* or *Why does the author include this detail?* Based on your reflections, formulate ideas about what the author's purpose might be.

DIRECTIONS: *Write one or two sentences telling why, in your opinion, James Thurber might have included each of the following details or events in "The Secret Life of Walter Mitty."*

1. Mrs. Mitty scolds her husband for driving too fast and for not wearing his gloves. He does what she tells him to do.

   _____

   _____

2. Walter Mitty daydreams, imagining that he is an important surgeon who repairs a piece of medical equipment and saves a patient's life.

   _____

   _____

3. Walter Mitty tells his wife that he does not need overshoes, but his wife insists that he does. He buys the overshoes.

   _____

   _____

4. Walter Mitty daydreams, imagining that he is a heroic air force captain about to fly a two-man bomber into heavy combat by himself.

   _____

   _____

5. Walter Mitty daydreams, imagining himself heroically facing a firing squad—"proud and disdainful, Walter Mitty the Undefeated, inscrutable to the last."

   _____

   _____

   _____

"The Secret Life of Walter Mitty" by James Thurber
Vocabulary Builder

Word List

derisive   distraught   inscrutable   insinuatingly
insolent   pandemonium

A. DIRECTIONS: *Each item consists of a related pair of words in CAPITAL LETTERS followed by four pairs of words. Write the letter of the pair that best expresses a relationship similar to the one expressed by the pair of words in capital letters.*

____ 1. INSOLENT : RESPECTFUL ::
   A. ancient : old
   B. backward : forward
   C. curious : eager
   D. incredible : unbelievable

____ 2. INSCRUTABLE : PUZZLING ::
   A. tardy : early
   B. precise : careless
   C. circular : round
   D. energetic : exhausted

____ 3. DISTRAUGHT : CAREFREE ::
   A. dangerous : treacherous
   B. alien : stranger
   C. mammoth : enormous
   D. casual : formal

____ 4. INSINUATINGLY : DIRECTLY ::
   A. surprisingly : predictably
   B. quickly : rapidly
   C. enormously : hopefully
   D. judiciously : cautiously

____ 5. DERISIVE : RESPECTFUL ::
   A. thoughtful : philosophical
   B. anxious : nervous
   C. courageous : cowardly
   D. practical : obvious

____ 6. PANDEMONIUM : NOISE ::
   A. silence : confusion
   B. affection : resentment
   C. boredom : freedom
   D. appreciation : gratitude

B. WORD STUDY The Latin suffix *-able* means "can or will" or "capable of being." Rewrite each sentence. Use the underlined word plus the suffix *-able* in the new sentence.

1. The runner was running too fast and would not be able to <u>sustain</u> the pace.

   _____

2. I cannot <u>predict</u> how this story is going to end.

   _____

3. He can <u>attain</u> his goal of getting a college degree and then starting his own business.

   _____

"**Uncle Marcos**" by Isabel Allende
Writing About the Big Question

Can truth change?

Big Question Vocabulary

assumption	belief	circumstance	context	convince
credible	distort	evidence	manipulate	perceive
perspective	skeptics	speculate	truth	verify

A. *Use one or more words from the list above to complete each sentence.*

1. The most magical stories look at truth from a different _____.

2. An author may _____ reality to reveal the truth.

3. In the story, Allende's _____ is that there can be many truths.

4. Uncle Marcos trusted his _____ in flying even though it was not strongly supported by the evidence.

B. *Follow the directions in responding to each item below.*

1. What person whom you know has lived the most unusual or exciting life?
   _____

2. How is the person's perspective on life similar to or different from your own? Write three sentences explaining your answer. Use two of the Big Question vocabulary words.
   _____
   _____
   _____

C. *In "Uncle Marcos," the narrator describes the fantastic escapades of an uncle who's not satisfied with the ordinary. Complete the sentence below. Then, write a short paragraph in which you connect this experience to the Big Question.*

A person who believes strongly in impractical and impossible things _____
_____
_____
_____
_____
_____

Name _____ Date _____

Literary Analysis: Character

A **character** is a person or an animal that takes part in the action of a literary work.

- A **round character** is complex, showing many different qualities—revealing faults as well as virtues. For example, a character might be sensitive in some situations but insensitive in others. A **flat character** is one-dimensional, showing a single trait.
- A **dynamic character** develops, changes, and learns something during the course of a story, unlike a **static character,** who remains the same.

The main character of a story is almost always a round character and is usually dynamic. The main character's development and growth are often central to a story's plot and theme. As you read, consider the traits that make characters seem round or flat, dynamic or static.

A. DIRECTIONS: *For each numbered item, write a sentence telling what character trait or traits the passage reveals.*

1. After a short time, bored with having to appear at ladies' gatherings where the mistress of the house played the piano, with playing cards, and with dodging all his relatives' pressures to pull himself together and take a job as a clerk in Severo del Valle's law practice, he bought a barrel organ and took to the streets with the hope of seducing his Cousin Antonieta and entertaining the public in the bargain.

   Character traits of Uncle Marcos: _____

   _____

2. In the face of this stain to the family reputation, Marcos was forced to give up organ grinding and resort to less conspicuous ways of winning over his Cousin Antonieta, but he did not renounce his goal.

   Character traits of Uncle Marcos: _____

   _____

3. He had lost his airplane and had to return on foot, but he had not broken any bones and his adventurous spirit was intact.

   Character traits of Uncle Marcos: _____

   _____

B. DIRECTIONS: *Write a brief character analysis of Uncle Marcos. Tell whether he is flat or round and dynamic or static. Give examples from the story to support your statements.*

_____

_____

_____

_____

_____

_____

Name _____ Date _____

"Uncle Marcos" *from* **The House of the Spirits** by Isabel Allende
Reading: Reflect on Details and Events to Determine an Author's Purpose

An **author's purpose** is his or her main reason for writing. In fiction, the specific purpose is often to convey the story's theme, message, or insight. Pause periodically while reading and **reflect** on the story's details and events to determine the author's purpose. Ask questions such as, *What significance might this event have?* or *Why does the author include this detail?*

Based on your reflections, formulate ideas about what the author's purpose might be.

A. DIRECTIONS: *Write one or two sentences telling why, in your opinion, Isabel Allende might have included each of the following details or events in "Uncle Marcos."*

1. Uncle Marcos sleeps during the day, stays up all night, and performs strange experiments in the kitchen.

   _____

   _____

2. He refuses to take a job in his brother-in-law's law firm.

   _____

   _____

3. He embarrasses the family by serenading Cousin Antonieta with a barrel-organ and a parrot.

   _____

   _____

4. He builds an airplane and takes off in it.

   _____

   _____

5. He gives up the fortune-telling business when he realizes that it is affecting people's lives.

   _____

   _____

B. DIRECTIONS: *Think back over the events and details of the story and your answers to the questions above. Then, in a sentence or two, write what you think the author's purpose is in "Uncle Marcos."*

_____

_____

_____

"Uncle Marcos" *from* The House of the Spirits by Isabel Allende
Vocabulary Builder

Word List

conspicuous   disconsolately   impassive   pallid   pertinent   unrequited

A. DIRECTIONS: *Each item consists of a related pair of words in CAPITAL LETTERS followed by four pairs of words. Write the letter of the pair that best expresses a relationship similar to the one expressed by the pair in capital letters.*

____ 1. PALLID : PALE ::
    A. tense : relaxed   C. anxious : worried
    B. organized : messy   D. stubborn : mule

____ 2. JOYFULLY : DISCONSOLATELY ::
    A. methodically : carefully   C. static : unchanged
    B. overflowing : empty   D. common : familiar

____ 3. UNREQUITED : RETURNED ::
    A. tamed : wild   C. tiny : molecule
    B. wrinkled : rumpled   D. exceptional : unusual

____ 4. CONSPICUOUS : CONCEALED ::
    A. forgotten : remembered   C. preferred : practical
    B. sorrowful : sincere   D. simplified : straightforward

____ 5. PERTINENT : RELEVANT ::
    A. timely : recent   C. elegant : graceful
    B. confident : doubtful   D. determined : uncertain

     6. IMPASSIVE : EMOTIONAL ::
    A. willful : stubborn   C. confused : puzzled
    B. passionate : romantic   D. careful : impulsive

B. WORD STUDY The Latin suffix *-ive* means "of, belonging to, quality of." Answer each of the following questions. Add the suffix *-ive* to the underlined word and use it in your new sentence.

1. Why would someone <u>reflect</u> on a poem?

_____

2. Why would you take a CD player back to the store if it had a <u>defect</u>?

_____

3. Why should government leaders <u>cooperate</u>?

_____

"The Secret Life of Walter Mitty" by James Thurber
"Uncle Marcos" *from* **The House of the Spirits** by Isabel Allende
Integrated Language Skills: Grammar

Relative, Interrogative, and Indefinite Pronouns

Pronouns are words that stand for nouns or for words that take the place of nouns. There are a number of different kinds of pronouns.

A **relative pronoun** begins a subordinate clause and connects it to another idea in the sentence. The five relative pronouns are *that, which, who, whom,* and *whose.*

Uncle Marcos is a person *who* likes adventure.

An **interrogative pronoun** begins a question. The five interrogative pronouns are *what, which, who, whom,* and *whose.*

Who is Clara?

Indefinite pronouns refer to people, places, or things, often without specifying which ones. Words that are or can function as indefinite pronouns include *anyone, everybody, nobody,* and *somebody; anything, nothing,* and *something; any, all, few, many, most, one,* and *some; little* and *much;* and *another, both,* and *either.*

Everybody came out to watch Uncle Marcos take off in the airplane.

A. PRACTICE: *Underline the relative, interrogative, or indefinite pronoun in each sentence. On the line or lines following the sentence, identify each pronoun you underlined as* relative, interrogative, *or* indefinite.

1. Trunks, animals in jars of formaldehyde, and Indian lances are some of the items that Uncle Marcos brought home from his travels. _____, _____

2. In whose house did Marcos spend his time, sleeping during the day and conducting experiments at night? _____

3. Marcos's departure by airplane was a remarkable event, which virtually everyone in town had come out to witness. _____, _____

4. Who were the explorers and mountain climbers who claimed to have found the body? _____, _____

5. Everyone was saddened when they appeared with the coffin that they claimed held Uncle Marcos's body (but which actually contained bags of sand). _____, _____, _____

B. Writing Application: *Write a paragraph that summarizes what happens when Uncle Marcos courts Cousin Antonieta. Use at least one relative pronoun, one interrogative pronoun, and one indefinite pronoun in your paragraph, and underline each.*

_____

_____

_____

_____

_____

Name _____ Date _____

"The Secret Life of Walter Mitty" by James Thurber
"Uncle Marcos" by Isabel Allende
Integrated Language Skills: Support for Writing a Character Profile

If you read "The Secret Life of Walter Mitty," choose one of the heroic characters in Mitty's daydreams (commander of a navy seaplane, famous surgeon, defendant at a trial, or captain of a bomber). If you read "Uncle Marcos," write your profile on that character. Gather ideas for your **character profile** by completing this cluster diagram.

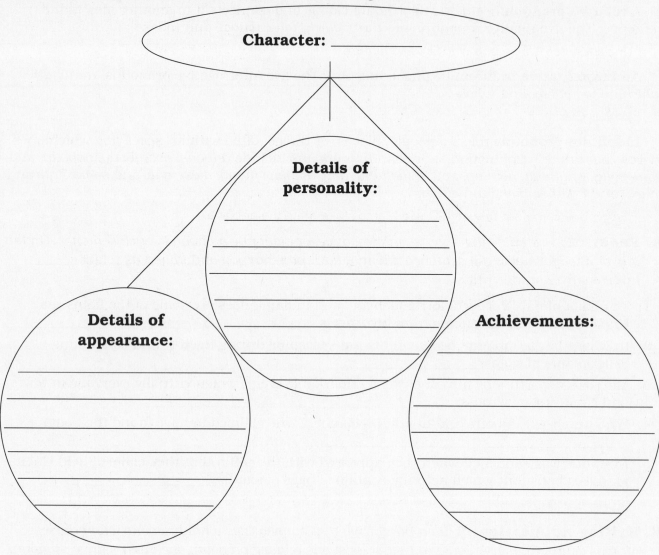

1. What single impression of the character do you want to convey?

   _____

2. Place a check mark next to the details in your diagram that will help you convey that impression.

3. Briefly list ideas in the order in which you will present them in your character profile.

   _____

   _____

Now, use your notes to draft a character profile of the character.

Name _____ Date _____

Writing About the Big Question

Can truth change?

Big Question Vocabulary

assumption	belief	circumstance	context	convince
credible	distort	evidence	manipulate	perceive
perspective	skeptics	speculate	truth	verify

A. *Use one or more words from the list above to complete each sentence.*

1. If we _____ on future events, we may see how truth changes.

2. Never make the _____ that people in the future will see the same truth we do.

3. Sometimes, it can be difficult to _____ people that the truth changes.

4. To convince someone of the truth, we must gather _____.

B. *Follow the directions in responding to each item below.*

1. What is happening in today's world that must change? List one thing.

   _____

   _____

2. What truth must change before the change you described above can happen? Use at least two of the Big Question vocabulary words.

   _____

   _____

C. *Some people feel that the condition of Earth is a constant, unchangeable truth. Complete the sentences below. Then, write a short paragraph in which you connect this experience to the Big Question.*

   I speculate that in 100 years, the Earth will be _____.

   My assumptions are based on _____.

"If I Forget Thee, Oh Earth . . ." by Arthur C. Clarke
from Silent Spring by Rachel Carson
Literary Analysis: Theme

The **theme** of a literary work is the central message or insight about life that is conveyed through the work. Sometimes, the theme is stated directly. More often, it is suggested indirectly through the words and experiences of the characters or through the events of a story.

How the theme is developed depends in part on the genre, or form, of the work. In nonfiction literature, such as essays, the theme is usually stated directly as a main idea. Then, the writer supports the idea with facts, details, and examples to prove the point.

In most fiction—short stories, novels, poetry, and plays—the theme is implied, or suggested. Readers must figure out the theme by looking at the ideas expressed through story events and character actions.

DIRECTIONS: *Read the following passages, and describe how each passage relates to the selection's theme.*

from "If I Forget Thee, Oh Earth . . ."

He was looking upon the funeral pyre of a world—upon the radioactive aftermath of Armageddon. Across a quarter of a million miles of space, the glow of dying atoms was still visible, a perennial reminder of the ruinous past. It would be centuries yet before that deadly glow died from the rocks and life could return again to fill that silent, empty world.

1. What does this passage imply about what has happened to Earth?

   _____

2. How does this passage relate to the theme of the story?

   _____

3. How would you state the theme of this story?

   _____

from Silent Spring

In the gutters under the eaves and between the shingles of the roofs, a white granular powder still showed a few patches; some weeks before it had fallen like snow upon the roofs and lawns, the fields and streams.

No witchcraft, no enemy action had silenced the rebirth of new life in this stricken world. The people had done it themselves.

1. What might the "white granular powder" be? What are the effects of the powder?

   _____

2. How does this passage relate to the theme of the selection?

   _____

3. How would you state the theme of this selection?

   _____

Name _____ Date _____

Vocabulary Builder

Word List

blight   maladies   moribund   perennial   purged

A. DIRECTIONS: *Revise each sentence so that the underlined vocabulary word is used logically. Be sure not to change the vocabulary word.*

1. I <u>purged</u> the wound on my foot, thereby increasing the chances of infection.

   _____

2. Those flowers are <u>perennials</u>, so you will need to plant them again next year.

   _____

3. Because of the <u>blight</u>, the potatoes we grew were especially fine this year.

   _____

4. Due to various <u>maladies</u>, they became more vigorous and cheerful.

   _____

5. The fact that her garden was <u>moribund</u> filled her with delight.

   _____

B. DIRECTIONS: *Write the letter of the word or phrase that is the best synonym for the Word List word.*

___ 1. perennial
    A. occasional
    B. temporary
    C. perpetual
    D. unusual

___ 2. maladies
    A. complaints
    B. diseases
    C. mistakes
    D. theories

___ 3. moribund
    A. depressing
    B. upsetting
    C. cheering
    D. dying

___ 4. purged
    A. cleansed
    B. destroyed
    C. manufactured
    D. created

"If I Forget Thee, Oh Earth . . ." by Arthur C. Clarke
from **Silent Spring** by Rachel Carson
Support for Writing to Compare Literary Works

Use a chart like the one below to make prewriting notes for your essay of comparison and contrast. Then, answer the two questions following the chart.

Points of Comparison/Contrast	"If I Forget Thee . . ."	*from* **Silent Spring**
My response to each selection		
Statement of each selection's theme		
Possible reasons why author chose genre		

1. In general, do you think fiction or nonfiction is more effective in expressing a theme? Explain.

   _____

   _____

   _____

2. Which of these two selections do you think is more effective in expressing its theme? Explain.

   _____

   _____

   _____

Time Out, performed by Natalia DiSario

Gotta get myself back on track /

Can't let anything ever ruin me /

I won't let it go down like that /

Have to watch and protect myself completely /

Gotta try to keep things intact /

Make sure I don't lose control over me /

I won't let it go down like that /

Need to nurture all the life within me /

Don't know why I thought it was funny when I heard it could happen but I'm standing here now without a reason for laughing /

Can't **articulate** or express where I am but lemme tell you this feeling isn't something I planned /

A **grievance** that you get down deep in your soul, a gripe so deep it'll make you feel old /

It even gives me chills when I try to explain just how this **issue** can conquer your brain /

Now you have a problem with every thought you convey, you didn't even know that you could function that way /

And it makes no **difference** even though you're alive, things are not the same, you got no will to **survive** /

The only thing you got left is a voice inside that **mediates** what's really going on and why / It makes sure that your body don't take over your mind so the roles of your system don't become intertwined /

I really wish there were words I could use to describe, how **antagonizing** this could be to the mind /

I know it sounds silly, but it'll upset you inside and before you know it, wipe the smile from your eyes /

At that point you start to think of all the times in your life that led up to this feeling that just doesn't seem right /

Could it have been all them people you considered your friends? Did you make a mistake by letting everyone in? /

Was it all the **controversy** you got yourself in? /

Was it really that important to ensure that you win? /

Not every **argument** can come **amicably** to an end /

Can't be nice and **cooperate** just to fit in /

Continued

I mean, how could you confuse who's at the top of your list?

Compete against the world and somehow become this? /

Strive against it all just to make it this far /

All them **battles** you won you can't be losing the **war** /

All that conflict and struggle, all the times you've been scarred, not everybody gets to live life, love who you are /

How about them people that never get a chance to experience life the way you do first hand? /

Not able to see things as clear as you can /

Not able to hear things all their sense impaired /

I don't think you understand what we dealing with here, before you were brave there had to be something you feared /

So be grateful for your life before it disappears cause you can't lose it and **appreciate** being here /

Life's not **equitable,** not fair, not right, but nothing is worth sacrificing my life /

The day you feel like that, ya life begins, and if you stay like that, ya life never ends /

So somewhere along the way you gotta take time out, take time to look around and see what life's about /

Song Title: **Time Out**
Artist / Performed by Natalia DiSario
Lyrics by Natalia DiSario
Music composed by Jason Martinez
Produced by Mike Pandolfo, Wonderful
Executive Producer: Keith London, Defined Mind

Unit 2: Short Stories
Big Question Vocabulary—1

The Big Question: Is conflict necessary?

When conflicts are discussed in a friendly, constructive way, sometimes we may begin to see the other side and to learn something.

amicably: acting in a friendly or peaceful way

appreciate: to understand how important or valuable something is

argument: a situation in which people disagree, often angrily

articulate: to express what you are thinking or feeling

differences: disagreements or controversies

DIRECTIONS: *Think of or invent a conflict that got resolved in a positive way. Write each step of the conflict using the vocabulary words. (For example, Step I could be Jason and I **argued** because he was late and kept me waiting.)*

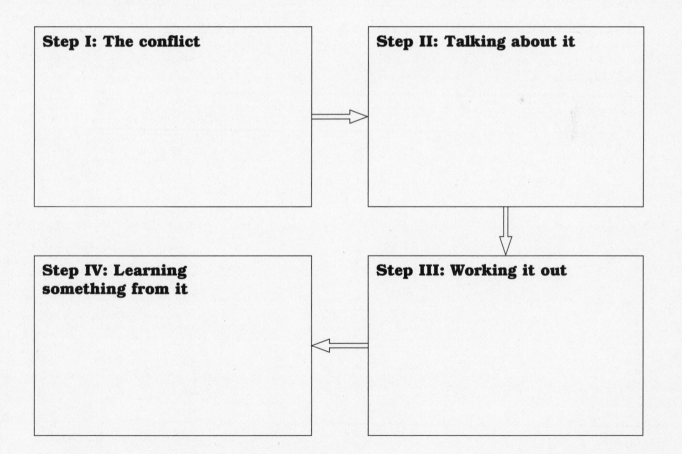

Step I: The conflict

Step II: Talking about it

Step IV: Learning something from it

Step III: Working it out

Name _____ Date _____

Unit 2: Short Stories
Big Question Vocabulary—2

The Big Question: Is conflict necessary?

Sometimes the actions of others can annoy or upset us. Some people have trouble expressing their displeasure in a constructive way. It is worth practicing this skill—working out differences in a productive way leads to a better atmosphere for everyone.

antagonize: to act in a way that annoys others; to act in opposition

compete: to try to be better or more successful than someone else

cooperate: to work together toward a common goal

grievance: a belief that you have been treated unfairly; a complaint about an unfair situation

mediate: to try to resolve or settle a conflict

DIRECTIONS: *Use the space below to write to someone who can help you resolve a complaint that you have. It can be real or imagined. Use all of the vocabulary words in your note.*

Unit 2: Short Stories
Big Question Vocabulary—3

The Big Question: Is conflict necessary?

battle: a fight or competition between people or groups in which each side has the goal of winning

controversy: a serious argument about something that continues for a long time

equity: the state or quality of being fair and impartial

issue: a problem or topic that people discuss, especially a topic that affects a lot of people

survival: the state of continuing to exist where there is a risk of death

DIRECTIONS: *Use all of the vocabulary words to write a newspaper article describing what happened at Gesco Inc. after this sign was posted for all employees to see.*

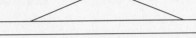

Notice to All Employees

It is everyone's responsibility to help the homeless. Therefore, Gesco Inc. will be deducting 10% of the pay of each employee to donate to the homeless.
Thank You.

Trouble at Gesco Inc.

Name _____ Date _____

Unit 2: Short Stories
Applying the Big Question

The Big Question: Is conflict necessary?

DIRECTIONS: *Complete the chart below to apply what you have learned about conflict and whether or not it is necessary. One row has been completed for you.*

Example	Conflict	Outcome	Was the Conflict Necessary for the Outcome?	What I Learned
From Literature	In "The Interlopers," bitter enemies are trapped under a tree together.	The two men talk and decide to end their feud.	Yes, because it forced the two men to **cooperate**.	A conflict can be an opportunity to resolve **differences**.
From Literature				
From Science				
From Social Studies				
From Real Life				

Wayson Choy
Listening and Viewing

Segment 1: Meet Wayson Choy
- How did Wayson Choy's experience growing up in Chinatown influence his writing?
- In what way are Choy's stories a bridge between two worlds?

_____

_____

_____

_____

Segment 2: The Short Story
- What do windchimes symbolize in "The Jade Peony"?
- Why would a writer build a short story around a symbol?

_____

_____

_____

_____

Segment 3: The Writing Process
- According to Wayson Choy, how is the process of a caterpillar turning into a butterfly similar to the writing process?
- How is your writing process similar to the process Choy describes?

_____

_____

_____

_____

Segment 4: The Rewards of Writing
- According Wayson Choy, literature is important to all people.
- Why does he think that?
- What have you learned from or identified with in a particular piece of literature?

_____

_____

_____

_____

Unit 2
Learning About Short Stories

A **short story** is a work of fiction meant to be read in one sitting. It is crafted in a concise manner so that it accomplishes its purpose in relatively few words—usually 500 to 10,000.

The **plot** is the series of related events that take place in the story. During the course of the plot, events unfold. They build to a **climax** (the point of greatest tension, or the turning point) and then, during the **resolution,** come to a conclusion.

At the core of the plot is a **conflict,** or struggle. An **external conflict** occurs between characters, between an individual and a group, or between a character and a force of nature. An **internal conflict** takes place within the mind of a character.

The **characters,** the personalities who participate in the action, are usually human beings, but they may be animals or even objects. Characters are described by means of **characterization:** descriptions of characters' appearance and actions, dialogue in which characters interact with other characters and reveal information about themselves and others, and descriptions of characters' thoughts and feelings.

The **setting** is the time and place of the action. It may be the past, the present, or the future. It may be unspecific, or it may name a particular season, year, or even hour of the day. It may refer to a social, an economic, or a cultural environment, and it may specify a geographic location—a country, town, or neighborhood. The setting sets the stage for the action. It may also create a mood or an atmosphere or present a character with a conflict.

The **theme** is a story's central message or insight into life. A **stated theme** is expressed directly by the author. An **implied theme** is suggested by the experiences of the characters or the events and the setting of the work.

DIRECTIONS: *Write the letter of the short-story element that best describes each numbered item.*

_____ 1. A freestyle swimmer finishes in first-place at an important meet.
     A. setting   B. character   C. climax

_____ 2. A woman struggles against discrimination at her job.
     A. setting   B. conflict   C. resolution

_____ 3. Two rivals grow to admire each other.
     A. plot   B. climax   C. resolution

_____ 4. A neighborhood in San Francisco's Chinatown is described.
     A. setting   B. character   C. theme

_____ 5. An obscure individual longs to become powerful and respected.
     A. internal conflict   B. external conflict   C. resolution

_____ 6. A young person learns that self-confidence is a powerful quality.
     A. character   B. setting   C. theme

_____ 7. A research station in Antarctica is described.
     A. theme   B. plot   C. setting

_____ 8. An elderly woman recalls a long-lost love.
     A. characterization   B. theme   C. resolution

_____ 9. A grandfather teaches his grandson about the respect owed to all creatures.
     A. climax   B. theme   C. characterization

"The Jade Peony" by Wayson Choy
Model Selection: Short Story

The **plot** of a short story is the series of related events that take place in the course of the story. At the core of a story's plot is usually a **conflict,** or struggle. The conflict may be **external,** in which case it features a clash between the main character and another character, between the main character and a group or society as a whole, or between the main character and a force of nature. If the conflict is **internal,** the struggle takes place within the character's mind.

The conflicts in a story typically build to a **climax,** or turning point. The events following the climax make up the outcome of the story, or the **resolution.**

Writers of short stories use methods of **characterization** to show what the characters are like. For example, writers may describe the characters' appearance and actions, quote their words, show them interacting with other characters, and describe their thoughts and feelings.

Another essential element of a short story is its setting. The **setting** is the time and place of the action. It may be general or specific, and it may include the social, economic, or cultural environment. Sometimes, the setting contributes to the **atmosphere,** or overall emotional mood, of a story. Sometimes, the setting creates a conflict.

A story's **theme** is its central message or insight about life. A **stated theme** is directly expressed by the writer. An **implied theme** is suggested by the characters' experiences, the setting, the author's tone or attitude, and/or the style of the work as a whole.

DIRECTIONS: *On the lines provided, answer these questions about "The Jade Peony."*

1. What conflicts, or problems, does Grandmama face?

   _____

   _____

2. What conflicts, or problems, does Sek-Lung (the narrator) face?

   _____

   _____

3. What conflicts, or problems, do the other members of the family face?

   _____

   _____

4. What is the setting of the story? _____

   _____

5. What role does the cultural environment play? _____

   _____

6. What is the climax of the story? Explain your answer. _____

   _____

7. In your opinion, what is the story's message about life and behavior?

   _____

Name _____ Date _____

"The Most Dangerous Game" by Richard Connell
Writing About the Big Question

Is conflict necessary?

Big Question Vocabulary

amicably	antagonize	appreciate	argument	articulate
compete/competition	controversy	cooperate	differences	equity
grievance	issue	mediate	survival	war/battle

A. *Use one or more words from the list above to complete each sentence.*

1. When Kim and her parents came to an agreement about her curfew, they resolved the conflict _____.

2. After Joe and Mark talked about a pressing political _____, they realized they had big _____ of opinion.

3. Todd and José built a model volcano to _____ in the science fair.

B. *Follow the directions in responding to each item below.*

1. Write two sentences describing a grievance you have had.

   _____

   _____

2. Write two sentences explaining how you dealt with the grievance. Use at least two of the Big Question vocabulary words.

   _____

   _____

C. *In "The Most Dangerous Game," a hunter faces a life-threatening conflict. Complete the sentence below. Then, write a short paragraph in which you connect this experience to the Big Question.*

To succeed in a fight for survival, a person needs to _____

_____

_____

_____

"The Most Dangerous Game" by Richard Connell
Literary Analysis: Conflict

Conflict is a struggle between opposing forces. There are two types of conflict: internal and external.

- In **internal conflict,** a character struggles with his or her own opposing feelings, beliefs, needs, or desires.
- In **external conflict,** a character struggles against an outside force, such as another character, society, or nature.

Conflict and the search for a solution are the mainspring of a story's plot. The solution, which usually occurs near the end of a story, is called the **resolution.** In some stories, the conflict is not truly resolved. Instead, the main character experiences an **epiphany,** or sudden flash of insight. Although the conflict is not resolved, the character's thoughts about it change.

A. DIRECTIONS: *"The Most Dangerous Game" contains a number of conflicts. On the following lines, briefly describe the story situations surrounding each conflict.*

1. Rainsford vs. nature _____

_____

_____

2. General Zaroff vs. the "visitors" to his island _____

_____

_____

3. Rainsford vs. General Zaroff _____

_____

_____

4. Rainsford within himself _____

_____

_____

B. DIRECTIONS: *On the following lines, briefly discuss the story's ending. Does the ending contain a resolution that solves the story's main conflict? Have Rainsford's experiences changed his views about hunting? Explain your answer by citing details from the story.*

_____

_____

_____

_____

_____

_____

Name _____ Date _____

Reading: Use Details to Make Inferences

An **inference** is a logical guess that you make based on details in a story. When you make inferences, you read between the lines to understand information that is not stated directly. To make inferences, ask yourself questions about the feelings and behavior of the characters. Here are some helpful questions to ask:

- What does this detail show about a character's motivation, or the reasons for his or her behavior?
- What does this passage say about the character's unspoken feelings and thoughts?

Example from "The Most Dangerous Game":

Detail from the story: "I can't believe you are serious, General Zaroff. This is a grisly joke."

Inference: Rainsford has just begun to realize that Zaroff hunts humans.

A. DIRECTIONS: *Use the following chart to make inferences from the details listed. The first item has been done for you.*

Details in the Story	My Inferences About Motivations/ Feelings
1. Rainsford tells Whitney that there are only two classes of people: hunters and huntees.	Rainsford begins the story with a matter-of-fact, almost hard-boiled attitude.
2. Rainsford asks Zaroff to excuse him for the night because he feels sick.	
3. Zaroff tells Rainsford how upset he was at the death of his dog Lazarus.	
4. Rainsford is able to rig up several ingenious traps, such as the Burmese tiger pit and a Malay mancatcher.	

B. DIRECTIONS: *Do you think "The Most Dangerous Game" has a serious theme, or message about human nature or behavior? Or, is it primarily a suspenseful adventure story intended to entertain readers rather than to make a point? Explain your answer with specific references to details in the story.*

_____

_____

_____

_____

_____

_____

"The Most Dangerous Game" by Richard Connell
Vocabulary Builder

Word List

futile   grotesque   indolently   naive   palpable   scruples

A. DIRECTIONS: *In each of the following items, think about the meaning of the italicized word, and then answer the question.*

1. What is the danger if you approach a research paper assignment *indolently*?

   _____

   _____

2. How are you feeling if you have *scruples* about doing something?

   _____

   _____

3. How would you feel if you make a long and *futile* journey?

   _____

4. If the tension during the final two minutes of a game is *palpable,* do you think the spectators feel suspense or not? Explain.

   _____

5. What is another word that can be used to describe something that is *grotesque*?

   _____

6. Is it easy to fool someone who is *naive*? Explain.

   _____

B. WORD STUDY: The French suffix *-esque* means "in the style or manner of." Use the context of the sentences and what you know about the **French suffix -esque** to explain your answer to each question.

1. Who directly influenced *Romanesque* architecture?

   _____

2. Is calling someone *statuesque* a compliment? Explain.

   _____

   _____

Name _____ Date _____

Writing About the Big Question

Is conflict necessary?

Big Question Vocabulary

amicably	antagonize	appreciate	argument	articulate
compete/competition	controversy	cooperate	differences	equity
grievance	issue	mediate	survival	war/battle

A. *Use one or more words from the list above to complete each sentence.*

1. Some people cannot get past their _____.

2. If you have a _____, you should speak to the person in charge.

3. Sometimes conflict can be avoided if you _____.

4. However, addressing an important _____ directly is often most productive.

5. In a conflict, it is necessary to clearly _____ your position.

B. *Follow the directions in responding to each item below.*

1. Write two sentences explaining how competition relates to conflict.

   _____

   _____

2. Write two sentences explaining how to resolve a conflict. Use at least two of the Big Question vocabulary words.

   _____

   _____

C. *In "American History," a teenage girl wrestles with personal feelings while adults around her try to grasp a tragic historic event. Complete the sentence below. Then, write a short paragraph in which you connect this experience to the Big Question.*

For both individuals and countries, important events often involve conflict because

_____

_____

_____

Name _____ Date _____

Literary Analysis: Conflict

Conflict is a struggle between opposing forces. There are two types of conflict: internal and external.

- In **internal conflict,** a character struggles with his or her own opposing feelings, beliefs, needs, or desires.
- In **external conflict,** a character struggles against an outside force, such as another character, society, or nature.

Conflict and the search for a solution are the mainspring of a story's plot. The solution, which usually occurs near the end of a story, is called the **resolution.** In some stories, the conflict is not truly resolved. Instead, the main character experiences an **epiphany,** or sudden flash of insight. Although the conflict is not resolved, the character's thoughts about it change.

A. DIRECTIONS: *"American History" contains a number of conflicts. On the following lines, briefly describe the story situation surrounding each conflict.*

1. Elena vs. Gail _____

_____

2. Elena and Eugene vs. their classmates _____

_____

3. Elena vs. her mother _____

_____

4. Elena within herself _____

_____

5. Elena vs. Eugene's mother _____

_____

B. DIRECTIONS: *On the following lines, briefly discuss the story's ending. Does the ending contain a resolution that solves the story's main conflict, or does it contain an epiphany, a sudden flash of insight? Explain your answer by citing details from the story.*

_____

_____

_____

_____

_____

_____

Name _____ Date _____

"American History" by Judith Ortiz Cofer
Reading: Use Details to Make Inferences

An **inference** is a logical guess that you make based on details in a story. When you make inferences, you read between the lines to understand information that is not stated directly. To make inferences, ask yourself questions about the feelings and behavior of the characters. Here are some helpful questions to ask:

- What does this detail show about a character's motivation, or the reasons for his or her behavior?
- What does this passage say about the character's unspoken feelings and thoughts?

Detail from the story: But the day President Kennedy was shot there was a profound silence in El Building.

Inference: The residents of El Building are deeply shocked by the assassination of President Kennedy.

DIRECTIONS: *Use the following chart to make inferences about the characters' motivations and feelings from the details listed. The first item has been done for you.*

Details in the Story	My Inferences About Motivations/ Feelings
1. There was only one source of beauty and light for me that school year.	Elena likes Eugene very much.
2. Eugene was in honors classes for all his subjects; classes that were not open to me because English was not my first language, though I was a straight A student.	
3. Since I had turned fourteen . . . my mother had been more vigilant than ever.	
4. "You are going out today?" The way she said 'today' sounded as if a storm warning had been issued.	
5. "You live there?" She pointed up to El Building, which looked particularly ugly, like a gray prison with its many dirty windows and rusty fire escapes.	

"American History" by Judith Ortiz Cofer
Vocabulary Builder

Word List

dilapidated   elation   discreet   profound   tenement   vigilant

A. DIRECTIONS: *For each of the following items, think about the meaning of the italicized word, and then answer the question.*

1. How does a typical *tenement* look—elegant or run-down? _____
   _____

2. If your aunt expresses *profound* misgivings about moving to Puerto Rico, how does she feel about the move? _____
   _____

3. If a watchdog is *vigilant,* is the dog doing its job well or badly? Explain. _____
   _____

4. If you want to move into a house in good condition, would you be likely to choose a *dilapidated* one? Explain why or why not. _____
   _____

5. If a person is *discreet* about something, are they likely to attract attention? Explain.
   _____

6. What kind of event might cause you to feel *elation*? _____
   _____

B. WORD STUDY: The suffix-*ant* often means "performing an action of." Use the context of the sentences and what you know about the **Latin suffix -ant** to explain your answer to each question.

1. Would something be clean if you applied a *disinfectant*? _____
   _____

2. What job does *coolant* do in a car? _____
   _____

3. What does an *assistant* do? _____
   _____

"American History" by Judith Ortiz Cofer
"The Most Dangerous Game" by Richard Connell
Integrated Language Skills: Grammar

Regular Verbs

A verb has four principal parts: the present, the present participle, the past, and the past participle. Most verbs in English are regular. **Regular verbs** form the past and the past participle by adding *-ed* or *-d* to the present form.

The past and past participle of regular verbs have the same form. In the following chart of principal parts, *has* is in parentheses in front of the past participle to remind you that this verb form is a past participle only if it is used with a helping verb.

Notice that the final consonant is sometimes doubled to form the present participle (*tapping*) as well as the past and the past participle (*tapped*). Notice also that the final *e* may be dropped in forming the present participle (*wiping*).

Principal Parts of Regular Verbs			
Present	**Present Participle**	**Past**	**Past Participle**
play	(is) playing	played	(has) played
tap	(is) tapping	tapped	(has) tapped
wipe	(is) wiping	wiped	(has) wiped

A. PRACTICE: *Write the answer(s) to each of the following questions on the lines provided.*

1. Give the four principal parts of the following verbs:

    walk: _____

    hunt: _____

    place: _____

    rip: _____

2. What do you add to form the past tense of regular verbs? _____

B. Writing Application: *Read the following sentences and notice the verb in italics. If the verb is used correctly, write Correct in the space provided. If the verb is not used correctly, rewrite the sentence using the correct form of the verb.*

1. In Paterson, New Jersey, Elena *lived* in El Building with her family.

    _____

2. After school started, Elena *looking* for Eugene in all her classes.

    _____

3. Mr. DePalma has *ask* us to line up in front of him.

    _____

4. Rainsford was exhausted when he *arrive* on the island.

    _____

"American History" by Judith Ortiz Cofer
"The Most Dangerous Game" by Richard Connell

Integrated Language Skills:
Support for Writing an Alternative Ending

For your alternative ending, use the following lines to jot down notes under each heading.

New ending grows out of earlier sequence of events: "American History"

Elena's life at school → Elena's attraction to Eugene → Mother's warnings → Study date
with Eugene → Assassination of President Kennedy → _____

_____

New ending grows out of earlier sequence of events: "The Most Dangerous Game"

Rainsford falls off yacht and lands on island → Rainsford meets General Zaroff and learns
of Zaroff's "game" → Rainsford is forced to become the "huntee" → Rainsford confronts
Zaroff in the general's bedroom → _____

_____

New ending is consistent with portrayal of characters: "American History"

Elena's character traits: _____

Personality of Elena's mother: _____

Eugene's character traits: _____

Personality of Eugene's mother: _____

New ending is consistent with portrayal of characters: "The Most Dangerous Game"

Rainsford's character traits: _____

Zaroff's character traits: _____

New ending provides a resolution to the conflict:

_____

_____

_____

_____

_____

_____

_____

_____

Now, use your notes to write an alternative ending. Write your ending on a separate piece of
paper. Be sure that your new ending resolves the main conflict in the story.

"The Gift of the Magi" by O. Henry
Writing About the Big Question

Is conflict necessary?

Big Question Vocabulary

amicably	antagonize	appreciate	argument	articulate
compete/competition	controversy	cooperate	differences	equity
grievance	issue	mediate	survival	war/battle

A. *Use one or more words from the list above to complete each sentence.*

1. _____ about hot topics forms the basis of political debates.

2. If you _____ a person, you will likely end up in a conflict.

3. Sometimes it is necessary to engage in a(n) _____ .

4. The goal should be to resolve the problem _____ .

B. *Follow the directions in responding to each of the items below.*

1. Write two sentences describing a time when you entered a conflict.

_____

_____

2. Write two sentences about how you resolved that conflict. Use at least two of the Big Question vocabulary words.

_____

_____

C. *Complete the sentence below. Then, write a short paragraph in which you connect this experience to the Big Question.*

When money is tight, it is hard to show love because _____

_____

_____

_____

_____

All-in-One Workbook
78

Name _____ Date _____

Literary Analysis: Irony and Surprise Ending

Irony is a difference or a contradiction between appearance and reality or between what is expected and what actually happens.

- In **situational irony,** something happens in the story that directly contradicts the expectations of a character or the reader. For example, you would expect that if Jim works hard at his job for a year, he will get a raise. If he gets a pay cut instead, the situation is ironic.
- A **surprise ending** often helps to create situational irony through a turn of events that takes the reader by surprise. To make a surprise ending believable, the author builds clues into the story that make the ending logical.

A. DIRECTIONS: *For each of the following excerpts from "The Gift of the Magi," write **I** in the space provided if the excerpt is ironic. Write **N** if the excerpt is not ironic. On the lines following each item, briefly explain why the excerpt is or is not ironic.*

____ 1. "Tomorrow would be Christmas Day, and she had only $1.87 with which to buy Jim a present. She had been saving every penny she could for months, with this result."

_____

_____

____ 2. "Where she stopped the sign read: 'Mme. Sofronie. Hair Goods of All Kinds.' One flight up Della ran, and collected herself, panting. Madame, large, too white, chilly, hardly looked the 'Sofronie.'"

_____

_____

____ 3. "Grand as the watch was he sometimes looked at it on the sly on account of the old leather strap that he used in place of a chain."

_____

_____

____ 4. "They were expensive combs, she knew, and her heart had simply craved and yearned over them without the least hope of possession. And now they were hers, but the tresses that should have adorned the coveted adornments were gone."

_____

_____

B. DIRECTIONS: *On the following lines, briefly explain the surprise ending in "The Gift of the Magi." Then, explain how O. Henry makes the surprise ending seem logical.*

_____

_____

_____

_____

Name _____ Date _____

"The Gift of the Magi" by O. Henry
Reading: Use Prior Knowledge and Experience
to Make Inferences

An **inference** is an educated guess that you make based on details in a text. In addition to what the author tells you, you can also **use your own prior knowledge and experience** to make inferences.

- As you read, watch movies and plays, and observe the world every day, you gather knowledge and experience.
- When you read something new, look for ways in which the characters and situations resemble ones you have seen before.
- Then, apply that knowledge and experience to make inferences about what you are reading.

Example from "The Gift of the Magi":

Detail from the story: "A furnished flat at $8 per week."

Inference: Della and Jim do not have much money. They have to scrimp and save to get by.

DIRECTIONS: *Use the following chart to record information about the characters listed. Then, make three more inferences about each character based on the details from the story. Some examples are shown.*

Details About Della	Inferences I Can Make About Della
1. She hugs Jim every time he comes home.	Della is deeply in love with her husband.
2. _____	_____
3. _____	_____

Details About Jim	Inferences I Can Make About Jim
1. He greatly values his watch, which was handed down to him.	He has strong feelings for his family.
2. _____	_____
3. _____	_____

Name _____ Date _____

"The Gift of the Magi" by O. Henry
Vocabulary Builder

Word List

cascade   depreciate   discreet   faltered   instigates   prudence

A. DIRECTIONS: *Decide whether each of the following statements is true or false, and write **T** or **F** on the line provided. Then, explain your answer.*

1. A person who *instigates* conflict might be called a "problem solver." _____
_____

2. After 6 years of hard use, a car will *depreciate* in value. _____
_____

3. Only a *discreet* person should be trusted with a secret. _____
_____

4. If a person *faltered*, he or she is likely confident. _____
_____

5. A person who practices *prudence* spends a lot of money. _____
_____

6. A waterfall can be described as a *cascade*. _____
_____

B. WORD STUDY: The prefix *de-* means "down." Use the context of the sentences and what you know about the **Latin prefix *de-*** to explain your answer to each question.

1. If you were to *devalue* a house, what would you do to it?
_____

2. What happens if a king is *deposed*?
_____

"The Interlopers" by Saki
Writing About the Big Question

Is conflict necessary?

Big Question Vocabulary

amicably	antagonize	appreciate	argument	articulate
compete/competition	controversy	cooperate	differences	equity
grievance	issue	mediate	survival	war/battle

A. *Use one or more words from the list above to complete each sentence.*

1. My little brother will _____ me until I pay attention to him.

2. Kemal's mother had to _____ the conflict between him and his sister.

3. Jane was so angry she could not _____ her position or feelings.

4. The _____ between Kate and Bryan was finally resolved.

B. *Follow the directions in responding to each item below.*

1. Tell about a time when you had to cooperate to resolve an argument.

   _____

   _____

2. Explain how you ended the argument. Use at least two of the Big Question vocabulary words.

   _____

   _____

C. *In "The Interlopers," men from feuding families face a situation that makes them rethink their hatred for each other. Complete the sentence below. Then, write a short paragraph in which you connect this experience to the Big Question.*

When a feud has been going on for a long time, the people involved may not know

   _____

   _____

   _____

Name _____ Date _____

Literary Analysis: Irony and Surprise Ending

Irony is a difference or a contradiction between appearance and reality or between what is expected and what actually happens.

- In **situational irony,** something happens in the story that directly contradicts the expectations of a character or the reader. For example, if long-standing enemies suddenly become friends, the situation would be ironic.
- A **surprise ending** often helps to create situational irony through a turn of events that takes the reader by surprise. To make a surprise ending believable, the author builds clues into the story that make the ending logical.

A. DIRECTIONS: *For each of the following excerpts from "The Interlopers," write* **I** *in the space provided if the excerpt is ironic. Write* **N** *if the excerpt is not ironic. On the lines following each item, briefly explain why the excerpt is or is not ironic.*

____ 1. If only on this wild night, in this dark, lone spot, he might come across Georg Znaeym, man to man, with one to witness—that was the wish that was uppermost in his thoughts. And as he stepped round the trunk of a huge beech he came face to face with the man he sought.

_____

_____

____ 2. Both had now given up the useless struggle to free themselves from the mass of wood that held them down.

_____

_____

____ 3. And each prayed a private prayer that his men might be the first to arrive, so that he might be the first to show honorable attention to the enemy that had become a friend.

_____

_____

____ 4. The two raised their voices in a prolonged hunting call.

_____

_____

B. DIRECTIONS: *On the following lines, briefly explain the surprise ending in "The Interlopers." Then, explain how Saki makes the surprise ending seem logical.*

_____

_____

_____

_____

_____

"The Interlopers" by Saki
Reading: Use Prior Knowledge and Experience to Make Inferences

An **inference** is an educated guess that you make based on details in a text. In addition to what the author tells you, you can also **use your own prior knowledge and experience** to make inferences.

- As you read, watch movies and plays, and observe the world every day, you gather knowledge and experience.
- When you read something new, look for ways in which the characters and situations resemble ones you have seen before.
- Then, apply that knowledge and experience to make inferences about what you are reading.

Example from "The Interlopers":

Detail from the story: "Ulrich von Gradwitz patrolled the dark forest in quest of a human enemy."

Inference: If he finds Georg, Ulrich will try to harm him.

DIRECTIONS: *Use the following chart to record information about the characters listed. Then, make three inferences about each character based on the details from the story. Some examples are shown.*

Details About Ulrich

1. He notices that the roebuck are running in an unusual way.

2. _____

_____

3. _____

_____

Inferences I Can Make About Ulrich

He is keenly observant.

_____

_____

_____

_____

Details About Georg

1. He says he cannot drink wine with an enemy.

2. _____

_____

3. _____

_____

Inferences I Can Make About Georg

He is stubborn and proud.

_____

_____

_____

_____

"The Interlopers" by Saki
Vocabulary Builder

Word List

acquiesced   condolences   disputed   feud   interlopers   precipitous

A. DIRECTIONS: *Replace each italicized word or group of words with a word from the Word List. Rewrite the sentence in the space provided.*

1. The movie star hired a security staff to protect her from the news media and other *intruders.* _____

_____

2. Ironically, Georg reassures Ulrich that he will send *expressions of sympathy.* _____

_____

3. The property in dispute is a narrow strip of *sheer, steeply inclined* woodland. _____

_____

4. Georg and Ulrich have been in a long-lasting *disagreement.* _____

_____

5. The families *fought over* the land and hunting rights. _____

_____

6. Neither *gave in* or tried to settle their disagreement civilly. _____

_____

B. WORD STUDY: The prefix *inter-* means "between." Use the context of the sentence and what you know about the Latin prefix *inter-* to explain your answer to each question.

1. Would people from more than one country attend an *international* conference?

_____

2. How would you describe an *interstate* highway?

_____

"The Gift of the Magi" by O. Henry
"The Interlopers" by Saki
Integrated Language Skills: Grammar

Irregular Verbs

Unlike regular verbs, the past tense and past participle of **irregular verbs** are not formed by adding -ed or -d to the present form. Instead, the past tense and past participle are formed in various ways. In some verbs, there is a change of vowels or consonants within the word. Other verbs change both vowels and consonants. Sometimes, the past and the past participle of an irregular verb are identical. In some irregular verbs, though, the past and the past participle have different forms.

Study the forms of the irregular verbs shown in the following chart.

Principal Parts of Irregular Verbs

Present	Present Participle	Past	Past Participle
run	(is) running	ran	(has) run
catch	(is) catching	caught	(has) caught
sit	(is) sitting	sat	(has) sat
fall	(is) falling	fell	(has) fallen
take	(is) taking	took	(has) taken

A. PRACTICE: *On the line provided, write the correct form of the verb in parentheses.*

1. Jim did not know that Della had (selled, sold) her hair.

   _____

2. If you had met Ulrich in the forest, would you have (ran, run) away?

   _____

3. The feud between Ulrich's and Georg's families (began, begun) long ago with a land dispute.

   _____

B. Writing Application: *Read the following sentences and notice the verbs in italics. If the verb is used correctly, write* Correct *in the space provided. If the verb is not used correctly, rewrite the sentence using the correct form.*

1. Although Saki wrote history, novels, and political satire, he is *knowed* especially for his short stories.

   _____

2. Born in Burma as H. H. Munro, he was *bringed* up in England by two aunts.

   _____

3. As a foreign correspondent, he *spended* time in Poland, Russia, and Paris.

   _____

"The Gift of the Magi" by O. Henry

"The Interlopers" by Saki

Integrated Language Skills: Support for Writing a News Story

To gather information for your brief news story, use the following graphic organizer. Jot down some notes that answer the six questions that reporters ask: *Who? What? When? Where? Why? How?*

Questions	Answers
Who?	
What?	
When?	
Where?	
Why?	
How?	

Use the most important, eye-catching details in your notes to write the lead (opening) paragraph of your human-interest news story on the following lines.

_____

_____

_____

_____

_____

_____

_____

On a separate piece of paper, write your revised lead paragraph and choose other details to write the remaining paragraphs of your story.

Name _____ Date _____

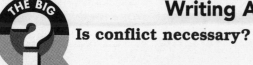

Writing About the Big Question

Is conflict necessary?

Big Question Vocabulary

amicably	antagonize	appreciate	argument	articulate
compete/competition	controversy	cooperate	differences	equity
grievance	issue	mediate	survival	war/battle

A. *Use one or more words from the list above to complete each sentence.*

1. What is another word for *conflict* or *fight*? _____

2. Which word names something you should do when in a conflict? It means "to describe clearly." _____

3. If a person helps two or more people resolve an argument, what word describes what that person has done? _____

B. *Follow the directions in responding to each item below.*

1. Write two sentences describing a controversy at your school or in your town.

   _____

   _____

2. Write two sentences describing the differences in opinion that sparked the controversy. Use at least two Big Question Vocabulary Words in your sentences.

   _____

   _____

C. *In both of these stories, the authors show the modern world in conflict with traditional ways. Complete the sentences below. Then, write a short paragraph in which you connect this experience to the Big Question.*

The modern world sometimes conflicts with traditional ways because _____

When these differences can be resolved, _____

_____

_____

_____

All-in-One Workbook
88

Name _____   Date _____

"The Man to Send Rain Clouds" by Leslie Marmon Silko
"Old Man of the Temple" by R. K. Narayan
Literary Analysis: Setting

The **setting** of a story is the time and place in which it occurs.

- The time may include not only the historical period but also a specific year, season, and hour of day.
- Place may involve not only geographical location but also the social, economic, and cultural environment.

The importance of setting varies from story to story.

- Sometimes, the setting simply furnishes a backdrop for the action. In such a story, the setting could change, but the characters, actions, and events would remain the same.
- Alternatively, the setting can shape the characters and events. For example, in a story set within a Native American culture, characters may make specific decisions and choices based on the rituals and expectations of the culture.
- Setting can play an important role in establishing or intensifying the atmosphere or over-all mood in a story.

DIRECTIONS: *As you read these stories, concentrate on the specific details about setting. List some of these details, and then describe why they are important to the story.*

"The Man to Send Rain Clouds"

1. Details of characters' physical surroundings: _____

   _____

2. Details that reflect the time in which the story takes place: _____

   _____

3. Details that reflect the characters' culture: _____

   _____

4. Overall importance of setting in the story: _____

   _____

"Old Man of the Temple"

5. Details of characters' physical surroundings: _____

   _____

6. Details that reflect the time in which the story takes place: _____

   _____

7. Details that reflect the characters' culture: _____

   _____

8. Overall importance of setting: _____

   _____

Name _____ Date _____

"The Man to Send Rain Clouds" by Leslie Marmon Silko
"Old Man of the Temple" by R. K. Narayan
Vocabulary Builder

Word List

awry   penetrated   perverse   venture

A. DIRECTIONS: *Revise each sentence so that the underlined vocabulary word is used logically. Be sure not to change the vocabulary word.*

1. His determination to break school rules is so <u>perverse</u> that the principal sent him a note of congratulations.

   _____

   _____

2. He was really happy when he discovered that his well-laid plans had gone <u>awry</u>.

   _____

   _____

3. When we saw how promptly they had taken their seats, we were impressed by their <u>venture</u>.

   _____

   _____

4. Her winter jacket is so well lined that the bitingly cold wind <u>penetrated</u> it easily.

   _____

   _____

B. DIRECTIONS: *Write the letter of the word or phrase that is the best antonym (word that means the opposite) for the Word List word.*

___ 1. perverse
   A. beneficial
   B. harmful
   C. useful
   D. ridiculous

___ 2. venture
   A. any action
   B. risky action
   C. safe action
   D. useless action

___ 3. awry
   A. crooked
   B. straight
   C. disastrous
   D. enormous

___ 4. penetrated
   A. went through
   B. did not go through
   C. acted carelessly
   D. carefully prepared

"The Man to Send Rain Clouds" by Leslie Marmon Silko
"Old Man of the Temple" by R. K. Narayan

Integrated Language Skills: Writing to Compare Literary Works

Use this chart to take prewriting notes for your essay comparing and contrasting the way the setting of each story influences the characters and story events.

Points of Comparison/Contrast	"The Man to Send Rain Clouds"	"Old Man of the Temple"
Daily lives of characters		
Cultural values and beliefs		
Effects of setting on characters		

Name _____ Date _____

"**Rules of the Game**" by Amy Tan
Writing About the Big Question

Is conflict necessary?

Big Question Vocabulary

amicably	antagonize	appreciate	argument	articulate
compete/competition	controversy	cooperate	differences	equity
grievance	issue	mediate	survival	war/battle

A. *Use one or more words from the list above to complete each sentence.*

1. Because Mrs. March had no bias, she was able to deal with the students' conflict with _____.

2. The team's _____ for the league championship was challenging.

3. After Amanda explained how she felt, Kyle said, "I _____ your honesty."

4. _____ in the woods without modern conveniences was the goal of the scouts' camping trip.

B. *Follow the directions in responding to each of the items below.*

1. Describe a conflict you were able to mediate with equity.

   _____

   _____

2. Articulate your opinion about a current event or issue.

   _____

   _____

C. *Complete the sentence below. Then, write a short paragraph in which you connect this experience to the Big Question.*

Competition can cause internal conflict because _____

_____

_____

_____

Name _____ Date _____

Literary Analysis: Character and Characterization

A **character** is a person, an animal, or even an object that participates in the action and experiences the events of a literary work. Writers communicate what characters are like through **characterization.** There are two main types of characterization:

- **Direct characterization:** The writer tells readers what a character is like.
- **Indirect characterization:** The writer gives readers clues to a character. The writer might show the character's behavior, present the character's words and thoughts, describe the character's physical appearance, or reveal what other characters say or think about the character. Often when a writer uses indirect characterization, it is up to the reader to draw logical conclusions about the character's personality and motivations.

> The next week I bit back my tongue as we entered the store with the forbidden candies. When my mother finished her shopping, she quietly plucked a small bag of plums from the rack and put it on the counter with the rest of the items.

In this example, we get a glimpse of the characters' personalities through their actions. Meimei's mother rewards her for learning the secret of invisible strength and biting back her tongue.

DIRECTIONS: *On the lines provided, briefly explain how each excerpt from the story helps to characterize one or more of the characters.*

1. My mother imparted her daily truths so she could help my older brothers and me rise above our circumstances.

   _____

   _____

2. When we got home, my mother told Vincent to throw the chess set away. "She not want it. We not want it," she said, tossing her head stiffly to the side with a tight, proud smile.

   _____

   _____

3. At the next tournament, I won again, but it was my mother who wore the triumphant grin. "Lost eight piece this time. Last time was eleven. What I tell you? Better off less!" I was annoyed, but I couldn't say anything.

   _____

   _____

4. My mother would proudly walk with me, visiting many shops, buying very little. "This my daughter Wave-ly Jong," she said to whoever looked her way.

   _____

   _____

"Rules of the Game" by Amy Tan

Reading: Ask Questions to Analyze Cause and Effect

A **cause** is an event, action, or feeling that produces a result. An **effect** is the result produced. As you read, **ask questions to analyze cause and effect.** Examining these relationships helps you follow the logic that moves a story forward. As you read, ask yourself the following questions:

- What happened?
- Why did it happen?
- What happens as a result?

A single cause may produce several effects. For example, a character who is saving to buy a bicycle takes a baby-sitting job with her neighbor's children. This leads to her starting a summer play group and starts her thinking about getting a college degree in early childhood education.

Effects may, in turn, become causes. That same character's successful experiences with young children leads her to volunteer on the pediatric floor of a local hospital.

DIRECTIONS: *Use the cause-and-effect chart below to keep track of events in "Rules of the Game."*

Cause	Effect
1. The Jong family goes to a church Christmas party.	Vincent gets a secondhand chess set.
2. Vincent and Winston play chess a lot.	_____ _____
3. _____ _____	_____ _____
4. _____ _____	_____ _____
5. _____ _____	_____ _____
6. _____ _____	_____ _____
7. _____ _____	_____ _____

Name _____ Date _____

"Rules of the Game" by Amy Tan
Vocabulary Builder

Word List

benevolently   concessions   malodorous   prodigy   pungent   retort

A. DIRECTIONS: *In each item below, think about the meaning of the italicized word, and then answer the question in a complete sentence.*

1. If a dish tastes *pungent,* is it spicy or bland? _____

   _____

2. If you reply to a person with a *retort,* are you speaking sweetly or sharply? _____

   _____

3. You enter a restaurant and notice that the air is *malodorous.* Explain whether or not you would choose to eat there. _____

   _____

4. If a classmate looks at you *benevolently,* do you feel happy or frightened? _____

   _____

5. Would a *prodigy* likely excel or fail? Explain. _____

   _____

6. Are *concessions* given to help or hurt a person? Explain. _____

   _____

B. WORD STUDY: The root *-bene-* means "good" or "well." Use the context of the sentences and what you know about the **Latin root *-bene-*** to explain your answer to each question.

1. Would a charity appreciate a *benefaction*? Why?

   _____

   _____

2. How is studying for an exam *beneficial*?

   _____

   _____

Name _____ Date _____

"The Necklace" by Guy de Maupassant
Writing About the Big Question

Is conflict necessary?

Big Question Vocabulary

amicably	antagonize	appreciate	argument	articulate
compete/competition	controversy	cooperate	differences	equity
grievance	issue	mediate	survival	war/battle

A. *Use one or more words from the list above to complete each sentence.*

1. If you cooperate with someone, any conflicts will likely be resolved _____.

2. It is possible to _____ someone's viewpoint but still disagree with it.

3. If you are fighting for _____, you will likely do anything to win.

4. _____ in opposing forces often leads to a fair argument.

B. *Answer each question using complete sentences. Use at least two Big Question vocabulary words.*

1. Is conflict always necessary? Why or why not?

   _____

   _____

2. What can we learn from conflict? How?

   _____

   _____

C. *In "The Necklace," a woman is jealous of people with greater wealth and social standing. Complete the sentence below. Then, write a short paragraph in which you connect this experience to the Big Question.*

Jealousy can lead to many conflicts. For example, _____

_____

_____

_____

"The Necklace" by Guy de Maupassant
Literary Analysis: Character and Characterization

A **character** is a person, an animal, or even an object that participates in the action and experiences the events of a literary work. Writers communicate what characters are like through **characterization.** There are two main types of characterization:

- **Direct characterization:** The writer tells readers what a character is like.
- **Indirect characterization:** The writer gives readers clues to a character. The writer might show the character's behavior, present the character's words and thoughts, describe the character's physical appearance, or reveal what other characters say or think about the character. Often, when a writer uses indirect characterization, it is up to the reader to draw logical conclusions about the character's personality and motivations.

When she sat down to dinner at her round table with its three-day-old cloth, and watched her husband opposite her lift the lid of the soup tureen and exclaim, delighted: "Ah, a good homemade beef stew! There's nothing better . . ." she would visualize elegant dinners with gleaming silver amid tapestried walls peopled by knights and ladies and exotic birds in a fairy forest.

This passage gives readers a glimpse of the personalities of both Madame and Monsieur Loisel through the characters' thoughts and words.

DIRECTIONS: *On the lines provided, briefly explain how each excerpt from the story helps to characterize one or more of the characters.*

1. She suffered constantly, feeling that all the attributes of a gracious life, every luxury, should rightly have been hers. _____

   _____

   _____

2. She looked at him, irritated, and said impatiently:
   "I haven't a thing to wear. How could I go?" _____

   _____

   _____

3. "Well, all right, then. I'll give you four hundred francs. But try to get something really nice."

   _____

   _____

4. Madame Forestier said in a faintly waspish tone: "You could have brought it back a little sooner! I might have needed it." _____

   _____

   _____

5. Madame Loisel started to tremble. Should she speak to her? Yes, certainly she should. And now that she had paid everything back, why shouldn't she tell her the whole story?

   _____

   _____

Name _____ Date _____

"The Necklace" by Guy de Maupassant
Reading: Ask Questions to Analyze Cause and Effect

A **cause** is an event, action, or feeling that produces a result. An **effect** is the result produced. As you read, **ask questions to analyze cause and effect.** Examining these relationships helps you follow the logic that moves a story forward. As you read, ask yourself:

- What happened?
- Why did it happen?
- What happens as a result?

A single cause may produce several effects. Effects may, in turn, become causes.

A. DIRECTIONS: *Use the cause-and-effect chart below to keep track of events in "The Necklace."*

Cause	Effect
1. Monsieur Loisel receives an invitation to a reception at the Ministry.	Madame Loisel complains that she has nothing to wear.
2.	
3.	
4.	
5.	
6.	

B. DIRECTIONS: *Is the cause of the catastrophe that overtakes Madame Loisel solely of her own making? Or does the author suggest that she is, to some extent, the product of a vain and materialistic society? Discuss your response on the lines below.*

_____

_____

_____

_____

_____

"The Necklace" by Guy de Maupassant
Vocabulary Builder

Word List

attributes   dejection   disheveled   profoundly   resplendent   rueful

A. DIRECTIONS: *In each item below, think about the meaning of the italicized word, and then answer the question in a complete sentence.*

1. How would a person with a *disheveled* appearance look? _____
_____

2. If you were *rueful* about one of your actions, how would you feel? _____
_____

3. Describe something that might move you *profoundly*, and tell how you would feel. _____
_____

4. Describe a *resplendent* scene that would impress you. _____
_____

5. What are your *attributes*? _____
_____

6. How would a person who is experiencing *dejection* likely act? _____
_____

B. WORD STUDY: The root *-jec(t)-* means "to throw." Use the context of the sentences and what you know about the **Latin root *-jec(t)-*** to explain your answer to each question.

1. What would happen to an item that was *rejected?*
_____

2. What do you do when you *project* into the future?
_____

All-in-One Workbook
99

"Rules of the Game" by Amy Tan
"The Necklace" by Guy de Maupassant
Integrated Language Skills: Grammar

Subjects and Predicates

Every sentence is made of two parts, a subject and a predicate. The complete **subject** includes all the words that tell whom or what a sentence is about. The complete **predicate** includes all the words that tell what the subject of a sentence does or is. The simple subject and simple predicate, underlined below, are the noun and verb that make a sentence complete. A subject and its verb should always agree in number.

Subject	Predicate
The <u>loss</u> of the necklace	<u>is</u> a great blow to the Loisels.
Many curious <u>people</u>	<u>gather</u> to watch Waverly play chess.

A. DIRECTIONS: *Write the answers to each of the following questions in the lines provided.*

1. What is the *subject* of a sentence?

   _____

   _____

2. Write an original sentence and underline the complete subject.

   _____

   _____

3. What is the *predicate* of a sentence?

   _____

   _____

4. Write an original sentence and underline the complete predicate.

   _____

   _____

5. What general rule applies to the agreement of subjects and predicates?

   _____

   _____

B. DIRECTIONS: *Draw a vertical line in each sentence to separate the subject from the predicate.*

1. Guy de Maupassant wrote "The Necklace."
2. As the writer of the story, de Maupassant examines the results of vanity.
3. The main characters borrow a necklace.
4. They are devastated when the necklace is lost.
5. The Loisels replace the necklace instead of telling the woman her necklace has been lost.
6. They learn later in the story that the original necklace was not real.

"The Necklace" by Guy de Maupassant
"Rules of the Game" by Amy Tan

Integrated Language Skills:
Support for Writing a Written Presentation

Use the lines below to jot notes about the issues the characters face and your suggestions for resolving them.

Issue 1: _____

_____

My suggestions on how to resolve this issue: _____

_____

_____

_____

Issue 2: _____

_____

My suggestions on how to resolve this issue: _____

_____

_____

_____

Issue 3: _____

_____

My suggestions on how to resolve this issue: _____

_____

_____

_____

Issue 4: _____

_____

My suggestions on how to resolve this issue: _____

_____

_____

_____

Now, use your notes to write your written presentation. Make a special effort not to favor one character over the other. Keep your tone neutral, and revise any language that sounds biased in favor of one of the characters.

"Blues Ain't No Mockin Bird" by Toni Cade Bambara
Writing About the Big Question

Is conflict necessary?

Big Question Vocabulary

amicably	antagonize	appreciate	argument	articulate
compete/competition	controversy	cooperate	differences	equity
grievance	issue	mediate	survival	war/battle

A. *Use one or more words from the list above to complete each sentence.*

1. If you _____ with someone, you try to win.

2. If you and another have _____ in opinion, you are likely to have conflict.

3. To _____ an argument, you must not be biased toward one side.

4. _____ resolving an argument can be achieved in many ways.

5. _____ often arises around social issues.

B. *Follow the directions in responding to each of the items below.*

1. Describe a time when you were antagonized.

_____

_____

2. Tell about how you resolved the conflict with the person who antagonized you.

_____

_____

C. *Complete the sentence below. Then, write a short paragraph in which you connect this experience to the Big Question.*

People will fight to protect _____

because _____

_____

_____

_____

All-in-One Workbook
102

"Blues Ain't No Mockin Bird" by Toni Cade Bambara
Literary Analysis: Dialogue and Dialect

Dialogue is a conversation between or among characters in a literary work. In prose, dialogue is usually set off by quotation marks, and a new paragraph indicates a change in speaker. Writers use dialogue to

- reveal character traits and relationships.
- advance the action of the plot and to develop the conflict.
- add variety, color, and realism to narratives.

To make characters even more vivid and to help establish a story's setting, authors may write dialogue that reflects characters' dialect. **Dialect** is a way of speaking that is common to people of a particular region or group. A dialect's words, pronunciations, and grammar are different from those used in the standard form of a language. In the dialect of the American South, for example, speakers often do not pronounce the *g* at the ends of *-ing* words. Dialect often makes characters' personalities, as well as the setting of a story, more vivid.

A. DIRECTIONS: *On the lines provided, briefly explain what each passage of dialogue from the story reveals about the speakers.*

1. "Now, aunty," Camera said, pointin' the thing straight at her.
   "Your mama and I are not related."

   _____

   _____

2. "So here comes . . . this person . . . with a camera, takin pictures of the man and the minister and the woman. Takin' pictures of the man in his misery about to jump, cause life so bad and people been messin' with him so bad. This person takin' up the whole roll of film practically. But savin a few, of course."

   _____

   _____

3. "You standin in the misses' flower bed," say Granddaddy. "This is our own place."

   _____

B. DIRECTIONS: *On the lines below, rewrite each of the passages in dialect in Standard English.*

1. Granny wasn't sayin nuthin.

   _____

2. Me and Cathy were waitin, too, cause Granny always got something to say.

   _____

3. And Granny just stare at the twins till their faces swallow up the eager and they don't even care any more about the man jumpin.

   _____

   _____

Name _____ Date _____

Reading: Visualize the Action to Analyze Cause and Effect

A **cause** is an event, an action, or a feeling that produces a result. An **effect** is the result produced. When reading a story, **visualize the action to analyze cause and effect.** Examining these relationships helps you follow the logic that drives the plot of a story.

- Based on details in the text, picture the setting, the characters, and the action.
- Use the details of your mental picture to help you identify the relationships between actions and events.

DIRECTIONS: *Use the lines provided to answer the following questions about cause-and-effect relationships in "Blues Ain't No Mockin Bird."*

1. **A.** Why does Granny tell the children a story about a photographer taking pictures of a man about to jump from a bridge?

   _____

   _____

   B. What is the effect of this story?

   _____

   _____

2. **A.** Why does the male hawk suddenly appear in the story?

   _____

   _____

   B. What effect does the hawk have on Smilin and Camera?

   _____

   _____

   C. How does Granddaddy Cain react to the hawk's appearance?

   _____

   _____

3. **A.** Why does Granddaddy Cain smash the reporters' camera?

   _____

   _____

   B. What effect does this action have on the reporters?

   _____

   _____

"Blues Ain't No Mockin Bird" by Toni Cade Bambara
Vocabulary Builder

Word List

formality   ladle   raggedy   reckless   reels   stalks

A. DIRECTIONS: *In each item below, think about the meaning of the italicized word, and then answer the question.*

1. If your older brother's driving is *reckless*, would you be nervous about riding in a car with him? Explain.

_____

_____

2. If someone treats you with *formality*, would your overall impression be of politeness or rudeness? Explain.

_____

_____

3. If your clothes are *raggedy*, would you wear them to dress up? Explain.

_____

_____

4. When would you use a *ladle*?

_____

_____

5. If a cat *stalks* a mouse, what is it doing?

_____

_____

6. If someone *reels* from bad news, what is his reaction like?

_____

_____

B. WORD STUDY: The suffix *-ity* means "having the quality of." Use the context of the sentences and what you know about the **Latin suffix *-ity*** to explain your answer to each question.

1. When a show is known for its *theatricality*, how could it be described?

_____

_____

2. If an issue is known for its *gravity*, how would you describe it?

_____

_____

"The Invalid's Story" by Mark Twain
Writing About the Big Question

Is conflict necessary?

Big Question Vocabulary

amicably	antagonize	appreciate	argument	articulate
compete/competition	controversy	cooperate	differences	equity
grievance	issue	mediate	survival	war/battle

A. *Use one or more words from the list above to complete each sentence.*

1. The _____ between the boys' and the girls' quiz teams was close.

2. Jason decided to _____ with his lab partner's plan for conducting the experiment.

3. The _____ of time arose as a result of the amount of studying Caleb needed to do.

4. The school board discussed the _____ about having co-ed gym classes.

B. *Follow the directions in responding to each item below.*

1. Write two sentences describing a reaction you appreciated during a conflict.

_____

_____

2. Write two sentences telling how you deal with competition. Use at least two of the Big Question vocabulary words.

_____

_____

C. *In "The Invalid's Story," the two main characters try to resolve a problem but do not have all the facts. Complete the sentence below. Then, write a short paragraph in which you connect this experience to the Big Question.*

A lack of information can lead to a humorous conflict; for example, _____

_____

_____

_____

"The Invalid's Story" by Mark Twain

Literary Analysis: Dialogue and Dialect

Dialogue is a conversation between or among characters in a literary work. In prose, dialogue is usually set off by quotation marks, and a new paragraph indicates a change in speaker. Writers use dialogue to

- reveal character traits and relationships.
- advance the action of the plot and to develop the conflict.
- add variety, color, and realism to narratives.

To make characters even more vivid and to help establish a story's setting, authors may write dialogue that reflects characters' dialect. **Dialect** is a way of speaking that is common to people of a particular region or group. A dialect's words, pronunciations, and grammar are different from those used in the standard form of a language. In the dialect of the American South, for example, speakers often do not pronounce the *g* at the ends of *-ing* words. Dialect often makes characters' personalities, as well as the setting of a story, more vivid.

A. DIRECTIONS: *Briefly explain what each passage of dialogue from the story reveals about the speaker.*

1. "We're all right, now! I reckon we've got the Commodore this time. I judge I've got the stuff here that'll take the tuck out of him."

   _____

   _____

2. "Cap, I'm a-going to chance him once more—just this once; and if we don't fetch him this time, the thing for us to do, is to just throw up the sponge and withdraw from the canvass. That's the way *I* put it up."

   _____

   _____

   _____

B. DIRECTIONS: *Use Standard English to rewrite each of the passages in dialect.*

1. "'Man that is born of woman is of few days and far between, as Scriptur' says.'"

   _____

   _____

2. "'Yes'ndeedy, it's awful solemn and cur'us; but we've all got to go, one time or another; they ain't no getting around it.'"

   _____

   _____

"The Invalid's Story" by Mark Twain

Reading: Visualize the Action to Analyze Cause and Effect

A **cause** is an event, action, or feeling that produces a result. An **effect** is the result produced. When reading a story, **visualize the action to analyze cause and effect.** Examining these relationships helps you follow the logic that drives the plot of a story.

- Based on details in the text, picture the setting, the characters, and the action.
- Use the details of your mental picture to help you identify the relationships between actions and events.

A. DIRECTIONS: *Use the lines provided to answer the following questions about cause-and-effect relationships in "The Invalid's Story."*

1. What is the effect on the narrator of his friend's death?

   _____

2. A. What causes the narrator to rush out from the eating room to the express car?

   _____

   B. What effect, unknown to the narrator at the time, results from confusion about the long white-pine boxes that are to be shipped by train?

   _____

3. As the train departs, a stranger places a package of Limburger cheese on one end of the coffin-box. What are the effects of this event?

   _____

   _____

4. A. What causes an evil odor to spread throughout the express car?

   _____

   B. What effects does the odor have on the narrator and the expressman?

   _____

B. DIRECTIONS: *Which part of the story created the most vivid impression in you? Describe and explain your choice on the lines below.*

_____

_____

_____

_____

_____

_____

Name _____ Date _____

"The Invalid's Story" by Mark Twain
Vocabulary Builder

Word List

deleterious   desultory   judicious   prodigious   placidly   ominous

A. DIRECTIONS: *In each item below, think about the meaning of the italicized word, and then answer the question.*

1. Describe someone who is acting *placidly*.

   _____

2. Does weather with *deleterious* effects tend to benefit or harm a building's exterior? Explain.

   _____

3. Would you ask advice from a person with a reputation for offering *judicious* advice? Explain.

   _____

4. How would you feel if you were climbing a *prodigious* mountain?

   _____

5. Would you choose a new computer in a *desultory* way?

   _____

6. Describe something that is *ominous*.

   _____

B. WORD STUDY: The suffix *-ous* means "like" or "pertaining to." Use the context of the sentences and what you know about the **Latin suffix *-ous*** (or ***-ious*** or ***-uous***) to explain your answer to each question.

1. If a person is *famous*, what does he have?

   _____

2. If a morning is *glorious*, what would the weather likely be?

   _____

Name _____ Date _____

"Blues Ain't No Mockin Bird" by Toni Cade Bambara
"The Invalid's Story" by Mark Twain
Integrated Language Skills: Grammar

Active and Passive Voice

A. DIRECTIONS: *Write the answers to each of the following questions on the lines provided.*

1. What is the *active voice*?

_____

_____

2. Write an original sentence using the active voice.

_____

_____

3. What is the *passive voice*?

_____

_____

4. Write an original sentence using the passive voice.

_____

_____

5. What general rule applies to using the active and passive voices?

_____

_____

B. DIRECTIONS: *Underline the verb or verbs in each sentence. Tell whether it is in the active or passive voice.*

1. "Blues Ain't No Mockin Bird" was written by Toni Cade Bambara.

_____

2. Mark Twain wrote "The Invalid's Story."

_____

3. Many short stories have been written by Mark Twain.

_____

4. *Tom Sawyer* and *Huckleberry Finn* name his most noted novels.

_____

5. Toni Cade Bambara not only wrote stories, she also made movies.

_____

Name _____ Date _____

"Blues Ain't No Mockin Bird" by Toni Cade Bambara
"The Invalid's Story" by Mark Twain

Integrated Language Skills: Support for Writing an Informal Letter

For your informal letter, use the lines below to jot down notes under each heading.

Personality Traits of This Character	Events and Details the Character Observed
_____	_____
_____	_____
_____	_____
_____	_____
_____	_____
_____	_____
_____	_____
_____	_____
_____	_____
_____	_____
_____	_____
_____	_____
_____	_____
_____	_____
_____	_____
_____	_____
_____	_____
_____	_____
_____	_____
_____	_____

Now, use your notes to write your informal letter. Be sure that the details you include and the language you use are consistent with the personality traits you have listed for the character.

Name _____ Date _____

"The Scarlet Ibis" by James Hurst
"The Golden Kite, the Silver Wind" by Ray Bradbury

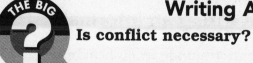

Writing About the Big Question

Is conflict necessary?

Big Question Vocabulary

amicably	antagonize	appreciate	argument	articulate
compete/competition	controversy	cooperate	differences	equity
grievance	issue	mediate	survival	war/battle

A. *Use one or more words from the list above to complete each sentence.*

1. It is important to _____ an argument's strengths and weaknesses.

2. If you carefully _____ your argument, you are likely to be better understood.

3. Resolving a(n) _____ before it escalates can lead to a more positive outcome.

4. Some governments see no other resolution to a conflict than _____.

B. *Follow the directions in responding to each item below.*

1. Write about a conflict in a story you have read. Use at least two of the Big Question vocabulary words.

_____

_____

2. Explain how the conflict was resolved. Use at least two of the Big Question vocabulary words.

_____

_____

C. *In both of these stories, competitiveness leads to conflict. Complete the sentences below. Then, write a sentence in which you connect this experience to the Big Question.*

Some people like to compete because _____

To prevent a competition from turning into a conflict, you might _____

_____

_____

_____

"The Scarlet Ibis" by James Hurst
"The Golden Kite, the Silver Wind" by Ray Bradbury
Literary Analysis: Symbolism and Allegory

A **symbol** is a person, a place, a thing, or an event that represents both itself and a larger idea or feeling. **Symbolism** is the use of symbols in literature. For example, a writer might use a journey as a symbol for the life of a human being.

An **allegory** is a poem or story that has parallel literal and symbolic meanings. On the literal level, the story appears simply as it is told. On the symbolic level, however, every element in the story—including the characters, events, descriptions, and features of the setting—has a symbolic meaning. While an allegory can be understood on the literal level, its full meaning is clear only on the symbolic level. Often, allegories may seem less realistic than nonallegorical works, and they may shed light on current events.

DIRECTIONS: *After you have read the selections, think about which of each work's details and events may be symbolic or allegorical. Then, read these key passages from the stories, and answer the questions that follow.*

"The Scarlet Ibis"

1. That summer, the summer of 1918, was blighted. In May and June there was no rain and the crops withered, curled up, then died under the thirsty sun.

   What is symbolic about the weather in this passage?

   _____

   _____

   _____

2. For a long long time, it seemed forever, I lay there crying, sheltering my fallen scarlet ibis from the heresy of rain.

   How is the symbolism in this passage related to a central theme or insight in the story?

   _____

   _____

   _____

"The Golden Kite, the Silver Wind"

3. And on every night of the year the inhabitants of the Town of the Kite could hear the good clear wind sustaining them. And those in the Town of the Wind could hear the kite singing, whispering, rising, and beautifying them.

   How does this outcome suggest the moral lesson to be drawn from the allegory in this story?

   _____

   _____

   _____

"The Scarlet Ibis" by James Hurst
"The Golden Kite, the Silver Wind" by Ray Bradbury
Vocabulary Builder

Word List

imminent   infallibility   precariously   ravenous   spurn

A. DIRECTIONS: *Revise each sentence so that the underlined vocabulary word is used logically. Be sure not to change the vocabulary word.*

1. A thunderstorm appears to be <u>imminent</u>, so we have decided to stay in the pool.

   _____

2. Josh made so many errors on the math test that we marveled at his <u>infallibility</u>.

   _____

3. A baby spider monkey is dangling <u>precariously</u> from the top of that tall tree, so we are not worried about its safety.

   _____

   _____

4. That tiger ate so little meat! It must have been <u>ravenous</u>.

   _____

5. To <u>spurn</u> a fellow guest at a party is a good way to make a new friend.

   _____

B. DIRECTIONS: *Write the letter of the word or phrase that means the opposite of the Word List word.*

___ 1. precariously
  A. dangerously
  B. securely
  C. insecurely
  D. ridiculously

___ 2. infallibility
  A. good behavior
  B. success
  C. probable failure
  D. impossibility

___ 3. ravenous
  A. polite
  B. full
  C. nervous
  D. pleasant

___ 4. spurn
  A. welcome
  B. reject
  C. introduce
  D. insult

"The Scarlet Ibis" by James Hurst
"The Golden Kite, the Silver Wind" by Ray Bradbury

Integrated Language Skills: Writing to Compare Literary Works

Use a chart like the one shown to make prewriting notes for your essay comparing and contrasting the use of symbolism in the two stories.

Points of Comparison/Contrast	"The Scarlet Ibis"	"The Golden Kite, the Silver Wind"
Message or lesson expressed in story		
Use of symbols to develop message		
If symbols were omitted, how would the message change?		

Knowledge Understanding, performed by Tavi Fields

We're hit with **statistics**, (numbers) created from patterns of some knowledge

Are we equipped with

The tools to **interpret,** convert it to understanding?

To understanding . . .

In life we learn many lessons

Obtain different **information** then we make **connections**

So we can see the relations and we gain perspective

Gotta read between the lines gotta play detective

And there's a process between taking something in as a **concept**

And making it a **feeling** you can touch like an object

Except it's a trigger that's inside that's your **instinct**

That's your **senses** on automatic you won't sink

If you trust that anchor in happiness and in anger

It's your guardian angel when you're safe or in danger

Like the difference in leaving a mark or branding

I guess knowledge ain't the same as understanding

(C'mon now help me out)

Well, knowledge plus understanding equals wisdom

And it can come from many different places

I believe in many truths don't think there is one

And that's because I've been in many different spaces (×2)

Please let me **clarify** let me make it clear

You gotta analyze what goes in your ears

Eyes nose mouth and what you touch

East west north south yo listen up

Everything in a textbook ain't always **fact**

You gotta do your **research** from front to back

Don't rely on just one source use many **sources**

Relying on one force? Use many forces

Continued

Power is endless remember these words when you feel defenseless

The more you know the less you gotta ride the fences

And when you understand that's focused lenses

Nod with your head if you **comprehend** this

(Yeah, Yo . . .)

Knowledge plus understanding equals wisdom

And it can come from many different places

I believe in many truths don't think there is one

And that's because I've been in many different spaces (×2)

I like being a nerd love reading and writing words

I live for nouns and verbs some say it's for the birds

And yes I wanna fly so I can touch the sky

I may not get as high but first I gotta try

We all got a light inside let's get bright

Let's share some advice let's give some **insight**

I'm serious don't fear ask questions if you're curious

Unlock the code it ain't gotta be mysterious

I ain't even being specific it's **ambiguous**

To what kind of knowledge that I'm referencing you figure it

Out for yourself and relate it to your experience

And sometimes you'll have to sacrifice your innocence

(C'mon)

Knowledge plus understanding equals wisdom

And it can come from many different places

I believe in many truths don't think there is one

And that's because I've been in many different spaces (×2)

Song Title: **Knowledge Understanding**
Artist / Performed by Tavi Fields
Lyrics by Tavi Fields
Music composed by Mike Pandolfo, Wonderful
Produced by Mike Pandolfo, Wonderful
Executive Producer: Keith London, Defined Mind

Unit 3: Types of Nonfiction
Big Question Vocabulary—1

The Big Question: Is knowledge the same as understanding?

Most people have had the experience of not fully understanding something. Sometimes this happens even when you have knowledge of facts.

ambiguous: unclear; having more than one meaning

clarify: to make something clearer and easier to understand

comprehend: to understand something that is complicated or difficult

concept: an idea of how something is or how something should be done

information: facts or details about something

DIRECTIONS: *Your teachers might as well be speaking a foreign language. You just do not understand! Use all of the vocabulary words to ask your teachers to explain their statements again and in more detail.*

The compounds combine to form a chemical reaction and ignite spontaneously.

1.

The health of the ecosystem is critical to the health of each species living within the ecosystem.

2.

The longest side of a right triangle is *always* directly across from the 90 degree angle. This side is called the hypotenuse.

3.

Unit 3: Types of Nonfiction
Big Question Vocabulary—2

The Big Question: Is knowledge the same as understanding?

Most students have had the experience of gathering data and ideas for a report or project. In the case of a complicated topic, students often must pore over the data they have gathered in order to gain understanding.

fact: a piece of information that is known to be true

interpret: to understand something to have a particular meaning

research: to study or investigate something in detail

sources: people, books, or documents that supply you with information

statistics: a set of numbers that represent facts or measurements

DIRECTIONS: *Write some guidelines for a young friend who is doing his first research project and is unsure how to research his topic. Use all of the vocabulary words in your instructions, and feel free to explain them to your young friend.*

1.
2.
3.
4.

Unit 3: Types of Nonfiction
Big Question Vocabulary—3

The Big Question: Is knowledge the same as understanding?

One way of getting information is experiencing it for ourselves. The only way to know if you like chocolate is to taste it. Similarly, we should pay attention to feelings, or "vibes," that we get about situations or people.

connection: the process or result of joining two or more things together

feeling: an opinion or a belief about something that is influenced by emotions

insight: clear or deep perception or understanding of something

instinct: the natural ability to think, behave, or react in a particular way without learning it or thinking about it first

sensory: involving one or more of the five senses: taste, touch, hearing, sight, and smell

DIRECTIONS: *Write your thoughts in a situation where you had a strong feeling about something but couldn't really explain why. Use all of the vocabulary words.*

Unit 3: Types of Nonfiction
Applying the Big Question

The Big Question: Is knowledge the same as understanding?

DIRECTIONS: *Complete the chart below to apply what you have learned about knowledge and understanding. One row has been completed for you.*

Example	What facts and information the author had	What knowledge the author gained	What the author came to understand	What I Learned
From Literature	In "On Summer," the author's friend has cancer.	Her friend faced life courageously.	We understand life better when others share their knowledge and experience.	Taking the time to understand others gives life more meaning.
From Literature				
From Science				
From Social Studies				
From Real Life				

Rebecca Walker
Listening and Viewing

Segment 1: Meet Rebecca Walker
- What early experiences with literature inspired Rebecca Walker to become a writer?
- What is your favorite piece of literature, and why is it important to you? Explain.

_____

_____

_____

_____

Segment 2: Types of Nonfiction
- How can music influence other art forms, especially literature?
- How do you think the emergence of hip-hop has influenced the nonfiction literature that people write today and will write in the future?

_____

_____

_____

_____

Segment 3: The Writing Process
- Which method in Rebecca Walker's writing process would you most likely adopt? Why?

_____

_____

_____

_____

Segment 4: The Rewards of Writing
- What does Rebecca Walker want to convey to young people who read her writing?
- Why do you think it is important for young people to be well-informed about current events?

_____

_____

_____

_____

Learning About Nonfiction

Three important types of nonfiction are essays, articles, and speeches. An **essay** examines and discusses a focused topic, often including the writer's personal viewpoints. In an **article,** a writer gives information about a specific topic, person, or event. In a **speech,** a speaker addresses a topic in front of a live audience. Like essays and articles, speeches may be informative, persuasive, or entertaining.

In nonfiction, just as in fiction, the author's style and tone are important elements. A writer's **style** is the particular way that he or she uses language. Here are some factors that contribute to a writer's distinctive style:

- level of language (formal vs. dialect or slang)
- use of figurative language (simile, metaphor, personification, hyperbole, symbol)
- diction, or word choice
- sentence patterns (long or short, variety in types of sentences, repetition)
- sensory imagery

The **tone** of a work is the author's attitude toward the subject matter, the characters, or the audience of readers or listeners. A work's tone can often be summed up in one word: *playful, solemn, mysterious, ominous, personal,* or *enthusiastic.* Be alert to shifts in tone. Different parts of a single work may deliberately exhibit different tones.

DIRECTIONS: *Circle the letter of the answer that best matches each numbered item.*

1. the style of a letter you write to your local school board
   A. formal   B. chatty   C. slangy

2. the tone of a birthday card you write to your little sister
   A. playful   B. scholarly   C. pessimistic

3. the tone of a speech urging support for a candidate for public office
   A. relaxed   B. persuasive   C. hesitant

4. the style of an essay focusing on one of your childhood experiences
   A. formal   B. informal   C. neutral

5. the tone of an after-dinner speech at an awards ceremony
   A. solemn   B. entertaining   C. poetic

6. the style of a descriptive essay focusing on a field of sunflowers in bloom
   A. sensory   B. persuasive   C. narrative

7. the style of a letter to a childhood friend who now lives in a foreign country
   A. complex   B. remote   C. conversational

8. the tone of an article summarizing the Civil War for high school students
   A. reflective   B. factual   C. humorous

Name _____ Date _____

"Before Hip-Hop Was Hip-Hop" by Rebecca Walker
Model Selection: Nonfiction

An **essay** is a brief work of nonfiction that discusses a focused topic and often includes the writer's personal experiences and opinions. An essayist's **style,** or distinctive way of using language, often reflects his or her personality. The **tone** of the essay, or the writer's attitude toward the subject matter and the audience, is also key to understanding an essay.

Essays can be classified by the author's **purpose,** or reason for writing. A **narrative** essay tells a story of actual events or the life experiences of an individual. A **descriptive** essay builds an overall impression of a person, an object, or an experience by using images that appeal to the senses. An **expository** essay provides information, discusses ideas, or explains a process. A **persuasive** essay attempts to convince readers to take a course of action or adopt the writer's viewpoint. A **reflective** essay expresses the writer's thoughts and feelings in response to a personal experience or to an idea.

DIRECTIONS: *Read the following passages from "Before Hip-Hop Was Hip-Hop." In the space provided in the chart, comment briefly on the style, tone, or purpose of each passage.*

Passage from the Essay	Comments on Style, Tone, or Purpose
1. I noted what they wore and how they wore it: the razor sharp creases of their Jordache jeans, the spotless sneakers with the laces left loose and untied.	
2. Intuitively, kids were making a community where there was none; we were affirming our sameness in a world that seemed to only emphasize our difference.	
3. I hope they will marvel at the fact that in the early days of hip-hop, young people were making it up as they went along, following their hearts, following what felt good. I hope they will think about what it takes to create culture that is unique and transcendent and honest, and I hope they will begin to dream about creating a new world for themselves.	

Name _____ Date _____

"A Celebration of Grandfathers" by Rudolfo A. Anaya
Writing About the Big Question

Is knowledge the same as understanding?

Big Question Vocabulary

ambiguous	clarify	comprehend	concept	connection
fact	feeling	information	insight	instinct
interpret	research	senses/sensory	sources	statistics

A. *Use one or more words from the list above to complete each sentence.*

1. The narrator describes his deep _____ to his grandfather.

2. In his essay, Anaya tries to _____ his knowledge of his grandfather so that we can understand who he was.

3. Facts about people's lives can _____ our understanding of them.

4. Megan's _____ for her aunt had more to do with her understanding of her than with what she actually knew about the mysterious relative.

B. *Follow the directions in responding to each item below.*

1. List two facts you know about someone you like and care about.

   _____

   _____

2. Write two sentences telling how the facts you listed above help you understand that person. Use at least two of the Big Question vocabulary words.

   _____

   _____

C. *"A Celebration of Grandfathers" explains how the author's grandfather and people of his generation lived and what they valued. Complete the sentence below. Then, write a short paragraph in which you connect this experience to the Big Question.*

Knowing what people do and how they live can give insight into who they are because

_____

_____

_____

_____

_____

_____

Name _____ Date _____

"A Celebration of Grandfathers" by Rudolfo Anaya

Literary Analysis: Style

An author's **style** is his or her unique way of writing. Style includes every feature of a writer's use of language. Some elements that contribute to an author's style are

- **Diction:** the kinds of words the author uses.
- **Syntax:** the way in which the author arranges words in sentences.
- **Tone:** the author's attitude toward his or her audience or subject.

A writer's diction and syntax might be described as formal or informal, technical or ordinary, sophisticated or down-to-earth. A writer's tone might be described as serious or playful, friendly or distant, sympathetic or scathing.

DIRECTIONS: *Consider the diction and syntax in the italicized passages from "A Celebration of Grandfathers" in the left-hand column. Then write notes or a sentence in the right-hand column to describe the tone produced by these features of Anaya's style.*

Passage	Tone
1. The old ones had looked deep into *the web that connects all animate and inanimate forms of life*, and they recognized the *great design* of the creation.	1. _____ _____ _____
2. Their faith shone in their eyes; it was in the *strength of their grip*, in the *creases time wove into their faces.*	2. _____ _____ _____
3. All this they passed on to the young, *so that a new generation would know what they had known, so the string of life would not be broken.*	3. _____ _____ _____
4. After he had covered my wells with the cool mud from the irrigation ditch, my grandfather calmly said: *"Know where you stand."*	4. _____ _____ _____
5. *He was a man; he died.* Not in his valley, but nevertheless cared for by his sons and daughters and flocks of grandchildren.	5. _____ _____ _____

Name _____ Date _____

"A Celebration of Grandfathers" by Rudolfo Anaya
Reading: Generate Prior Questions to Identify Main Idea and Details

The **main idea** is the central message, insight, or opinion in a work of nonfiction. **Supporting details** are the pieces of evidence that a writer uses to prove the main idea. These details can include facts, statistics, quotations, or anecdotes. To **identify the main idea and supporting details** in a work, **generate questions prior to reading.** Before you read, you can ask yourself questions such as

- Why did the author choose this title?
- How might events in the author's life influence his or her attitude toward the subject?

As you read, look for details that answer those questions and point to the main idea.

A. DIRECTIONS: *Answer the following questions to guide your reading of "A Celebration of Grandfathers."*

1. Consider the connotations or associations of the word *celebration* in Rudolfo Anaya's title. What expectations does this title create in you for the content and tone of the essay?

   _____

   _____

2. In the opening paragraph, Anaya uses a greeting in Spanish: "Buenos días le de Dios, abuelo." What does this greeting lead you to expect about the way in which elders were treated in the traditional culture in which Anaya grew up?

   _____

   _____

3. Anaya, who is considered the father of Chicano literature, has called himself "an oral story-teller" who now tells his tales "on the printed page." What does this self-characterization lead you to expect about the structure and content of his essay?

   _____

   _____

B. DIRECTIONS: *In an essay celebrating grandfathers, what kind of main idea might you expect? What sorts of supporting details might you find in such an essay? Support your answer with examples from your own experience or from your reading.*

_____

_____

_____

_____

_____

"A Celebration of Grandfathers" by Rudolfo Anaya
Vocabulary Builder

Word List

absurdity   anguish   nurturing   permeate   perplexes   revival

A. DIRECTIONS: *Revise each sentence so that the underlined vocabulary word is used logically. Be sure not to change the vocabulary word.*

1. After solving the problem brilliantly, she sadly admits how much it still <u>perplexes</u> her.

_____

2. Because their explanation seemed so logical, we were struck by its <u>absurdity</u>.

_____

3. The rain managed to <u>permeate</u> even the stoutest foul-weather gear, so our clothes were dry.

_____

4. What <u>anguish</u> she felt when her doctor told her that her dog was cured.

_____

5. They were <u>nurturing</u> the young tree and hoped to have it cut down soon.

_____

6. Few people visited the small town after its <u>revival.</u>

_____

B. WORD STUDY: The Latin root -*viv*- means "to live." Answer each of these questions using one of these words containing the root -*viv*-: *vivid, survive, convivial.*

1. Why might a *vivid* description help you visualize a setting?

_____

2. Why would you rather spend time with *convivial* friends than with sad ones?

_____

3. If you *survive* a bad case of the flu, do you begin to have more energy?

_____

Name _____ Date _____

Writing About the Big Question

Is knowledge the same as understanding?

Big Question Vocabulary

ambiguous	clarify	comprehend	concept	connection
fact	feeling	information	insight	instinct
interpret	research	senses/sensory	sources	statistics

A. *Use one or more words from the list above to complete each sentence.*

1. To try to understand summer, Hansberry recalls _____ gathered through her _____.

2. Her _____ with the woman in Maine added to her understanding.

3. Observing the woman's pain and laughter gave her the knowledge to partly _____ the meaning of the person's life.

4. However, she knows that a _____ about someone is only useful if we _____ it.

B. *Describe a time when you made a connection with someone. How did this connection help you understand him or her? Write three or four sentences. Use at least two of the Big Question vocabulary words.*

_____

_____

_____

_____

C. *In "On Summer," Lorraine Hansberry's growing understanding of life has changed her feelings about summer. Complete the sentence below. Then, write a short paragraph in which you connect this experience to the Big Question.*

Learning the facts of people's lives may change how we comprehend them because

_____

_____

_____

_____

Name _____ Date _____

"On Summer" by Lorraine Hansberry
Literary Analysis: Style

An author's **style** is his or her unique way of writing. Style includes every feature of a writer's use of language. Some elements that contribute to an author's style are

- **Diction:** the kinds of words the author uses
- **Syntax:** the way in which the author arranges words in sentences
- **Tone:** the author's attitude toward his or her audience or subject

A writer's diction and syntax might be described as formal or informal, technical or ordinary, sophisticated or down-to-earth. A writer's tone might be described as serious or playful, friendly or distant, sympathetic or scathing.

DIRECTIONS: *Consider the diction and syntax in the italicized passages from "On Summer" in the left-hand column below. Then write notes or a sentence in the right-hand column to describe the tone produced by these features of Hansberry's style.*

Passage	Tone
1. The adolescence, admittedly lingering still, brought the traditional passionate commitment to melancholy autumn—*and all that.*	1. _____ _____ _____
2. By duration alone, for instance, a summer's day seemed *maddeningly excessive, an utter overstatement.*	2. _____ _____ _____
3. And it was also *cool and sweet* to be on the grass and there was usually the scent of freshly cut lemons or melons in the air.	3. _____ _____ _____
4. The woman that I met was *as wrinkled as a prune and could hardly hear and barely see and always seemed to be thinking of other times.*	4. _____ _____ _____
5. I heard later that she did live to see another summer. *And I have retained my respect for the noblest of the seasons.*	5. _____ _____ _____

"**On Summer**" by Lorraine Hansberry
Reading: Generate Prior Questions to Identify Main Idea and Details

The **main idea** is the central message, insight, or opinion in a work of nonfiction. **Supporting details** are the pieces of evidence that a writer uses to prove the main idea. These details can include facts, statistics, quotations, or anecdotes. To **identify the main idea and supporting details** in a work, **generate questions prior to reading.** Before you read, you can ask yourself questions such as

- Why did the author choose this title?
- How might events in the author's life influence his or her attitude toward the subject?

As you read, look for details that answer those questions and point to the main idea.

A. DIRECTIONS: *Answer the following questions to guide your reading of "On Summer."*

1. The word *on,* meaning "concerning" or "about," has been used in the titles of many essays. What expectations does Hansberry's title create in you, the reader?

   _____

   _____

2. In her first sentence, Hansberry declares, "It has taken me a good number of years to come to any measure of respect for summer." What does this opening sentence lead you to expect about the structure of Hansberry's essay?

   _____

   _____

3. A crucial fact about Hansberry's own life was her struggle against cancer and her premature death from the disease at age thirty-four. How do you think this biographical fact might affect the writer's attitude toward the seasons and the passage of time?

   _____

   _____

B. DIRECTIONS: *In an essay about summer, what kind of main idea might you expect? What sorts of supporting details might you find in such an essay? Support your answer with examples from your own experience or from your reading.*

   _____

   _____

   _____

   _____

"On Summer" by Lorraine Hansberry
Vocabulary Builder

Word List

aloofness   apex   bias   duration   melancholy   pretentious

A. DIRECTIONS: *Revise each sentence so that the underlined vocabulary word is used logically. Be sure not to change the vocabulary word.*

1. Because she mingles easily with her classmates, she has a reputation for <u>aloofness</u>.

   _____

2. The team's unexpected victory created intense feelings of <u>melancholy</u> in the stands.

   _____

3. Thoroughly <u>pretentious</u>, he always dresses casually and simply.

   _____

4. He felt that this failure was surely bound to be the <u>apex</u> of his career.

   _____

5. The chairperson acted with clear <u>bias</u> when she chose the best qualified person.

   _____

6. I knew I was out for the <u>duration</u> of the season when the doctor said my injury wasn't serious.

   _____

B. WORD STUDY: The Latin root *-dur-* means "to harden, hold out, last." Answer each of these questions using one of these words containing the root *-dur-*: *endure, durable, duress.*

1. Why is a stone sculpture more <u>durable</u> than an ice sculpture?

   _____

2. What might someone with a toothache have to <u>endure</u>?

   _____

3. Why isn't it fair to use <u>duress</u> to get someone to do something for you?

   _____

"A Celebration of Grandfathers" by Rudolfo Anaya
"On Summer" by Lorraine Hansberry
Integrated Language Skills: Grammar

Direct Object and Indirect Object

A **direct object** is the noun or pronoun that receives the action of a verb. You can determine whether a word is a direct object by asking *whom?* or *what?* after an action verb.

> In her essay, Hansberry praises *summer*. [praises *what?*]

> Every morning, Rudolfo greeted his *grandfather.* [greeted *whom?*]

An **indirect object** is a noun or pronoun that names the person or thing that receives the action of the verb. You can tell whether a word is the indirect object by finding the direct object and asking *to / for whom?* or *to / for what?* after the action verb. An indirect object always comes between the subject and the direct object, and it never appears in a sentence without a direct object.

> His grandfather gave *Rudolfo* some wise advice. [*gave advice to whom?*]

A. DIRECTIONS: *Identify each direct object and indirect object in the sentences below by writing the objects on the line provided. After each object, write* D.O. *for direct object and* I.O. *for indirect object. Note: Some sentences will have both a direct and an indirect object.*

1. In her essay "On Summer," Lorraine Hansberry tells several anecdotes.

   _____

2. Hansberry's observations offer us a subtle portrait of summer.

   _____

3. Clearly, Rudolfo Anaya greatly admired his grandfather.

   _____

4. Anaya's grandfather offered the younger generation an inspiring model.

   _____

B. Writing Application: *On the lines below, write a paragraph in which you compare and contrast Lorraine Hansberry's "On Summer" with Rudolfo Anaya's "A Celebration of Grandfathers." Use at least two direct objects and two indirect objects in your writing. Underline each direct object once and each indirect object twice.*

_____

_____

_____

_____

_____

_____

_____

Name _____ Date _____

"A Celebration of Grandfathers" by Rudolfo Anaya
"On Summer" by Lorraine Hansberry

Integrated Language Skills: Support for Writing Book-Jacket Copy

For your book-jacket copy, use the chart below to jot down notes under each heading.

Older Person You Admire: _____

Biographical Highlights

_____
_____
_____
_____
_____
_____
_____

Reasons to Admire the Person

_____
_____
_____
_____
_____
_____
_____

Now, use your notes to write copy for your book jacket. Be sure that the details you include will make readers want to know more about your subject.

Name _____ Date _____

Writing About the Big Question

Is knowledge the same as understanding?

Big Question Vocabulary

ambiguous	clarify	comprehend	concept	connection
fact	feeling	information	insight	instinct
interpret	research	senses/sensory	sources	statistics

A. *Use one or more words from the list above to complete each sentence.*

1. Every example and _____ Postman gives about TV news helps us understand how that medium works.

2. If news is _____, it cannot help us understand what is happening.

3. Adam does _____ to gain knowledge and come to an understanding.

4. He wants to gain _____ into how laws are passed.

B. *Follow the directions in responding to each item below.*

1. List three ways that you get news about current events.

_____

_____

2. Pick one of the methods you listed above. Tell how the information helps you understand how events in the news affect your personal life. Use at least two of the Big Question vocabulary words.

_____

_____

C. *In "The News," the author describes the presentation of television news. Complete the sentence below. Then, write a short paragraph in which you connect this experience to the Big Question.*

We react in different ways to the presentations of news information on television and to the presentations in other media because _____

_____

_____

_____

_____

"The News" by Neil Postman
Literary Analysis: Expository Essay

An **expository essay** is a short piece of nonfiction that presents information, discusses ideas, or explains a process. In a good expository essay, the writer provides evidence and examples to present an accurate and complete view of the topic. The writer may also use one or more of the following techniques to provide support, depth, and context.

- **Description:** including language that appeals to the senses
- **Comparison and contrast:** showing similarities and differences among two or more items
- **Cause and effect:** explaining the relationship between events, actions, or situations by showing how one can result in another

DIRECTIONS: *Use the lines provided to answer the questions about Neil Postman's expository essay.*

1. What is the topic that Postman discusses in his essay "The News"?

   _____

2. In paragraphs 7–10, Postman discusses the "structure" of a typical television newscast. Give three specific details that Postman includes in his description of a typical television newscast.

   _____
   _____
   _____

3. How does this description relate to Postman's main idea in the essay?

   _____
   _____

4. Postman compares and contrasts TV news and print media (newspapers and magazines). Briefly summarize three ways in which they are alike or different.

   _____
   _____
   _____
   _____

5. How does this comparison and contrast support the writer's main idea in the essay?

   _____
   _____

6. According to Postman, what underlying cause explains the fact that the national evening news has not expanded from a half-hour format to a full hour?

   _____
   _____

"The News" by Neil Postman

Reading: Reread to Identify Main Idea and Details

The **main idea** is the central message, insight, or opinion in a work of nonfiction. The **supporting details** in a work help to prove the writer's point. These details can include facts, statistics, quotations, or anecdotes. To help you **identify the main idea and supporting details** in a work, **reread** passages that do not seem to support the work's main idea.

- As you read, note key details to form ideas about what the main idea might be.
- If a detail does not seem to support that main idea, reread the passage to be sure you have not misinterpreted it.
- If necessary, revise your assumptions about the main idea.

DIRECTIONS: *Answer the following questions to guide your reading of "The News."*

1. Reread paragraphs three and four of the essay. Why does Postman describe moving pictures of a burning aircraft carrier as "interesting" and pictures of toppling buildings as "exciting"?

   _____

   _____

   _____

2. According to Postman, why do visual changes on TV have to be more dramatic to be interesting? (Reread the paragraph beginning, "The television screen is smaller than life.")

   _____

   _____

   _____

3. What does Postman mean when he connects television news broadcasts to the "realm of the symbolic"? (Reread the seventh and eighth paragraphs of the essay.)

   _____

   _____

   _____

4. How does the author support his claim that "it is the trivial event that is often best suited for television coverage"? (Reread the long paragraph that begins, "While the form of a news broadcast emphasizes tidiness and control. . . .")

   _____

   _____

   _____

"The News" by Neil Postman
Vocabulary Builder

Word List

compensation   daunting   imposition   medium   revered   temporal

A. DIRECTIONS: *Revise each sentence so that the underlined vocabulary word is used logically. Be sure not to change the vocabulary word.*

1. She settled her lawsuit for a substantial amount, refusing all <u>compensation</u> for her injuries.

   _____

2. The climb to the summit seemed <u>daunting</u>, and we thought it would be an easy hike.

   _____

3. Ray is devoted to the <u>temporal</u> realities of his job and is therefore late for work more often than not.

   _____

4. "It is because you are a <u>revered</u> expert," she said, "that we feel free to disregard your opinion."

   _____

5. No <u>medium</u> reported the interview, but it was covered in newspapers.

   _____

6. The <u>imposition</u> of a rule against leaving early gave students greater freedom.

   _____

B. WORD STUDY: The Latin root *-temp-* means "time." Answer each of these questions using one of these words containing the root *-temp-*: *temporary* (for a short time), *temporize* (to do something to gain time), *contemporary* (at the current time).

1. Why isn't President Washington a <u>contemporary</u> president?

   _____

2. When can you tell that a situation is not <u>temporary</u>?

   _____

3. Why would someone <u>temporize</u> if he were caught doing something wrong?

   _____

Name _____ Date _____

"Single Room, Earth View" by Sally Ride
Writing About the Big Question

Is knowledge the same as understanding?

Big Question Vocabulary

ambiguous	clarify	comprehend	concept	connection
fact	feeling	information	insight	instinct
interpret	research	senses/sensory	sources	statistics

A. *Use one or more words from the list above to complete each sentence.*

1. Alana didn't understand the _____ of space travel until she read Ride's essay.

2. "My _____ is that we benefit from space exploration," Mark said.

3. Ride helps _____ what it's like to actually travel in space.

4. Each _____ she gives is based on personal knowledge.

B. *Follow the directions in responding to each item below.*

1. List two things you think people gain from America's space program.

   _____

   _____

2. Choose one thing you listed and explain how Americans benefit from it. Use two Big Question vocabulary words in your answer.

   _____

   _____

C. *In "Single Room, Earth View," astronaut Sally Ride explains what it is like to see Earth from the space shuttle. Complete the sentence below. Then, write a short paragraph in which you connect this experience to the Big Question.*

Looking at Earth from space may change how we comprehend the world because

   _____

   _____

   _____

   _____

   _____

   _____

Name _____   Date _____

"Single Room, Earth View" by Sally Ride
Literary Analysis: Expository Essay

An **expository essay** is a short piece of nonfiction that presents information, discusses ideas, or explains a process. In a good expository essay, the writer provides evidence and examples to present an accurate and complete view of the topic. The writer may also use one or more of the following techniques to provide support, depth, and context.

- **Description:** including language that appeals to the senses
- **Comparison and contrast:** showing similarities and differences among two or more items
- **Cause and effect:** explaining the relationship between events, actions, or situations by showing how one can result in another

DIRECTIONS: *Use the lines provided to answer the questions about Sally Ride's expository essay.*

1. What is the topic that Ride discusses in her essay "Single Room, Earth View"?

   _____

2. How does Ride use comparison and contrast in the second paragraph of the essay, where she discusses airplane travel and spaceflight?

   _____

   _____

   _____

3. How does this discussion relate to Ride's main idea in the essay?

   _____

   _____

4. Give three examples of "civilization's more unfortunate effects on the environment" that Ride describes from space.

   _____

   _____

   _____

5. The space shuttle orbits the Earth once every 90 minutes. Name one effect of that 90-minute orbit.

   _____

   _____

   _____

6. In her conclusion, what does Ride say about comparing airplane travel to spaceflight?

   _____

   _____

   _____

Name _____ Date _____

"**Single Room, Earth View**" by Sally Ride
Reading: Reread to Identify Main Idea and Details

The **main idea** is the central message, insight, or opinion in a work of nonfiction. The **supporting details** help to prove the writer's point. These details can include facts, statistics, quotations, or anecdotes. To help you **identify the main idea and supporting details** in a work, **reread** passages that do not seem to support the work's main idea.

- As you read, note key details to form ideas about what the main idea might be.
- If a detail does not seem to support that main idea, reread the passage to be sure you have not misinterpreted it.
- If necessary, revise your assumptions about the main idea.

DIRECTIONS: *Answer the following questions to guide your reading of "Single Room, Earth View."*

1. Reread paragraph three, which begins with "While flying over the Hawaiian Islands." Explain why Ride describes the scene as "surreal" in the last sentence of the paragraph.

   _____

   _____

   _____

2. In paragraph four, why does Ride say that she found it "almost impossible to keep track of where we were at any given moment"?

   _____

   _____

3. Reread paragraph six, in which Ride mentions plate tectonics. Why does she become an instant believer in this scientific theory?

   _____

   _____

   _____

4. What does Ride mean by "the signatures of civilization" in paragraph nine? Reread the paragraph, and then explain the writer's figure of speech.

   _____

   _____

   _____

   _____

"**Single Room, Earth View**" by Sally Ride
Vocabulary Builder

Word List

articulate   diffused   extrapolating   muted   novice   surreal

A. DIRECTIONS: *Each of the following questions consists of a related pair of words in CAPITAL LETTERS followed by four lettered pairs of words. Choose the pair that best expresses a relationship* similar *to that expressed in the pair in capital letters.*

1. NOVICE : PROFESSIONAL ::
   A. casual : informal
   B. student : professor
   C. manager : director
   D. athlete : catcher

2. DIFFUSED : SPREAD OUT ::
   A. careful : reckless
   B. anxious : confident
   C. cautious : prudent
   D. unpopular : likable

3. EXTRAPOLATING : CONCLUSION ::
   A. summary : statistics
   B. creating : writer
   C. scientist : evidence
   D. observing : fact

4. ARTICULATE : INCOMPREHENSIBLE
   A. fierce : savage
   B. tranquil : tempestuous
   C. pretentious : ostentatious
   D. prejudiced : biased

5. SURREAL : COMMON ::
   A. historic : famous
   B. confused : puzzled
   C. idealistic : practical
   D. relieved : comforted

6. VIVID : MUTED ::
   A. loud : noisy
   B. serious : refined
   C. successful : accomplished
   D. courageous : cowardly

B. WORD STUDY: The Latin root *-nov-* means "new, recent." Words containing the root *-nov-* include *novelty, novice,* and *renovation.* Consider the meaning of these words and the root *-nov-* as you revise the following sentences so that they make sense.

1. The <u>novelty</u> of the situation comedy is that it was like so many others.

   _____

2. The <u>novice</u> mechanic had been working on cars for ten years.

   _____

3. After the <u>renovation</u>, the house was in great need of repairs.

   _____

Name _____ Date _____

Integrated Language Skills: Grammar

A **predicate nominative** is a noun or pronoun that appears with a linking verb. (Linking verbs include *become, grow, look, seem,* and all forms of *be.*) A predicate nominative renames, identifies, or explains the subject of the sentence. In a sentence with a predicate nominative, the linking verb acts as an equal sign between the subject and the predicate nominative. They refer to the same person or thing. In the following examples, the subject is in boldface, the linking verb is in italics, and the predicate nominative is underlined.

Sally Ride *was* the first American <u>woman</u> in space.

This *is* the <u>problem</u> with television news.

A **predicate adjective** is an adjective that appears with a linking verb and describes the subject of the sentence. In the following examples, the subject is in bold type, the linking verb is in italics, and the predicate adjective is underlined.

The **aircraft carrier** *seemed* <u>enormous</u>.

Through the pollutant haze, some **colors** *looked* <u>muted</u>.

A. DIRECTIONS: *In each of the following sentences, circle the linking verb. Then, underline each predicate nominative once and each predicate adjective twice.*

1. The television screen is smaller than life.
2. In the cinema, the situation is somewhat different.
3. But they are also symbols of a dominant theme of television news.
4. Another severe limitation on television is time.
5. I also became an instant believer in plate tectonics.
6. The Great Wall of China is *not* the only man-made object visible from space.
7. In space, night is very, very black.
8. Part of the fascination with space travel is the element of the unknown.

B. Writing Application: *On the lines below, write a paragraph in which you describe either your favorite natural landscape or your favorite television show. In your paragraph, use at least two predicate nominatives and two predicate adjectives. Underline each predicate nominative once and each predicate adjective twice.*

_____

_____

_____

_____

_____

_____

_____

Name _____ Date _____

"The News" by Neil Postman
"Single Room, Earth View" by Sally Ride

Integrated Language Skills: Support for Writing
an Announcement Script

For your commercial or public-service announcement script, use the chart below to jot down notes under each heading. Include reasons, photos, and quotations to support your purpose.

Details That Might Persuade People to Agree	Persuasive Photos and Other Visuals	Direct Quotation and Visual
_____	_____	_____
_____	_____	_____
_____	_____	_____
_____	_____	_____
_____	_____	_____
_____	_____	_____
_____	_____	_____
_____	_____	_____
_____	_____	_____
_____	_____	_____
_____	_____	_____
_____	_____	_____
_____	_____	_____
_____	_____	_____
_____	_____	_____
_____	_____	_____
_____	_____	_____

Now, use your notes to write the script for your announcement. Be sure that the words and visuals all contribute to your central purpose.

Name _____ Date _____

from **A Lincoln Preface** by Carl Sandburg
"Arthur Ashe Remembered" by John McPhee

Writing About the Big Question

Is knowledge the same as understanding?

Big Question Vocabulary

ambiguous	clarify	comprehend	concept	connection
fact	feeling	information	insight	instinct
interpret	research	senses/sensory	sources	statistics

A. *Use one or more words from the list above to complete each sentence.*

1. To _____ another person's life, we must get to know the person.

2. Brian studies _____ on Lincoln's war decisions and tries to _____ his motives.

3. What _____ and other information show how good Ashe was?

4. Lincoln's directions to his commanders could not be _____.

B. *Follow the directions in responding to each item below.*

1. Describe a difficult problem you had to solve.

   _____

   _____

2. When you solved the problem, did you rely on facts and information, or did you use your instincts? Explain your answer. Use at least two of the Big Question vocabulary words.

   _____

   _____

C. *Complete the sentence below. Then, write a short paragraph in which you connect this experience to the big question.*

Both of these biographers give factual descriptions and details to add to both our knowledge and our understanding of the subjects. Complete this sentence:

When a biographer presents facts fairly and truthfully, _____

_____

_____

_____

_____

Name _____   Date _____

from **A Lincoln Preface** by Carl Sandburg
"Arthur Ashe Remembered" by John McPhee
Literary Analysis: Biographical Writing

Biographical writing is a form of nonfiction in which a writer tells the life story of another person. Biographies are often written about historical figures. The best biographies do not just list the facts, events, or accomplishments in the subject's life. Although factual information is important, a good biography presents the writer's interpretation of those pieces of information. The biographer shows why an understanding of the subject's life is meaningful to readers.

In biographical writing, the details that an author chooses to describe help create our impression of the subject. Biographers often focus on one or all of the following aspects of a subject's life:

- personality
- relationships
- major life events

- upbringing
- role in important events
- influence on others

DIRECTIONS: *Write your answers to the following questions on the lines provided.*

1. In the excerpt from "A Lincoln Preface," what does the following anecdote reveal about Lincoln's personality?

   "While the war drums beat, he liked best of all the stories told of him, one of two Quakeresses heard talking in a railway car. 'I think that Jefferson will succeed.' 'Why does thee think so?' 'Because Jefferson is a praying man.' 'And so is Abraham a praying man.' 'Yes, but the Lord will think Abraham is joking.'"

   _____

   _____

   _____

2. In a sentence or two, sum up the portrait of Lincoln's personality that Carl Sandburg creates in the excerpt from *A Lincoln Preface.*

   _____

   _____

   _____

3. In "Arthur Ashe Remembered," what are two ways in which John McPhee supports his belief that "When things got tough, [Ashe] had control"?

   _____

   _____

   _____

4. In "Arthur Ashe Remembered," what writing techniques does John McPhee use to give readers a detailed portrait of Arthur Ashe?

   _____

   _____

   _____

from **A Lincoln Preface** by Carl Sandburg
"Arthur Ashe Remembered" by John McPhee
Vocabulary Builder

Word List

censure   despotic   droll   enigma   legacy   lithe

A. DIRECTIONS: *Revise each sentence so that the underlined vocabulary word is used logically. Be sure not to change the vocabulary word.*

1. Most of the people enjoy their ruler's use of <u>despotic</u> power.

   _____

2. Mary's personality is an <u>enigma</u>, so we have no difficulty discovering her true motives.

   _____

3. A successful athlete typically has no need of a <u>lithe</u> body.

   _____

4. The movie was so <u>droll</u> that we found ourselves falling asleep in our seats.

   _____

5. In our opinion, the team leader's admirable conduct deserves <u>censure</u>.

   _____

6. The brand-new temple is a <u>legacy</u> from a bygone civilization.

   _____

B. DIRECTIONS: *On the line, write the letter of the choice that is the best synonym for each numbered word.*

___ 1. despotic
   A. temporary
   B. verifiable
   C. tyrannical
   D. true

___ 2. legacy
   A. memento
   B. heirloom
   C. legal document
   D. bracelet

___ 3. lithe
   A. flexible
   B. affluent
   C. devious
   D. permanent

___ 4. enigma
   A. award
   B. joke
   C. advertisement
   D. riddle

All-in-One Workbook
147

Name _____ Date _____

from A Lincoln Preface by Carl Sandburg
"Arthur Ashe Remembered" by John McPhee
Support for Writing to Compare

Use a chart like the one shown to make prewriting notes for an essay comparing your reactions to these two biographical selections.

	from A Lincoln Preface	**"Arthur Ashe Remembered"**
Importance of subject		
My response to each selection		
Main impression author wants to convey		

Name _____ Date _____

"**Carry Your Own Skis**" by Lian Dolan
Writing About the Big Question

Is knowledge the same as understanding?

Big Question Vocabulary

ambiguous	clarify	comprehend	concept	connection
fact	feeling	information	insight	instinct
interpret	research	senses/sensory	sources	statistics

A. *Use one or more words from the list above to complete each sentence.*

1. Emily understands the _____ of carrying her own skis.

2. Her _____ is that people who don't know how to take care of themselves won't be successful.

3. Dolan uses an example to help people _____ her meaning.

4. Albert will try to _____ his understanding by asking for facts.

B. *Follow the directions in responding to each item below.*

1. Describe an experience you have found meaningful.

   _____

   _____

2. How did the experience you describe above teach you a lesson about life? Use at least two Big Question vocabulary words in your answer.

   _____

   _____

C. *In "Carry Your Own Skis," the author draws an analogy between carrying your own skis and taking responsibility for yourself. Complete the sentence below. Then, write a short paragraph in which you connect this experience to the Big Question.*

Personal responsibility is a concept that many people do not understand because

_____

_____

_____

_____

_____

_____

_____

"Carry Your Own Skis" by Lian Dolan
Literary Analysis: Persuasive Essay

A **persuasive essay** is a short nonfiction work that tries to persuade a reader to think or act in a particular way. Persuasive essays usually include one or both of the following:

- **Appeals to reason:** logical arguments based on verifiable evidence, such as facts, statistics, or expert testimony
- **Appeals to emotion:** statements intended to affect listeners' feelings about a subject. These statements often include charged language—words with strong positive or negative associations.

DIRECTIONS: *Use the lines provided to answer the questions about Lian Dolan's persuasive essay.*

1. What opinion or course of action is summed up in the title of the essay, "Carry Your Own Skis"? State the writer's position in your own words.

   _____

   _____

2. In paragraph 2, Dolan mentions luxuries that were not available in the mid-1960s when she learned to ski—for example, valet parking, condos, clothing that keeps you warm and dry. How do these details about what skiing was like in the 1960s support Dolan's main idea?

   _____

   _____

   _____

3. Reread the following excerpt from the essay:

   The real world is riddled with people who have never learned to carry their own skis—the blame-shifters, the no-RSVPers, the coworkers who never participate in those painful group birthdays except if it's their own. I admit it: I don't really get these people.

   In this passage, what are two words or phrases with strong emotional associations? Are these emotional associations positive or negative? Explain your answer.

   _____

   _____

   _____

4. Does Dolan's use of repetition in the essay appeal primarily to reason or to emotion? Write a brief paragraph analyzing the writer's use of repetition. Support your main idea with specific references to the text.

   _____

   _____

   _____

   _____

   _____

   _____

"Carry Your Own Skis" by Lian Dolan

Reading: Reread to Analyze and Evaluate Persuasive Appeals

Persuasive appeals in an essay are the arguments the author makes to persuade readers or listeners to think or act in a particular way. To **analyze and evaluate persuasive appeals,** identify passages in which the author makes an argument in support of his or her position. Then, **reread** those passages to test the logic and reasoning of the author's arguments. Ask yourself these questions:

- Is the author's argument supported by evidence, or is it based on faulty assumptions?
- Does the author demonstrate clear connections between ideas, or does the author make leaps in logic?

A. DIRECTIONS: *Answer the following questions about Lian Dolan's use of persuasive appeals in "Carry Your Own Skis."*

1. Reread the first three paragraphs of the essay. Why do you think Dolan chose to begin her essay about the importance of responsibility with a description of how and why her mother and aunt took up skiing?

_____

_____

_____

2. According to Dolan, what are two of the consequences of *not* taking responsibility for yourself and your stuff? How does she support her argument?

_____

_____

_____

3. Reread the next-to-last paragraph in the essay, beginning, "Now I have a life that includes a husband, two children, a dog, a house." What analogy (comparison) does Dolan draw in this paragraph? Does this analogy support her case effectively, in your view? Why or why not?

_____

_____

_____

B. DIRECTIONS: *Think of two more persuasive appeals that Dolan might have included to support her main idea in this persuasive essay. The persuasive appeals might be appeals to reason or appeals to emotion. In the space below, list and comment on two persuasive appeals that you think might effectively support Dolan's main idea.*

_____

_____

_____

_____

"Carry Your Own Skis" by Lian Dolan
Vocabulary Builder

Word List

collective   entailed   forgo   inevitability   potential   riddled

A. DIRECTIONS: *On the line, write the letter of the choice that is the best synonym for each word.*

___ 1. riddled
   A. exposed
   B. permeated
   C. tainted
   D. polished

___ 2. inevitability
   A. certainty
   B. credibility
   C. ambiguity
   D. complexity

___ 3. potential
   A. possibility
   B. desire
   C. probability
   D. withdrawal

___ 4. entailed
   A. required
   B. endured
   C. profited
   D. released

___ 5. collective
   A. individual
   B. supportive
   C. collaborative
   D. substitute

___ 6. forgo
   A. reveal
   B. complain
   C. indulge
   D. abstain

B. WORD STUDY: The Latin root -*potens*- means "able" or "having the essence of." Answer each of the following questions using one of these words containing -*potens*-: *potency, omnipotence, potential.*

1. How can you determine the <u>potency</u> of a medicine?

   _____

2. Why might a king believe he has <u>omnipotence</u>?

   _____

3. What would you do if a talent scout claimed you had the <u>potential</u> to become a big star?

   _____

"Libraries Face Sad Chapter" by Pete Hamill
Writing About the Big Question

Is knowledge the same as understanding?

Big Question Vocabulary

ambiguous	clarify	comprehend	concept	connection
fact	feeling	information	insight	instinct
interpret	research	senses/sensory	sources	statistics

A. *Use one or more words from the list above to complete each sentence.*

1. _____ alone only tell us facts; they do not help us understand.

2. Libraries are _____ of _____ that leads us toward knowledge and understanding.

3. John went to the library to do _____ on the Carnegie libraries.

4. He wanted to gain _____ into Carnegie's motive for donating so much money.

B. *Follow the directions in responding to each item below.*

1. Describe two recent occasions when you used the library to do research.

   _____

   _____

2. How could you make better use of your time in the library? Give one example. Use at least two of the Big Question vocabulary words.

   _____

   _____

C. *In "Libraries Face Sad Chapter," the author urges readers to contribute to a fund to support public libraries, a source of knowledge. Complete the sentence below. Then, write a short paragraph in which you connect this experience to the Big Question.*

Libraries, as a source of information and a place for research, are still important because _____

_____

_____

_____

_____

_____

_____

Name _____ Date _____

"Libraries Face Sad Chapter" by Pete Hamill
Literary Analysis: Persuasive Essay

A **persuasive essay** is a short nonfiction work that tries to persuade a reader to think or act in a particular way. Persuasive essays usually include one or both of the following:

- **Appeals to reason:** logical arguments based on verifiable evidence, such as facts, statistics, or expert testimony
- **Appeals to emotion:** statements intended to affect listeners' feelings about a subject. These statements often include charged language—words with strong positive or negative associations.

DIRECTIONS: *Answer these questions about Pete Hamill's persuasive essay.*

1. What is Pete Hamill's opinion and suggested course of action in his essay "Libraries Face Sad Chapter"? State the writer's position in your own words.

   _____

   _____

2. Identify two logical arguments Hamill uses to support his case for the importance of libraries and freely circulating books.

   _____

   _____

   _____

   _____

3. Reread the following excerpt from the essay:

   No teacher sent us to those leathery cliffs of books. Reading wasn't an assignment; it was a pleasure. We read for the combined thrills of villainy and heroism, along with the knowledge of the vast world beyond the parish. Living in those other worlds, we could become other people

   In this passage, what are two words or phrases with strong emotional associations? Are these emotional associations positive or negative? Explain your answer.

   _____

   _____

   _____

   _____

4. At the end of his essay on libraries, Hamill stresses a "debt" that must be honored. On the lines below, explain how Hamill conceives of this "debt" and why it does (or does not) constitute an effective conclusion for his persuasive essay.

   _____

   _____

   _____

   _____

Name _____ Date _____

Reading: Reread to Analyze and Evaluate Persuasive Appeals

Persuasive appeals in an essay are the arguments the author makes to persuade readers or listeners to think or act in a particular way. To **analyze and evaluate persuasive appeals,** identify passages in which the author makes an argument in support of his or her position. Then, **reread** those passages to test the logic and reasoning of the author's arguments. Ask yourself these questions:

- Is the author's argument supported by evidence, or is it based on faulty assumptions?
- Does the author demonstrate clear connections between ideas, or does the author make leaps in logic?

A. DIRECTIONS: *Answer the following questions about Pete Hamill's use of persuasive appeals in "Libraries Face Sad Chapter."*

1. Reread the first section of the essay. Why do you think Hamill chose to open this essay with a reminiscence of how he and his friends used libraries in their childhood?

_____

_____

_____

_____

2. According to Hamill, why are libraries more important than ever in hard times? In the section "Built by Carnegie," what arguments does Hamill use to support this opinion?

_____

_____

_____

_____

3. Reread the section entitled "Immigrants' Appreciation." In your opinion, does Hamill appeal primarily to reason or to emotion in this section? Use specific references to the text to explain your answer.

_____

_____

_____

_____

B. DIRECTIONS: *On the lines below, explain how Hamill uses a mixture of idealism and realism to appeal to his audience. Is this combination effective, in your opinion? Why or why not?*

_____

_____

_____

Name _____ Date _____

"Libraries Face Sad Chapter" by Pete Hamill
Vocabulary Builder

Word List

> curtailed   duration   emulate   medium   presumed   volumes

A. DIRECTIONS: *Revise each sentence so that the underlined vocabulary word is used logically. Be sure not to change the vocabulary word.*

1. We were extremely upset to find out that the <u>duration</u> of the exam was only half an hour.

   _____

2. The championship tennis match was <u>curtailed</u> by rain, leaving the spectators certain about the outcome.

   _____

3. Since e-mail is a rapid and cheap <u>medium</u>, its popularity today is hard to explain.

   _____

4. If the author wrote so many books, why are so many <u>volumes</u> of his work in the library?

   _____

5. We <u>presumed</u> he was going with us, so we left before he met us.

   _____

6. Alexandra likes to <u>emulate</u> her sister, so she never wears the same kind of clothes.

   _____

B. WORD STUDY: The Latin root -*sum*- means "to take." Answer each of the following questions using one of these words containing -*sum*-: *consumer, assumption,* and *resume.*

1. How does a <u>consumer</u> usually get what he or she wants?

   _____

   _____

2. What happened as a result of Columbus's <u>assumption</u> that the world is round?

   _____

   _____

3. When do TV programs <u>resume</u> when commercials interrupt the broadcast?

   _____

   _____

"Carry Your Own Skis" by Lian Dolan
"Libraries Face Sad Chapter" by Pete Hamill
Integrated Language Skills: Grammar

Adjectives

An **adjective** is a word used to describe a noun or pronoun or to give a noun or pronoun a more specific meaning. Adjectives modify nouns and pronouns by telling *what kind, which one, how many,* or *how much.* Sometimes a noun, pronoun, or verb may serve as an adjective.

Adjective:	the *typical* lodge (modifies *lodge*)
Noun as Adjective:	a *rope* tow (noun *rope* modifies *tow*)
Pronoun as Adjective:	carried *her* skis (pronoun *her* modifies *skis*)
Verb as Adjective:	children *left* in the lodge (past participle *left* modifies *children*)

A prepositional phrase may function as an adjective: for example, "rows *of picnic tables.*"

A. DIRECTIONS: *Read the following sentences from "Carry Your Own Skis" and "Libraries Face Sad Chapter." Write all the adjectives in each sentence. You can omit the adjectives* a, an, *and* the, *but do not forget to list any nouns, pronouns, and verbs used as adjectives.*

1. Getting across the icy parking lot and back seemed a small price to pay for the potential of great fun.

   _____

2. Most days, skiing for me was about freezing rain and constantly trying to catch up to my older, faster, more talented siblings.

   _____

3. We passed into that library between two mock-Corinthian columns that gave the building a majestic aura.

   _____

4. Since those ancient nights around prehistoric campfires, we have needed myth. And heroes. And moral tales.

   _____

B. Writing Application: *Write a brief paragraph describing your school or local library. Include specific details. Use at least five adjectives in your writing and underline each one.*

_____

_____

_____

_____

_____

_____

_____

"Carry Your Own Skis" by Lian Dolan
"Libraries Face Sad Chapter" by Pete Hamill

Integrated Language Skills: Support for Writing an Abstract

For your abstract, use the chart below to jot down notes under each heading.

Topic: _____
_____

Main Idea: _____
_____
_____

Supporting Details:

1. _____
_____
_____
_____

2. _____
_____
_____
_____

3. _____
_____
_____
_____

4. _____
_____
_____
_____
_____

Now, use your notes to write your abstract. Give enough information so that someone who has not yet read the essay can get a clear understanding of what the essay is about.

Name _____ Date _____

"I Have a Dream" by Martin Luther King, Jr.
Writing About the Big Question

 Is knowledge the same as understanding?

Big Question Vocabulary

ambiguous	clarify	comprehend	concept	connection
fact	feeling	information	insight	instinct
interpret	research	senses/sensory	sources	statistics

A. *Use one or more words from the list above to complete each sentence.*

1. The ___information___ helped Jill understand the civil rights movement.

2. King spoke with great ___feeling___ that helped people understand his message.

3. He made a powerful ___connection___ with his audience as he gave them information on the injustices suffered by many people.

4. Andrew better understood King's appeal when he read ___sources___ about all the people who went to hear King speak.

B. *Follow the directions in responding to each item below.*

1. When have you heard a good speaker? Describe the occasion.
   when I'am in My church, My pastor speak about God
   very well, and he is a good speaker.

2. How did the speaker help you understand the topic? What techniques or methods did the speaker use? Use at least two of the Big Question vocabulary words.
   Maybe he research sources about of what his gonna say,
   with that he can clarify his speech.

C. In "I Have a Dream," Martin Luther King makes a logical and emotional speech to help listeners understand his dream of freedom and equality. Complete the sentence below. Then, write a short paragraph in which you connect this experience to the Big Question.

The concept of equality might be ambiguous to some people because ___There are___
different things that can be equal, but to understand
the purpose of King its necessary to know the
equality that he want for the people in U.S.

"I Have a Dream" by Martin Luther King, Jr.
Literary Analysis: Persuasive Speech

A **persuasive speech** is a speech that tries to convince listeners to think or act in a certain way. Persuasive speeches may appeal to reason or emotion or both. In order to engage the audience, speakers often include **rhetorical devices,** special patterns of words and ideas that create emphasis and stir emotion in the audience. Common rhetorical devices include the following:

- **Parallelism:** repeating a grammatical structure or arrangement of words to create a sense of rhythm and momentum
- **Restatement:** expressing the same idea in different words to clarify and stress key points
- **Repetition:** expressing different ideas using the same words or images in order to reinforce concepts and unify the speech

DIRECTIONS: *Read each of the following passages from King's "I Have a Dream" speech. On the lines provided, identify the rhetorical device or devices in each passage. (You may find more than one rhetorical device.) Then briefly explain your answer by citing the words and phrases that exemplify the device.*

1. But one hundred years later, the Negro still is not free. One hundred years later, the life of the Negro is still sadly crippled by the manacles of segregation and the chains of discrimination. One hundred years later, the Negro lives on a lonely island of poverty in the midst of a vast ocean of material prosperity.

   Rhetorical Device(s): _repetition_

   Explanation: _He keeps reating thefact that no_
   equality to Negros

2. When the architects of our republic wrote the magnificent words of the Constitution and the Declaration of Independence, they were signing a promissory note to which every American was to fall heir. This note was a promise that all men . . . would be guaranteed the unalienable rights of life, liberty, and the pursuit of happiness.

   Rhetorical Device(s): _restatement_

   Explanation: _He restate the constitution of_
   declaration of independence

3. It is obvious today that America has defaulted on this promissory note insofar as her citizens of color are concerned. Instead of honoring this sacred obligation, America has given the Negro people a bad check; a check which has come back marked "insufficient funds."

   Rhetorical Device(s): _pallarelism_

   Explanation: _He used rhythm._

Name _____   Date _____

"I Have a Dream" by Martin Luther King, Jr.
Reading: Analyze Persuasive Techniques

Persuasive techniques are devices used to influence the audience in favor of the author's argument. In addition to presenting evidence in a persuasive speech, a speaker may use the following:

- emotionally charged language
- rhetorical devices, such as parallelism, restatement, and repetition

To analyze and evaluate persuasive techniques, **read aloud** to hear the effect. Notice the emotional impact of the sounds of certain words, as well as the rhythm and momentum created by the word patterns that the author uses. Consider both the purpose and effect of these persuasive techniques and evaluate the author's success in using them to make a convincing argument.

DIRECTIONS: *Read the following excerpts from "I Have a Dream." Then, on the lines provided, answer the questions that follow.*

1. Five score years ago, a great American, in whose symbolic shadow we stand today, signed the Emancipation Proclamation.

    A. To which "great American" does King allude in this sentence? _Abraham lincom_

    B. What place does King refer to in saying "in whose symbolic shadow we stand"?
    About lincom speech

    C. What well-known speech in American history does King echo in saying "five score years ago"? _He uses Rhythm with his meta phone_

2. Now is the time to make real the promises of Democracy.
   Now is the time to rise from the dark and desolate valley of segregation to the sunlit path of racial justice.

    A. How does this passage illustrate parallelism? _Now is the time to rise_

    _____

    B. What emotionally charged words or phrases does King use in this passage? _____
    Slavery.

3. This sweltering summer of the Negro's legitimate discontent will not pass until there is an invigorating autumn of freedom and equality.

    A. What image dominates this passage? _It used of somthing to_
    equality.

    B. How does the passage illustrate parallelism? _when he talk about_
    Freedom.

Name _____ Date _____

"I Have a Dream" by Dr. Martin Luther King, Jr.

Vocabulary Builder

Word List

creed   defaulted   degenerate   hallowed   momentous   oppression

A. DIRECTIONS: *In each item, think about the meaning of the underlined word and then answer the question.*

1. If you think that a certain place is <u>hallowed</u> ground, would you consider it with respect or indifference? Explain.

   respect because it is holy

2. Why is a <u>creed</u> something that most people take seriously?

   they take it seriosly, because it is a from of belief.

3. If the condition of your house were to <u>degenerate</u> over the next few years, what might you do?

   Because find away to get better

4. Why do people often take photographs during <u>momentous</u> occasions in their lives?

   To be remember

5. How would you feel if you loaned a friend some money and he <u>defaulted</u> on his promise to pay it back?

   Steal money Back

6. Why do you think many people dislike living under <u>oppression</u>?

   Because all people gonna to be free.

B. WORD STUDY: The Latin root *-cred-* means "to trust, to believe." Answer each of the following questions using one of these words containing *-cred-*: *credence* ("the act of believing"), *credible* ("believable"), *credulous* ("ready to believe").

1. Why isn't it wise to give <u>credence</u> to everything you hear on commercials?

   when you believe

2. Why do lawyers want <u>credible</u> witnesses to support their case?

   when he do this

3. What kind of trouble might someone who is too <u>credulous</u> get into?

   _____

All-in-One Workbook

162

"First Inaugural Address" by Franklin Delano Roosevelt
Writing About the Big Question

Is knowledge the same as understanding?

Big Question Vocabulary

ambiguous	clarify	comprehend	concept	connection
fact	feeling	information	insight	instinct
interpret	research	senses/sensory	sources	statistics

A. *Use one or more words from the list above to complete each sentence.*

1. When a person acts out of a natural _____, is that person relying on knowledge or understanding?

2. Roosevelt gave _____ and _____ so Americans would understand what needed to be done.

3. Roosevelt tried to _____ the causes of the Great Depression.

4. By reading Roosevelt's speech, Maya got a new _____ into his presidency.

B. *Follow the directions in responding to each item below.*

1. Why should our presidents explain their understanding of national events?

   _____

   _____

2. How did Roosevelt help you understand the Great Depression? Use two of the Big Question vocabulary words.

   _____

   _____

C. *In "First Inaugural Address," President Roosevelt acknowledges the cold realities of the Great Depression and he promises to do whatever is necessary to help the nation recover. Complete the sentence below. Then, write a short paragraph in which you connect this experience to the Big Question.*

For leaders to inspire confidence, they must comprehend _____

because _____

_____

_____

_____

"**First Inaugural Address**" by Franklin Delano Roosevelt
Literary Analysis: Persuasive Speech

A **persuasive speech** is a speech that tries to convince listeners to think or act in a certain way. Persuasive speeches may appeal to reason or emotion or both. In order to engage the audience, speakers often include **rhetorical devices,** special patterns of words and ideas that create emphasis and stir emotion in the audience. Common rhetorical devices include the following:

- **Restatement:** expressing the same idea in different words to clarify and stress key points
- **Repetition:** expressing different ideas using the same words or images in order to reinforce concepts and unify the speech
- **Analogy:** drawing a comparison that shows a similarity between unlike things
- **Parallelism:** repeating a grammatical structure or arrangement of words to create a sense of rhythm and momentum

DIRECTIONS: *Read each of the following passages from Roosevelt's "First Inaugural Address." On the lines provided, identify the rhetorical device or devices in each passage. (You may find more than one rhetorical device.) Then briefly explain your answer by citing the words and phrases that exemplify the device.*

1. Values have shrunken to fantastic levels; taxes have risen; our ability to pay has fallen

   Rhetorical Device(s): _____

   Explanation: _____

   _____

2. Nature still offers her bounty and human efforts have multiplied it. Plenty is at our door-step, but a generous use of it languishes in the very sight of the supply.

   Rhetorical Device(s): _____

   Explanation: _____

   _____

3. The money changers have fled from their high seats in the temple of our civilization. We may now restore that temple to the ancient truths.

   Rhetorical Device(s): _____

   Explanation: _____

   _____

4. In the field of world policy I would dedicate this nation to the policy of the good neighbor— the neighbor who resolutely respects himself and . . . the rights of others.

   Rhetorical Device(s): _____

   Explanation: _____

   _____

"**First Inaugural Address**" by Franklin Delano Roosevelt
Reading: Analyze Persuasive Techniques

Persuasive techniques are devices used to influence the audience in favor of the author's argument. In addition to presenting evidence in a persuasive speech, a speaker may use the following:

- emotionally charged language
- rhetorical devices, such as parallelism, restatement, and repetition

To analyze and evaluate persuasive techniques, **read aloud** to hear the effect. Notice the emotional impact of the sounds of certain words, as well as the rhythm and momentum created by the word patterns that the author uses. Consider both the purpose and effect of these persuasive techniques and evaluate the author's success in using them to make a convincing argument.

DIRECTIONS: *Read the following excerpts from Roosevelt's "First Inaugural Address." Then, on the lines provided, answer the questions that follow.*

1. Primarily, this is because the rulers of the exchange of mankind's goods have failed through their own stubbornness and their own incompetence, have admitted that failure and abdicated. Practices of the unscrupulous money changers stand indicted in the court of public opinion, rejected by the hearts and minds of men.

   A. How does the passage illustrate parallelism? _____

   _____

   B. What are three examples of emotionally charged language in the passage? Are the emotional associations positive or negative? _____

   _____

2. Small wonder that confidence languishes, for it thrives only on honesty, on honor, on the sacredness of obligations, on faithful protection, on unselfish performance. Without them it cannot live.

   A. How does this passage exemplify parallelism? _____

   _____

   B. How does Roosevelt use restatement in the passage? _____

   _____

3. We face the arduous days that lie before us in the warm courage of national unity; with the clear consciousness of seeking old and precious moral values; with the clean satisfaction that comes from the stern performance of duty by old and young alike.

   A. What are the emotional associations of the adjectives *warm, clear, precious,* and *clean?*

   _____

   B. How would you describe the rhythm of this passage? _____

   _____

All-in-One Workbook
165

"First Inaugural Address" by Franklin Delano Roosevelt
Vocabulary Builder

Word List

abdicated   arduous   candor   discipline   feasible   induction

A. DIRECTIONS: *Revise each sentence so that the underlined vocabulary word is used logically. Be sure not to change the vocabulary word.*

1. Because the task was so <u>arduous</u>, we completed it with little effort.

   _____

   _____

2. The people hoped that the queen's rule would last a lifetime, so it came as a welcome surprise that she <u>abdicated</u> the throne in the second year of her reign.

   _____

   _____

3. On my cousin's <u>induction</u> into the army, our family gathered to welcome him home.

   _____

   _____

4. Because she always spoke with <u>candor</u>, no one ever believed her.

   _____

   _____

5. The child didn't need any <u>discipline</u> because she was so frightfully disobedient.

   _____

   _____

6. If you are a good student, it is quite <u>feasible</u> that you'll never do well in college.

   _____

   _____

B. WORD STUDY: The Latin root *-duct/duc-* means "to lead" or "bring." Answer each of the following questions using one of these words containing *-duct/duc-*: *conduct, reduction, deduct.*

1. Why would anyone want to <u>conduct</u> an orchestra?

   _____

2. How would a price <u>reduction</u> help you buy more music CDs?

   _____

3. Why should you <u>deduct</u> what something costs from how much money you have before making a purchase?

   _____

"I Have a Dream" by Dr. Martin Luther King, Jr.
"First Inaugural Address" by Franklin Delano Roosevelt
Integrated Language Skills: Grammar

Adverbs

An **adverb** is a word that modifies a verb, an adjective, or another adverb. Adverbs answer the questions *Where? When? In what way?* and *To what extent?* about the words they modify. You can often make descriptions more meaningful by using adverbs. Look at these examples:

Modifying a Verb:	The audience listened to the speech *attentively*. (*Attentively* modifies the verb *listened*.)
Modifying an Adjective:	Dr. King made an *extremely* eloquent speech. (*Extremely* modifies the adjective *eloquent*.)
Modifying an Adverb:	Dr. King used language *very* persuasively. (*Very* modifies the adverb *persuasively*.)

A. PRACTICE: *Read the following passages from "I Have a Dream" and "First Inaugural Address." On the lines provided, write the adverb(s) in each sentence and the word that each adverb modifies. Then, in parentheses, tell whether the word modified by each adverb is a verb, an adjective, or another adverb.*

1. We must forever conduct our struggle on the high plane of dignity and discipline.

   _____

2. I say to you today, my friends, that in spite of the difficulties of today and tomorrow, I still have a dream. It is a dream deeply rooted in the American dream.

   _____

3. Nature still offers her bounty and human efforts have multiplied it.

   _____

4. We may now restore that temple to the ancient truths.

   _____

B. WRITING APPLICATION: *Write a brief paragraph focusing on a national issue that you think is important. Use at least three adverbs in your writing, and underline each adverb that you use.*

_____

_____

_____

_____

_____

_____

_____

_____

Name _____   Date _____

"I Have a Dream" by Dr. Martin Luther King, Jr.
"First Inaugural Address" by Franklin Delano Roosevelt

Integrated Language Skills: Support for Writing a Proposal

Use the chart below to make prewriting notes for your proposal.

Issues That Concern Students	**Possible Speakers and Topics**
1. _____	1. _____
_____	_____
_____	_____
_____	_____
2. _____	2. _____
_____	_____
_____	_____
_____	_____
3. _____	3. _____
_____	_____
_____	_____
_____	_____
4. _____	4. _____
_____	_____
_____	_____
5. _____	5. _____
_____	_____
_____	_____

My Choice of Speaker: _____

_____

Why This Speaker Can Inspire Students: _____

_____

_____

_____

Now use your notes to write your proposal.

All-in-One Workbook
168

"The Talk" by Gary Soto
"Talk" retold by George Herzog and Harold Courlander

Writing About the Big Question

Is knowledge the same as understanding?

Big Question Vocabulary

ambiguous	clarify	comprehend	concept	connection
fact	feeling	information	insight	instinct
interpret	research	senses/sensory	sources	statistics

A. *Use one or more words from the list above to complete each sentence.*

1. Jamie and Mike make a strong _____ by talking about all the things that happen in their lives.

2. If you _____ the conversation in "The Talk," you will understand much about the lives of the two boys.

3. Hannah thought her _____ were deceiving her when her chair began to speak.

4. When the fish trap talked, it gave the fisherman new _____ into the information the farmer gave him.

B. *Follow the directions in responding to each item below.*

1. List one or two people you like to talk to.

   _____

2. How does talking to someone help you clarify your feelings and ideas? Use at least two of the Big Question vocabulary words.

   _____

   _____

C. *Complete the sentence below. Then, write a short paragraph in which you connect this experience to the big question.*

Each of these selections builds our knowledge and understanding with facts and other details. Complete this sentence:

When a writer presents facts in a humorous way, _____

_____

_____

_____

_____

Name _____ Date _____

Literary Analysis: Comparing Humorous Writing

A **humorous essay** is a form of nonfiction writing intended to make the reader laugh. Some humorous writing, often described as harsh or biting, ridicules its subjects. Other humorous writing, often described as gentle, treats its subjects with affection even as it makes fun of them.

Humorous writers often include one or more of the following figures of speech:

- **hyperbole:** intentional (and often outrageous) overstatement, or exaggeration
- **understatement:** the presentation of something in a restrained or subtle manner; the opposite of hyperbole

In addition to these techniques, the comic writer's **diction,** or word choice, may include funny names, slang, or other examples of verbal humor.

Although humorous writing is meant to entertain, it can have other purposes as well. For example, humor can be used to convey a serious message.

DIRECTIONS: *Write your answers to the following questions on the lines provided.*

1. Read this passage from "The Talk" by Gary Soto:

   The eyes stayed small as well, receding into pencil dots on each side of an unshapely nose that cast remarkable shadows when we turned sideways.

   What humorous technique does the passage exemplify? Briefly explain your answer.

   _____

   _____

2. What serious issue concerning childhood and adolescence does "The Talk" raise? How does the writer's tone in the essay help you to gain perspective on that issue?

   _____

   _____

3. What examples of the authors' diction stand out to you in the folk tale "Talk"? How does the diction contribute to the humor of the story?

   _____

   _____

4. What important message is conveyed in "Talk"?

   _____

   _____

5. Which story, "The Talk" or "Talk," makes the most use of hyperbole? Of understatement? Explain your answer and give examples.

   _____

   _____

All-in-One Workbook
170

"Talk" retold by Harold Courlander and George Herzog
"The Talk" by Gary Soto
Vocabulary Builder

Word List

bulging   feisty   refrain   renegade   wheezed

A. DIRECTIONS: *Revise each sentence so that the underlined vocabulary word is used logically. Be sure not to change the vocabulary word.*

1. We worried about the laziness of the <u>feisty</u> dog.

    _____

2. The group of <u>renegade</u> fans loyally cheered the home team whenever it scored.

    _____

3. The <u>bulging</u> balloon grew smaller and smaller before our eyes.

    _____

4. She could not <u>refrain</u> from leaving the luscious dessert untouched.

    _____

5. The runner <u>wheezed</u> loudly and smiled as he thought how strong he felt after this race.

    _____

B. DIRECTIONS: *On the line, write the letter of the choice that is the best answer for each analogy question.*

___ 1. RENEGADE : DISLOYAL ::
    A. prudent : cautious
    B. honest : deceptive
    C. reckless : cautious
    D. rude : loyal

___ 2. FEISTY : LAZY ::
    A. hostile : unfriendly
    B. nimble : athletic
    C. aggressive : peaceful
    D. talkative : chatty

___ 3. BULGING : STUFFED ::
    A. thin : narrow
    B. relaxed : zealous
    C. deprived : privileged
    D. willful : stubborn

___ 4. WHEEZED : GASPED ::
    A. shuddered : shivered
    B. perspired : panted
    C. lunged : withdrew
    D. restricted : extended

___ 5. PERSIST : REFRAIN ::
    A. identify : recognize
    B. unite : isolate
    C. resist : achieve
    D. sacrifice : resistant

"Talk" retold by Harold Courlander and George Herzog
"The Talk" by Gary Soto

Support for Writing to Compare Literary Works

Use a chart like the one shown to make prewriting notes for your essay analyzing why the authors chose to discuss their subjects in a humorous fashion.

	"The Talk"	"Talk"
Characters' current challenges		
Contributing circumstances		
Clues that challenges can be overcome		
Why authors chose to use humor		

All-in-One Workbook
172

 **BQ Tunes**

Communication, performed by Blip Blip Bleep

We're kicking off the **communication**

by talking 'bout the things that we think about
And the words are open to **interpretation,**

Yeah we just try to listen as we're hanging out

And think about the **meanings** of all of these things
Discuss all our feelings of what is going on here
And we start to become **aware,** of what goes on around us
and the things we share

We can **exchange**

For a little bit of an **understanding,**

illuminate why sometimes we whisper, sometimes we shout,
Sometimes you'll disagree but find **resolution,**

And kid I know you'll work it out, work it out

React and put yourself in someone else's shoes
and feel some **empathy** for someone else's blues

And **respond** with your point of view
That shows some **comprehension** and shows some understanding
We're kickin off the **communication,**

so we can stay **informed** of what's happening
With all our friends and all of our family,

relationships that help us learn how to live

We think about the **meanings** of all of these things
discuss and we talk about what is going on here,

What is going on here . . .

Song Title: **Communication**
Artist / Performed by Blip Blip Bleep
Vocals: Sean Han
Backing vocals: Sarah Lee
Drums: Brett Thomson
Lyrics by Sean Han
Music composed by Sean Han and Mike Pandolfo, Wonderful
Produced by Mike Pandolfo, Wonderful
Executive Producer: Keith London, Defined Mind

All-in-One Workbook
173

Name _____ Date _____

Unit 4: Poetry
Big Question Vocabulary—1

The Big Question: How does communication change us?

Honest and frequent communication is important to keep relationships healthy. When you are in doubt about the meaning of somebody's words or actions, the best thing to do is open a dialogue with him or her and ask.

discuss: to talk about something and exchange ideas

empathy: understanding and identifying with another's feelings

interpretation: an explanation or understanding of something

relationship: a connection or association between people

resolution: a final solution to a problem or difficulty

DIRECTIONS: *Leave a message on the answering machine of a close friend or relative, telling them that you want to talk about something he or she did that upset you. Use all of the vocabulary words.*

Unit 4: Poetry
Big Question Vocabulary—2

The Big Question: How does communication change us?

When we read a newspaper or watch television, we receive information, but we do not usually contribute information. In some cases, though, it is possible to take some action that communicates a message in response to news.

communication: the act of speaking or writing to share ideas

comprehension: the ability to understand something

informed: having knowledge gained through study, communication, research, and so on

respond: to reply; to react favorably

understanding: *n.* a grasp of the meaning of something;

adj. having compassion or showing sympathy

DIRECTIONS: *Think about a news story or issue that you care about, and then answer the questions below. Use the vocabulary words in parentheses in each of your answers.*

1. Where did you hear about the news story or issue? (*communication*)

_____

_____

_____

2. What new knowledge did you gain when you heard the story or issue? (*informed*)

_____

_____

_____

3. What are you confused about related to the story or issue? (*understanding*)

_____

_____

_____

4. What would clarify the story for you? (*comprehension*)

_____

_____

_____

5. Is there any action you can take to improve or change this issue? (*respond*)

_____

_____

_____

Name _____ Date _____

Unit 4: Poetry
Big Question Vocabulary—3

The Big Question: How does communication change us?

Sometimes a conversation with someone can cause you to understand things in a new way and, as a result, take action.

aware: informed; knowledgeable

exchange: to give something for something else, as in an exchange of ideas

illuminate: to make clear; to give light to

meaning: what is expressed or what is intended to be expressed; the purpose or significance of something

react: to act in response to an agent or influence

DIRECTIONS: *Use the vocabulary words to help Douglas understand the newspaper strike.*

Douglas had no idea why his paper was not delivered this morning. It had ruined his morning. On his way to work, he stopped at a newsstand and was told about a strike at the newspaper office. Sure enough, as he passed the newspaper office, there were picketers, holding signs.

One of the picketers stopped Douglas and asked him to sign a petition to help the newspaper staff get a raise in pay.

They had the following conversation:

Douglas:

Striker:

Douglas:

Striker:

Name _____ Date _____

Unit 4: Poetry
Applying the Big Question

The Big Question: How does communication change us?

DIRECTIONS: *Complete the chart below to apply what you have learned about communication. One row has been completed for you.*

Example	The subject	What happens	The writer's response	How my ideas changed
From Literature	Making decisions in "The Road Not Taken"	The speaker makes a decision about a small matter.	The decision may change his life forever.	I realize that small decisions may affect my entire life.
From Literature				
From Science				
From Social Studies				
From Real Life				

Pat Mora
Listening and Viewing

Segment 1: Meet Pat Mora
- According to Pat Mora, why is it important to use one's "home" language when writing?
- What two languages does Mora use when writing? Why?

_____

_____

_____

_____

Segment 2: Poetry
- How does the shape of "Uncoiling" help you visualize the poem?
- How does the poem's shape add to its intensity?

_____

_____

_____

_____

Segment 3: The Writing Process
- What does Pat Mora do when she revises a poem?
- Do you agree with Pat Mora that revising is an important part of the writing process? Why or why not?

_____

_____

_____

_____

Segment 4: The Rewards of Writing
- Pat Mora believes that writing should be viewed as an exploration. What can you gain from using writing as a tool to explore?

_____

_____

_____

_____

Name _____   Date _____

Learning About Poetry

Poetry is a literary form that relies on the precise meanings of words, their emotional associations, their sounds, and the rhythms they create. **Figurative language,** or language that is not intended to be interpreted literally, helps poets to express ideas and feelings in a fresh way.

- A **metaphor** compares two apparently unlike things without using the words *like, as, than,* or *resembles:* "My love is a red, red rose."
- A **simile** uses a connecting word to make such comparisons.
- In **personification,** human qualities are given to nonhuman or inanimate things.
- **Imagery** is descriptive language poets use to create word pictures, or **images.** Images appeal to one or more of the five senses: sight, hearing, touch, taste, and smell.

Poets also use various **sound devices** to give their works a musical quality.

- **Rhythm** is the pattern created by the stressed and unstressed syllables of words.
- **Rhyme** is the repetition of identical or similar sounds in stressed syllables of words.
- **Alliteration** is the repetition of the initial consonant sounds of words. **Assonance** is the repetition of vowel sounds in nearby words. **Consonance** is the repetition of consonants within nearby words in which the separating vowels differ.
- **Onomatopoeia** is the use of a word whose sound imitates its meaning, such as *clank, crackle,* and *sputter.*

The following are some major types and forms of poetry.

Narrative poetry tells a story in verse.

- **Ballad:** a relatively brief, songlike narrative about an adventure or a romance
- **Epic:** a long narrative poem about gods or heroes

Dramatic poetry tells a story using a character's own thoughts or statements.

Lyric poetry expresses the feelings of a single speaker, creating a single effect.

- **Haiku:** a poem containing three lines and seventeen syllables and using imagery to convey a single, vivid emotion
- **Sonnet:** a fourteen-line lyric poem with formal patterns of rhyme, rhythm, and line structure

DIRECTIONS: *Circle the letter of the answer that best matches each numbered item.*

1. words not meant literally
   A. figurative language   B. onomatopoeia   C. quatrain
2. sonnet
   A. narrative poem   B. dramatic poem   C. lyric poem
3. pattern of stressed and unstressed syllables
   A. rhythm   B. free verse   C. tercets
4. "their eyes are lasers"
   A. simile   B. metaphor   C. personification
5. "fear of a frightful fiend"
   A. assonance   B. consonance   C. alliteration

The Poetry of Pat Mora
Model Selection: Poetry

Poets use **sound devices**—such as rhyme, rhythm, alliteration, assonance, and onomatopoeia—to create musical, appealing effects with words. Poets also create unexpected insights and perspectives by using words in fresh ways. **Figurative language**—such as simile, metaphor, and personification—goes beyond the literal meanings of words to express ideas and feelings in a fresh way. A poem also becomes vivid and memorable through the use of **imagery,** sensory language that appeals to one or more of the five senses (sight, hearing, smell, taste, and touch).

DIRECTIONS: *Read the passages from "Uncoiling" and "A Voice." Then, answer the questions that follow each passage.*

1. With thorns, she scratches
   on my window, tosses her hair dark with rain . . . ("Uncoiling")

   A. What figure of speech do these lines contain?

   _____

   B. To which sense(s) does the imagery in these lines appeal?

   _____

2. She spews gusts and thunder,
   spooks pale women who scurry to
   lock doors, windows
   when her tumbleweed skirt starts its spin. ("Uncoiling")

   A. Identify one example of alliteration in these lines.

   _____

   B. Identify one example of assonance in the passage.

   _____

3. In your house that smelled like
   rose powder, you spoke Spanish formal
   as your father, the judge without a courtroom
   in the country he floated to in the dark
   on a flatbed truck. ("A Voice")

   A. Which lines in the passage illustrate the use of simile? (Hint: There are two similes.)

   _____

   B. Explain the metaphor contained in the words "the judge without a courtroom."

   _____

   _____

Name _____ Date _____

Poetry Collection: Langston Hughes, William Wordsworth, Gabriela Mistral, Jean de Sponde

Writing About the Big Question

 How does communication change us?

Big Question Vocabulary

aware	communication	comprehension	discuss	empathy
exchange	illuminate	informed	interpretation	meaning
react	relationship	resolution	respond	understanding

A. *Use one or more words from the list above to complete each sentence.*

1. Two people who do not speak the same language may find _____ difficult.

2. Because we shared their feelings deeply, we wanted to communicate our _____ to them.

3. A good dictionary is a valuable resource for determining the _____ of an unfamiliar word.

4. Sometimes you need courage and patience when you _____ a difficult issue or conflict with others.

5. To communicate with others effectively, you need to remain _____ of their point of view.

B. *Follow the directions in responding to each of the items below.*

1. List two different times when you have found **communication** with another person difficult.

   _____

   _____

2. Write two sentences to explain one of these experiences, and describe how it made you feel. Use at least two of the Big Question vocabulary words.

   _____

   _____

C. *Complete the sentence below. Then, write a short paragraph in which you connect the sentence to the Big Question.*

When the speaker of a poem asks the audience to **respond** to a question, the audience is encouraged to _____

_____

_____

_____

Name _____ Date _____

Literary Analysis: Figurative Language

Figurative language is language that is used imaginatively rather than literally. Figurative language includes one or more **figures of speech,** literary devices that make unexpected comparisons or change the usual meanings of words. The following are figures of speech:

- **Simile:** a comparison of two apparently unlike things using *like, as, than,* or *resembles*
- **Metaphor:** a comparison of two apparently unlike things without using *like, as, than,* or *resembles*
- **Personification:** giving human characteristics to a nonhuman subject
- **Paradox:** a statement, an idea, or a situation that seems contradictory but actually expresses a truth

DIRECTIONS: *Read the following passages and then use the lines provided to identify each example of figurative language. Briefly indicate the reason for your answer.*

1. "Does it stink like rotten meat?" ("Dream Deferred")

   _____

   _____

2. "Life is a broken-winged bird / That cannot fly." ("Dreams")

   _____

   _____

3. "Ten thousand saw I at a glance,
   Tossing their heads in sprightly dance." ("I Wandered Lonely as a Cloud")

   _____

   _____

4. "They flash upon that inward eye
   Which is the bliss of solitude." ("I Wandered Lonely as a Cloud")

   _____

   _____

5. "The wind wandering by night
   rocks the wheat.
   Hearing the loving wind,
   I rock my son." ("Meciendo")

   _____

   _____

6. "What becomes more and more secure, the longer
   it is battered by inconstancy . . .?" ("Sonnets on Love XIII")

   _____

   _____

Poetry Collection: Langston Hughes, William Wordsworth,
Gabriela Mistral, Jean de Sponde

Reading: Read Fluently

Reading fluently is reading smoothly and continuously while also comprehending the text and appreciating the writer's artistry. To improve your fluency when reading poetry, **read in sentences.** Use punctuation—periods, commas, colons, semicolons, and dashes—rather than the ends of lines to determine where to pause or stop reading.

DIRECTIONS: *Read the following passages and then answer the questions on the lines provided.*

1. "God, the Father, soundlessly rocks
   his thousands of worlds.
   Feeling His hand in the shadow,
   I rock my son." ("Meciendo")

   At the ends of which lines would you make major pauses in reading? Minor pauses? No pause at all?

   _____

   _____

2. "But if that dead
   sage could return to life, he would find a clear
   demonstration of his idea, which is not
   pure theory after all. That putative spot
   exists in the love I feel for you, my dear." ("Sonnets on Love XIII")

   After which words would you make a minor pause? After which words would you make a major pause?

   _____

   _____

3. "The waves beside them danced; but they
   Outdid the sparkling waves in glee;
   A poet could not but be gay,
   In such a jocund company;
   I gazed—and gazed—but little thought
   What wealth the show to me had brought:" ("I Wandered Lonely as a Cloud")

   After which words at the end of lines should you not make any pause at all?

   _____

   _____

Poetry Collection: Langston Hughes, William Wordsworth,
Gabriela Mistral, Jean de Sponde
Vocabulary Builder

Word List

barren   deferred   fester   paradoxical   pensive   solitude

A. DIRECTIONS: *Answer each of the following questions.*

____ 1. Which of the following is the best synonym for *deferred*?
   A. postponed   B. analyzed   C. replaced   D. completed

____ 2. Which of the following most nearly means the opposite of *pensive*?
   A. deliberate   B. thoughtless   C. envious   D. cautious

____ 3. Which of the following is the best synonym for *barren*?
   A. plentiful   B. sterile   C. elegant   D. wealthy

____ 4. Which of the following most nearly means the opposite of *solitude*?
   A. linkage   B. loneliness   C. sadness   D. relaxation

B. DIRECTIONS: *For each of the following items, think about the meaning of the italicized word and then answer the question.*

1. Would most of the people at a lively party be likely to be in a *pensive* mood? Why or why not?

   _____

2. Would you be happy if your salary or the fee for a job you had completed was unexpectedly *deferred*? Why or why not?

   _____

3. Would a *paradoxical* statement be easy to understand at first? Why or why not?

   _____

4. If a wound is allowed to *fester*, will it heal quickly? Why or why not?

   _____

C. WORD STUDY: *Match the word with the latin root -fer- in Column A with its meaning in Column B by writing the correct letter on the line provided.*

____ 1. transfer   A. meet with
____ 2. conifer   B. carry across
____ 3. confer   C. greater liking
____ 4. preference   D. pine or spruce tree

Poetry Collection: Richard Brautigan, Emily Dickinson, Stanley Kunitz

Writing About the Big Question

How does communication change us?

Big Question Vocabulary

aware	communication	comprehension	discuss	empathy
exchange	illuminate	informed	interpretation	meaning
react	relationship	resolution	respond	understanding

A. *Use one or more words from the list above to complete each sentence.*

1. Experienced public speakers know that repeating an important point improves their audience's _____ of it.

2. In small discussion groups, you can _____ ideas with your classmates.

3. In any _____ with another person, good _____ is very valuable.

4. We read newspapers and magazines to stay _____ about current events.

5. It often happens that no two readers have exactly the same _____ of a poem.

B. *Follow the directions in responding to each of the items below.*

1. List two different times when your **understanding** of another person's point of view helped improve your **relationship** with him or her.

    _____

    _____

2. Write two sentences to explain one of these experiences, and describe how it made you feel. Use at least two of the Big Question vocabulary words.

    _____

    _____

C. *Complete the sentence below. Then, write a short paragraph in which you connect the sentence to the Big Question.*

As a result of advances in computer technology, **communication** between people has become _____

_____

_____

_____

All-in-One Workbook
185

Name _____ Date _____

Literary Analysis: Figurative Language

Figurative language is language that is used imaginatively rather than literally. Figurative language includes one or more **figures of speech,** literary devices that make unexpected comparisons or change the usual meanings of words. The following are figures of speech:

- **Simile:** a comparison of two apparently unlike things using *like, as, than,* or *resembles*
- **Metaphor:** a comparison of two apparently unlike things without using *like, as, than,* or *resembles*
- **Personification:** giving human characteristics to a nonhuman subject
- **Paradox:** a statement, an idea, or a situation that seems contradictory but actually expresses a truth

DIRECTIONS: *Read the following passages and then use the lines provided to identify each example of figurative language. Briefly indicate the reason for your answer. Note that some passages may exemplify more than one figure of speech.*

1. "Where mammals and computers
   live together in mutually
   programming harmony
   like pure water
   touching pure sky" ("All Watched Over by Machines of Loving Grace")

   _____

   _____

2. "I've heard it in the chillest land—
   And on the strangest Sea—
   Yet, never, in Extremity,
   It asked a crumb—of Me." ("Hope is the thing with feathers—")

   _____

   _____

3. "The man who sold his lawn to standard oil
   Joked with his neighbors come to watch the show
   While the bulldozers, drunk with gasoline,
   Tested the virtue of the soil
   Under the branchy sky
   By overthrowing first the privet-row." ("The War Against the Trees")

   _____

   _____

4. "Much madness is divinest Sense—
   To a discerning Eye—
   Much Sense—the starkest Madness—" ("Much Madness is divinest Sense")

   _____

   _____

Poetry Collection: Richard Brautigan, Emily Dickinson, Stanley Kunitz
Reading: Read Fluently

Reading fluently is reading smoothly and continuously while also comprehending the text and appreciating the writer's artistry. To improve your fluency when reading poetry, **read in sentences.** Use punctuation—periods, commas, colons, semicolons, and dashes—rather than the ends of lines to determine where to pause or stop reading.

DIRECTIONS: *Read the following passages and then answer the questions on the lines provided.*

1. "I like to think
   (it has to be!)
   of a cybernetic ecology
   where we are free of our labors
   and joined back to nature,
   returned to our mammal
   brothers and sisters,
   and all watched over
   by machines of loving grace." ("All Watched Over by Machines of Loving Grace")

   At the ends of which lines would you make major pauses in reading? Minor pauses? No pauses at all?

   _____

   _____

   _____

2. "All day the hireling engines charged the trees,
   Subverting them by hacking underground
   In grub-dominions, where dark summer's mole
   Rampages through his halls,
   Till a northern seizure shook
   Those crowns, forcing the giants to their knees." ("The War Against the Trees")

   After which words would you make a minor pause? After which words would you make no pause at all?

   _____

   _____

   _____

Poetry Collection: Richard Brautigan, Emily Dickinson, Stanley Kunitz
Vocabulary Builder

Word List

abash   discerning   preliminaries   prevail   seizure   subverting

A. DIRECTIONS: *Answer each of the following questions.*

___ 1. Which of the following is the best synonym for *discerning*?
   A. differentiating
   B. insightful
   C. despising
   D. prepared

___ 2. Which of the following most nearly means the opposite of *preliminaries*?
   A. consequences
   B. circumstances
   C. details
   D. considerations

___ 3. Which of the following is the best synonym for *subverting*?
   A. expanding   B. reducing   C. encouraging   D. undermining

___ 4. Which of the following most nearly means the opposite of *prevail*?
   A. be defeated   B. praise   C. endure   D. analyze

B. DIRECTIONS: *In each of the following items, think about the meaning of the italicized word and then answer the question.*

1. Would you want the pilot of an airplane flight to possess a *discerning* eye? Why or why not?

   _____

2. Do *preliminaries* take place before, during, or after the main event?

   _____

3. Would a warm, gentle breeze be likely to *abash* a person? Why or why not?

   _____

4. Does a *seizure* suggest a violent or a gentle action or event? Explain your answer.

   _____

C. WORD STUDY: Use the context of the sentences and what you know about the Latin root *-vert-* to explain your answer to each question.

1. If people *subvert* the government, do they support it or undermine it?

   _____

   _____

2. If you have an *aversion* to turnips, do you like them or dislike them?

   _____

   _____

3. If a statement is *incontrovertible,* can it be disproved or refuted?

   _____

   _____

Poetry Collections: Langston Hughes, William Wordsworth, Gabriela Mistral, Jean de Sponde; Richard Brautigan, Emily Dickinson, Stanley Kunitz

Integrated Language Skills: Grammar

Prepositions and Prepositional Phrases

A **preposition** is a word that relates a noun or pronoun that appears with it to another word in the sentence. Although most prepositions, such as *at, by, in,* and *with,* are single words, some prepositions, such as *because of* and *in addition to,* are compound. In the following example from "The War Against the Trees," the prepositions are in italics.

"Ripped *from* the craters much too big *for* hearts

The club-roots bared their amputated coils"

The **object of a preposition** is the noun or pronoun at the end of a prepositional phrase. In the following example, the prepositional phrase is underlined and the object of the preposition is in italics.

Gabriela Mistral wrote many poems <u>about *children*</u>.

A. PRACTICE: *Read the following passages from the poems in these collections. On the lines provided, write each prepositional phrase. Then, circle the object of the preposition.*

1. "'Hope is the thing with feathers—
   That perches in the soul—"

   _____

2. "Where we are free of our labors
   and joined back to nature . . ."

   _____

3. "That putative spot
   exists in the love I feel for you, my dear."

   _____

B. Writing Application: *Write a brief paragraph in which you describe the way you get to school in the morning. Use at least five prepositional phrases in your writing, and underline each prepositional phrase you use.*

_____

_____

_____

_____

_____

_____

Poetry Collections: Langston Hughes, William Wordsworth, Gabriela Mistral, Jean de Sponde, Richard Brautigan; Emily Dickinson, Stanley Kunitz

Support for Writing a Description of a Scene

Use the following lines to make prewriting notes for your description of a scene in nature.

Choice of Scene: _____

_____

Sensory Details:

1. **Sight:** _____

_____

_____

2. **Sound:** _____

_____

_____

3. **Touch:** _____

_____

_____

4. **Smell:** _____

_____

_____

5. **Taste:** _____

_____

_____

Unified Impression: _____

_____

Now, use your notes to write a few paragraphs or a poem describing a scene in nature.

Name _____ Date _____

Writing About the Big Question

How does communication change us?

Big Question Vocabulary

aware	communication	comprehension	discuss	empathy
exchange	illuminate	informed	interpretation	meaning
react	relationship	resolution	respond	understanding

A. *Use one or more words from the list above to complete each sentence.*

1. Discussing a difficult poem with friends can often help _____ the poet's purpose.

2. My _____ of a poem is often improved if I read the poem aloud.

3. Sal made a New Year's _____ to start learning a foreign language this year.

4. People's facial expressions often signal how they _____ to a statement or question.

5. If you _____ to a question too abruptly, people may think you are being rude.

B. *Follow the directions in responding to each of the items below.*

1. List two different times when your senses—sight, hearing, touch, taste, and smell—played an important part in your **relationship** with the world around you.

   _____

   _____

2. Write two sentences to explain one of these experiences, and describe how it made you feel. Use at least two of the Big Question vocabulary words.

   _____

   _____

C. *Complete the sentence below. Then, write a short paragraph in which you connect the sentence to the Big Question.*

By reading someone else's **interpretation** of a common experience, a reader can learn to _____

   _____

   _____

   _____

All-in-One Workbook
191

Poetry Collection: Walter Dean Myers; Alfred, Lord Tennyson; May Swenson

Literary Analysis: Sound Devices

Poets use **sound devices** to emphasize the sound relationships among words. These devices include the following:

- **Alliteration:** the repetition of initial consonant sounds in stressed syllables: "*running and ripping*"
- **Consonance:** the repetition of final consonant sounds in stressed syllables with different vowel sounds, as in *bat* and *met*
- **Assonance:** the repetition of similar vowel sounds in stressed syllables that end with different consonant sounds, as in *please* and *steam*
- **Onomatopoeia:** the use of a word whose sound imitates its meaning, as in *hiss* and *buzz*

DIRECTIONS: *Analyze each poem. For each poem, give one or more examples of each of the following sound devices. If a poem does not use a particular sound device, write* None.

Sound Device	"Summer"	"The Eagle"	"Analysis of Baseball"
Alliteration			
Assonance			
Consonance			
Onomatopoeia			

Name Julieth Angarita   Date 02/18/16.

Poetry Collection: Walter Dean Myers; Alfred, Lord Tennyson; May Swenson
Reading: Read Fluently ✓

Reading fluently is reading smoothly and continuously while also comprehending the text and appreciating the writer's artistry. To avoid being tripped up by the meaning as you read, **use your senses.** To do so, notice language that appeals to the five senses:

- sight   • hearing   • smell   • taste   • touch

Using your senses will help you connect with a poem and appreciate the effects that the poet creates.

DIRECTIONS: *As you read each poem in this collection, note words and phrases that appeal to your senses. On the following chart, write sensory details in the appropriate section. (Copy the words or phrases exactly.) Because an image can appeal to more than one sense, you may enter a word or phrase more than once.*

Senses	"Summer"	"The Eagle"	"Analysis of Baseball"
Sight	Bugs buzzin from cousin To cousin	He watches From his mountain walls	Ball bounces off bat, flies air or thuds or bound
Hearing	Birds peeping	The wrinkled Sea beneath his clawls	sometime ball gets hit (pow)
Smell	No smell	No smell	No smell
Taste	Juices dripping	No Taste	No Taste
Touch	Catch the one you love days	He clasps The crag	Ball hits bat, or it hits mitt

Poetry Collection: Walter Dean Myers; Alfred, Lord Tennyson; May Swenson

Vocabulary Builder

Word List

analysis   azure   clasps

A. DIRECTIONS: *Answer each of the following questions.*

B 1. Which of the following is the best synonym for *clasps* as Tennyson uses it in the line "He clasps the crag with crooked hands"?
- A. handles
- (B) grips
- C. punches
- D. connects

C 2. Which of the following might be described as *azure*?
- A. a tiger
- B. autumn leaves
- (C) the sky
- D. a diamond

A 3. Which of the following is the best synonym for *analysis*?
- (A) thorough examination
- B. superficial argument
- C. temporary suspension
- D. reflective speech

B. DIRECTIONS: *For each of the following items, think about the meaning of the italicized word and then answer the question.*

1. Which of the following colors is closest to *azure*: gold, brown, blue-green, or gray? Explain.
blue green, because Blue is azure.

2. If you *clasp* someone's hand in greeting or farewell, is your gesture likely to be friendly or hostile? Explain.
I Think is Friendly because is a form to say hi.

3. Would an *analysis* of an issue help you to understand it better? Why or why not?
Yes, because its a examination or studying, that can help you.

C. WORD STUDY: Use the context of each sentence and what you know about the Greek prefix *ana-* to rewrite the sentence so that it makes sense. Be careful not to change the word in italics.

1. Because she felt the two theories were *analogous*, she couldn't wait to point out the differences between them.
Because she felt the two theories were analogous, she couldn't wait point out the similarities between them.

2. The *anachronisms* in that novel showed that the author was keenly aware of the historical setting.
The anachronisms in that novel showed that the author was no keenly aware of the historical

3. The *Analects* are a single teaching by the ancient Chinese philosopher Confucius.
The Analects are multiple teaching by the ancient Chinese philosopher confucius.

Name _____ Date _____

Writing About the Big Question

How does communication change us?

Big Question Vocabulary

aware	communication	comprehension	discuss	empathy
exchange	illuminate	informed	interpretation	meaning
react	relationship	resolution	respond	understanding

A. *Use one or more words from the list above to complete each sentence.*

1. Most of us _____ favorably when someone invites us to a party.

2. For good _____ in a foreign country, some knowledge of the language is helpful.

3. The committee met several times to _____ that issue before it made a final decision.

4. Otto was a man of few words, and it was sometimes hard to figure out his real _____.

5. Thelma's _____ of the poem had never occurred to me, but I had to admit that it made sense.

B. *Follow the directions in responding to each of the items below.*

1. List two different times when you had a disagreement with a friend.

   _____

   _____

2. Write two sentences to explain one of these experiences, and describe how it made you feel. Use at least two of the Big Question vocabulary words.

   _____

   _____

C. *Complete the sentence below. Then, write a short paragraph in which you connect the sentence to the Big Question.*

By reading about the **meaning** that someone finds in certain sounds, a reader can learn to _____

_____

_____

_____

Name _____ Date _____

Literary Analysis: Sound Devices

Poets use **sound devices** to emphasize the sound relationships among words. These devices include the following:

- **Alliteration:** the repetition of initial consonant sounds in stressed syllables: "_muffled monotone_"
- **Consonance:** the repetition of final consonant sounds in stressed syllables with different vowel sounds, as in _toll_ and _bell_
- **Assonance:** the repetition of similar vowel sounds in stressed syllables that end with different consonant sounds, as in "_mellow wedding bells_"
- **Onomatopoeia:** the use of a word whose sound imitates its meaning, as in _jangle_ and _knells_

DIRECTIONS: _Analyze each poem. For each poem, give one or more examples of each of the following sound devices. If a poem does not use a particular sound device, write_ None.

Sound Device	"Slam, Dunk, & Hook"	"Jabberwocky"	"The Bells"
Alliteration			
Assonance			
Consonance			
Onomatopoeia			

Name _____ Date _____

Poetry Collection: Yusef Komunyakaa, Lewis Carroll, Edgar Allan Poe
Reading: Read Fluently

Reading fluently is reading smoothly and continuously while also comprehending the text and appreciating the writer's artistry. To avoid being tripped up by the meaning of words as you read, **use your senses.** To do so, notice language that appeals to the five senses:

- sight
- hearing
- smell
- taste
- touch

Using your senses will help you connect with a poem and appreciate the effects that the poet creates.

DIRECTIONS: *As you read each poem in this collection, note words and phrases that appeal to your senses. On the following chart, write sensory details in the appropriate section. (Copy the words or phrases exactly.) Because an image can appeal to more than one sense, you may enter a word or phrase more than once.*

Senses	"Slam, Dunk, & Hook"	"Jabberwocky"	"The Bells"
Sight			
Hearing			
Smell			
Taste			
Touch			

Poetry Collection: Yusef Komunyakaa, Lewis Carroll, Edgar Allan Poe
Vocabulary Builder

Word List

endeavor   jibed   metaphysical
monotone   palpitating   voluminously

A. DIRECTIONS: *Match each word in Column A with the correct definition in Column B.*

Column A

___ 1. metaphysical
___ 2. palpitating
___ 3. voluminously
___ 4. jibed

Column B

A. fully
B. spiritual
C. changed direction
D. throbbing

B. DIRECTIONS: *Revise each sentence so that the underlined vocabulary word is used logically. Be sure not to change the vocabulary word.*

1. He spoke in a <u>monotone</u>, full of delightful and surprising shifts in tone and mood.

_____

2. He was determined to make an <u>endeavor</u> at finishing the assignment that evening, and so he went to bed early.

_____

3. My heart was <u>palpitating</u> as I awoke from a deep slumber to the sight of rays of morning sunlight dancing across my bed.

_____

C. WORD STUDY: Use the context of the sentences and what you know about the Greek prefix *mono-* to explain your answer to each question.

1. If the animals of a certain species are *monogamous*, do they have one mate or many?

_____

_____

2. Is a person with *monomania* interested in one subject or in many?

_____

_____

3. In a play, is a *monologue* spoken by one character or by many?

_____

_____

Poetry Collections: Walter Dean Myers; Alfred, Lord Tennyson; May Swenson; and Yusef Komunyakaa, Lewis Carroll, Edgar Allan Poe

Integrated Language Skills: Grammar

Prepositional Phrases as Modifiers

A **prepositional phrase,** such as *on the court* or *of the bells,* is made up of a preposition and a noun or pronoun, called the object of the preposition, with all of its modifiers. Prepositional phrases may function either as adjectives by modifying nouns or pronouns or as adverbs by modifying verbs, adjectives, and adverbs.

When acting as an adjective, a prepositional phrase is called an *adjective phrase.* **Adjective phrases** modify a noun or pronoun by telling *what kind* or *which one.*

Example: We enjoy the sounds *of summer.* (*of summer* modifies the noun *sounds*)

When functioning as an adverb, a prepositional phrase is called an *adverb phrase.* **Adverb phrases** modify a verb, an adjective, or an adverb by telling *where, when, in what way,* or *to what extent.*

Examples: In summer, we enjoy outdoor activities. (*in summer* modifies the verb *enjoy*)

The forest was quiet *before dawn.* (*before dawn* modifies the adjective *quiet*)

A. PRACTICE: *For each of the following sentences, use the space provided to write all the prepositional phrases. Classify each one as an adjective phrase or an adverb phrase. Then, write the word that each phrase modifies.*

1. Basketball is popular with many sports fans.

   _____

2. The game was invented in the late nineteenth century.

   _____

3. The inventor of basketball was a physical education instructor named James Naismith.

   _____

4. Naismith's new game originally involved two teams of nine players.

   _____

B. Writing Application: *Write a brief paragraph describing your favorite sport or game. In your paragraph, use at least two adjective phrases and two adverb phrases. Underline each prepositional phrase and label it as an adjective phrase or adverb phrase.*

_____

_____

_____

_____

_____

Poetry Collection: Walter Dean Myers; Alfred, Lord Tennyson; May Swenson;
Yusef Komunyakaa; Lewis Carroll; Edgar Allan Poe

Integrated Language Skills: Support for Writing an Editorial

Use the following chart to develop prewriting notes for an editorial that will be related to a poem in this collection.

Title of Poem: _____

Issue or Topic Related to Poem: _____

_____

_____

My Opinion Statement: _____

_____

_____

Supporting Details:

1. _____

_____

2. _____

_____

3. _____

_____

4. _____

_____

5. _____

_____

Opposing Arguments / Counterarguments:

_____

_____

_____

_____

Now, use your notes to write an editorial about the issue you have chosen.

Poetry by Mary Tall Mountain, Naomi Shihab Nye: Essays by Student Writers

Writing About the Big Question

How does communication change us?

Big Question Vocabulary

aware	communication	comprehension	discuss	empathy
exchange	illuminate	informed	interpretation	meaning
react	relationship	resolution	respond	understanding

A. *Use one or more words from the list above to complete each sentence.*

1. Because he was _____ that his audience was very young and inexperienced, Josh spoke slowly and carefully.

2. When Gina asked a rapid-fire series of questions, we didn't know how to _____ or _____.

3. Responsible politicians want the public to be _____ about important issues.

4. Although she came from a wealthy family, the mayor's _____ with the poor was evident in every speech she gave.

B. *Follow the directions in responding to each of the items below.*

1. List two different times when writing or talking about a topic has improved your **understanding** of it.

   _____

   _____

2. Write two sentences to explain one of these experiences, and describe how it made you feel. Use at least two of the Big Question vocabulary words.

   _____

   _____

C. *Complete the sentence below. Then, write a short paragraph in which you connect the sentence to the Big Question.*

When a writer **responds** strongly to an experience, _____

_____

_____

_____

_____

_____

Poetry by Mary Tall Mountain, Naomi Shihab Nye: Essays by Student Writers
Literary Analysis: Imagery

Imagery is language that appeals to one or more of the senses—sight, hearing, touch, taste, and smell. The use of imagery allows writers to express their ideas with vividness and immediacy. Images create mental pictures for readers and allow them to make connections between their own experiences and the ideas presented in poems. Some images have a universal appeal and appear in many poems, but most are unique to one poem. Here is an example from Naomi Shihab Nye's poem "Daily": "These T-shirts we fold into / perfect white squares." The words *white* and *squares* appeal to our sense of sight: We can see the folded T-shirts. The word *fold* also appeals to our sense of touch: We can feel the action of folding the shirts.

DIRECTIONS: *Tell which senses (there may be more than one) are appealed to in each of the following passages. Then, describe the complete image that each passage creates in your mind.*

1. "A shade of feeling rippled
   The wind-tanned skin." ("There Is No Word for Goodbye")

   _____

   _____

   _____

2. "Ah, nothing, she said,
   watching the river flash." ("There Is No Word for Goodbye")

   _____

   _____

   _____

3. "These tortillas we slice and fry to crisp strips
   This rich egg scrambled in a gray clay bowl" ("Daily")

   _____

   _____

   _____

4. "This table I dust till the scarred wood shines" ("Daily")

   _____

   _____

   _____

5. "Adam's reply was cut off by the crash of a huge oak tree being ripped out of the dirt and slamming into the ground . . . .". ("Hope")

   _____

   _____

   _____

Poetry by Mary Tall Mountain, Naomi Shihab Nye: Essays by Student Writers
Vocabulary Builder

Word List

amid	awestruck	emitting	miraculously
scarred	shriveled	submerged	succumbed

A. DIRECTIONS: *Revise each sentence so that the underlined vocabulary word is used logically. Be sure not to change the vocabulary word.*

1. The performance was so dull that we were <u>awestruck</u>.

   _____

2. After the storm had passed over, we were standing <u>amid</u> howling winds.

   _____

3. Because of the fine weather and the good amount of rain, the flowers in our garden look <u>shriveled</u>.

   _____

4. The furniture is so new that it looks <u>scarred</u> and unstable.

   _____

B. DIRECTIONS: *On the line, write the letter of the choice that is the best synonym, or word with a similar meaning, for each numbered word.*

___ 1. miraculously
   A. accidentally
   B. wonderfully
   C. fearfully
   D. horribly

___ 2. emitting
   A. leaving out
   B. returning
   C. sending out
   D. receiving

___ 3. succumbed
   A. yielded
   B. relaxed
   C. restrained
   D. interpreted

___ 4. submerged
   A. substituted
   B. reimbursed
   C. covered with water
   D. displaced

Poetry by Mary Tall Mountain, Naomi Shihab Nye: Essays by Student Writers
Support for Writing to Compare Literary Works

Use a chart like the one shown to make prewriting notes for an essay comparing and contrasting how the writer's use of imagery adds to the meaning of each selection.

"There Is No Word for Goodbye"
Images of Sokoya →
Speaker's feeling for her aunt: _____

_____

_____

_____

_____

_____

_____

"Daily"
Images of objects/tasks →
Speaker's affection for ordinary things: _____

_____

_____

_____

_____

_____

_____

"Hope" and "The Day of the Storm"
Images of sound and desertion →
Narrator's fear and loneliness: _____

_____

_____

_____

_____

_____

_____

Poetry Collection: Ernest Lawrence Thayer, William Stafford, Sandra Cisneros
Writing About the Big Question

How does communication change us?

Big Question Vocabulary

aware	communication	comprehension	discuss	empathy
exchange	illuminate	informed	interpretation	meaning
react	relationship	resolution	respond	understanding

A. *Use one or more words from the list above to complete each sentence.*

1. The chairperson announced, "We will not reach a _____ in this debate unless we all listen carefully to one another's viewpoints."

2. My _____ with Ken was damaged when I learned he was telling lies about me.

3. "It is my _____," Stacy said, "that the package will arrive at our office before 2 P.M."

4. "Let's _____ e-mail addresses," Matt urged, "so we can stay in touch."

5. That article helped a lot to _____ some obscure passages in the poem.

B. *Follow the directions in responding to each of the items below.*

1. List two different times when an **exchange** of ideas with someone else persuaded you to change your mind about someone or something.

   _____

   _____

2. Write two sentences to explain one of these experiences, and describe how it made you feel. Use at least two of the Big Question vocabulary words.

   _____

   _____

C. *Complete the sentence below. Then, write a short paragraph in which you connect the sentence to the Big Question.*

When a crowd communicates its support or disapproval, a person might **react** by

_____

_____

_____

Poetry Collection: Ernest Lawrence Thayer, William Stafford, and Sandra Cisneros
Literary Analysis: Narrative Poetry

Narrative poetry is verse that tells a story and includes the same literary elements as narrative prose:

- a plot, or sequence of events
- specific settings
- characters who participate in the action

Also like narrative prose, such as a short story, a narrative poem conveys a **mood,** or **atmosphere**—an overall feeling created by the setting, plot, words, and images. For example, a narrative poem's mood can be gloomy, joyous, or mysterious. Poetry's emphasis on precise words and images makes mood a powerful element in a narrative poem.

DIRECTIONS: *As you read "Casey at the Bat," "Fifteen," and "Twister Hits Houston," answer the following questions.*

"Casey at the Bat"

1. What story does this poem tell?

   _____

2. Who are the two most important characters in the poem?

   _____

3. Briefly describe the poem's outcome.

   _____

4. How does Thayer use details of sound to contribute to the poem's setting?

   _____

   _____

"Fifteen"

5. Who is the speaker in this poem, and what occasion does he recall?

   _____

6. What is the principal conflict in "Fifteen"?

   _____

   _____

"Twister Hits Houston"

7. What details create suspense in this narrative poem?

   _____

   _____

8. How would you describe the atmosphere, or mood, at the end of the poem?

   _____

   _____

Poetry Collection: Ernest Lawrence Thayer, William Stafford, and Sandra Cisneros
Reading: Paraphrasing

Paraphrasing is restating in your own words what someone else has written or said. A paraphrase retains the essential meaning and ideas of the original but is simpler to read.

Paraphrasing is especially helpful when reading poetry because poems often contain **figurative language,** words and phrases that are used imaginatively rather than literally. To paraphrase lines in a narrative poem, **picture the action:**

- Based on details in the poem, form a mental image of the setting, the characters, and the characters' actions.
- To be sure that your mental picture is accurate, pay close attention to the way that the poet describes elements of the scene.
- Then, use your own words to describe your mental image of the scene and the action taking place in it.

DIRECTIONS: *On the lines provided, paraphrase the following passages from the narrative poems in this collection. Remember that a paraphrase is a restatement in your own words.*

1. And now the leather-covered sphere came hurtling through the air,
   And Casey stood a-watching it in haughty grandeur there.
   Close by the sturdy batsman the ball unheeded sped;
   "That ain't my style," said Casey. "Strike one," the umpire said. ("Casey at the Bat")

   _____

   _____

   _____

2. I admired all that pulsing gleam, the
   shiny flanks, the demure headlights,
   fringed where it lay; I led it gently
   to the road and stood with that
   companion, ready and friendly. I was fifteen. ("Fifteen")

   _____

   _____

   _____

3. Papa who was sitting on his front porch
   when the storm hit
   said the twister ripped
   the big black oak to splinter . . . ("Twister Hits Houston")

   _____

   _____

   _____

Poetry Collection: Ernest Lawrence Thayer, William Stafford, and Sandra Cisneros
Vocabulary Builder

Word List

defiance   demure   multitude   pallor   preceded   writhing

A. DIRECTIONS: *Match each word in Column A with the correct definition in Column B.*

Column A	Column B
___ 1. pallor	A. twisting
___ 2. writhing	B. modest
___ 3. demure	C. paleness

B. DIRECTIONS: *In each of the following items, think about the meaning of the italicized word and then answer the question.*

1. A *multitude* of townspeople attended the parade. Why might it have been hard to see the marchers?

   _____

2. Jean reacted with *defiance* when we asked her to deliver her report. Why might we have felt angry and hurt?

   _____

3. Nathaniel *preceded* his piano recital with a few informal comments about the composer. Which came first: his comments or his performance?

   _____

C. WORD STUDY: Use the context of each sentence and what you know about the Latin prefix *pre-* to rewrite the sentence so that it makes sense. Be careful not to change the word in italics.

1. Lucy was greatly interested in the comments by the authors in the *preface* at the end of the report.

   _____

   _____

2. At the parade, Mayor Vargas was scarcely visible because she *preceded* all the other marchers.

   _____

   _____

3. Thinking about yesterday's history test, Mark has a *premonition* that several questions would relate to the chapter review.

   _____

   _____

All-in-One Workbook
208

Poetry Collection: Edgar Allan Poe, Edwin Muir, Richard Wilbur
Writing About the Big Question

How does communication change us?

Big Question Vocabulary

aware	communication	comprehension	discuss	empathy
exchange	illuminate	informed	interpretation	meaning
react	relationship	resolution	respond	understanding

A. *Use one or more words from the list above to complete each sentence.*

1. Reading an encyclopedia article usually improves your _____ of a topic.

2. During the debate, the candidates were each given a maximum of three minutes to _____ to the panel's questions.

3. The TV documentary made us keenly _____ of the worldwide problems of hunger and malnutrition.

4. I thought I understood that poem well, but Patrick presented a completely different _____.

5. When you _____ a problem or conflict with others, your _____ of ideas may often lead to a(n) _____.

B. *Follow the directions in responding to each of the items below.*

1. List two different times when another person's facial expression or body language has played an important part in your figuring out his or her real **meaning.**

   _____

   _____

2. Write two sentences to explain one of these experiences, and describe how it made you feel. Use at least two of the Big Question vocabulary words.

   _____

   _____

C. *Complete the sentence below. Then, write a short paragraph in which you connect the sentence to the Big Question.*

Having **empathy** for someone who is in a difficult situation might make a person realize that _____

_____

_____

_____

Poetry Collection: Edgar Allan Poe, Edwin Muir, and Richard Wilbur
Literary Analysis: Narrative Poetry

Narrative poetry is verse that tells a story and includes the same literary elements as narrative prose:

- a plot, or sequence of events
- specific settings
- characters who participate in the action

Also like narrative prose, such as a short story, a narrative poem conveys a **mood,** or **atmosphere**—an overall feeling created by the setting, plot, words, and images. For example, a narrative poem's mood can be gloomy, joyous, or mysterious. Poetry's emphasis on precise words and images makes mood a powerful element in a narrative poem.

DIRECTIONS: *As you read "The Raven," "The Horses," and "The Writer," answer the following questions.*

"The Raven"

1. Who is the speaker in the poem? What kind of person is this speaker?

   _____

2. Briefly describe the poem's setting.

   _____

3. What story does the poem tell?

   _____

"The Horses"

4. What events does the speaker in the poem recall?

   _____

   _____

5. Briefly describe the poem's setting.

   _____

6. On what emotional note does the poem end?

   _____

"The Writer"

7. What two stories are told by the poem's speaker?

   _____

   _____

8. How would you describe the atmosphere, or overall mood, of the poem?

   _____

Poetry Collection: Edgar Allan Poe, Edwin Muir, and Richard Wilbur
Reading: Paraphrasing

Paraphrasing is restating in your own words what someone else has written or said. A paraphrase retains the essential meaning and ideas of the original but is simpler to read.

Paraphrasing is especially helpful when reading poetry because poems often contain **figurative language,** words and phrases that are used imaginatively rather than literally. To paraphrase lines in a narrative poem, **picture the action:**

- Based on details in the poem, form a mental image of the setting, the characters, and the characters' actions.
- To be sure that your mental picture is accurate, pay close attention to the way that the poet describes elements of the scene.
- Then, use your own words to describe your mental image of the scene and the action taking place in it.

DIRECTIONS: *On the lines provided, paraphrase the following passages from the narrative poems in this collection. Remember that a paraphrase is a restatement in your own words.*

1. Eagerly I wished the morrow—vainly I had tried to borrow
   From my books surcease of sorrow—sorrow for the lost Lenore—
   For the rare and radiant maiden whom the angels name Lenore—
       Nameless here for evermore. ("The Raven")

   _____

   _____

   _____

2. Yet they waited,
   Stubborn and shy, as if they had been sent
   By an old command to find our whereabouts
   And that long-lost archaic companionship. ("The Horses")

   _____

   _____

   _____

3. I remember the dazed starling
   Which was trapped in that very room, two years ago;
   How we stole in, lifted a sash

   And retreated, not to affright it; ("The Writer")

   _____

   _____

   _____

Poetry Collection: Edgar Allan Poe, Edwin Muir, and Richard Wilbur
Vocabulary Builder

Word List

archaic   beguiling   impenetrable   iridescent   pondered   respite

A. DIRECTIONS: *Match each word in Column A with the correct definition in Column B.*

Column A

___ 1. beguiling

___ 2. respite

___ 3. archaic

Column B

A. relief

B. charming

C. old-fashioned

B. DIRECTIONS: *Revise each sentence so that the underlined vocabulary word is used logically. Be sure not to change the vocabulary word.*

1. The professor's lecture was so *impenetrable* that we all grasped his main ideas without difficulty.

   _____

2. The *iridescent* fabric of the tablecloth was boring and unattractive.

   _____

3. He *pondered* his dilemma, laughing and joking with friends at the party.

   _____

C. WORD STUDY: Use the context of the sentences and what you know about the Latin prefix *im-* to explain your answer to each question.

1. Can an *immutable* situation be changed? Why or why not?

   _____

   _____

2. If you speak in an *impersonal* tone, are people likely to feel that you care about them?

   _____

   _____

3. If someone acts with *impropriety*, is that person behaving politely?

   _____

   _____

Poetry Collection: Enest Lawrence Thayer, William Stafford, Sandra Cisneros; Edgar Allan Poe,
Edwin Muir, and Richard Wilbur

Integrated Language Skills: Grammar

Appositive Phrases

An **appositive** is a noun or pronoun placed near another noun or pronoun to identify, rename, or explain it. Notice in the following example that the appositive is set off by commas, which indicates that it is not essential to the meaning of the sentence and can be removed.

Example: The author of "The Raven," *Edgar Allan Poe,* was also a noted short-story writer.

In the following example, *Edgar Allan Poe* is not set off by commas because it is needed to complete the meaning of the sentence.

Example: The American writer *Edgar Allan Poe* is often credited with the invention of the modern short story.

When an appositive has its own modifiers, it forms an **appositive phrase.** Appositive phrases are placed next to a noun or pronoun to add information and details.

Example: We enjoyed reading Poe's "The Cask of Amontillado," *a thrilling tale of suspense.*

A. DIRECTIONS: *Underline the appositive phrase in each of the following sentences. Then, write the word or words that each appositive phrase renames.*

1. Hyperbole, a figure of speech involving deliberate exaggeration, appears in a wide variety of literary works.

   _____

2. For instance, Homer, the oral poet credited with composing the *Iliad* and the *Odyssey,* often uses hyperbole to describe the deeds of epic heroes.

   _____

3. Jonathan Swift employs the same device for fantastic effects in *Gulliver's Travels,* his pointed satire on human life and behavior.

   _____

B. Writing Application: *Write a brief paragraph in which you describe an appliance that you often use at home. Use at least three appositive phrases in your writing, and underline each appositive phrase you use.*

_____

_____

_____

_____

_____

_____

_____

Name _____ Date _____

Poetry Collection: Ernest Lawrence Thayer, William Stafford, Sandra Cisneros;
Edgar Allan Poe, Edwin Muir, and Richard Wilbur

Integrated Language Skills: Support for Writing a Movie Scene

For your movie scene, use the following lines to make notes.

Details from "The Raven"

1. Characters: _____

_____

2. Setting: _____

_____

3. Actions: _____

_____

4. Mood: _____

_____

Mood in Movie's Opening Scene: _____

_____

_____

_____

_____

_____

Details Contributing to Mood: _____

_____

_____

_____

_____

_____

Camera Angles, Lighting, and so on: _____

_____

_____

_____

_____

_____

Poetry Collection: Emily Dickinson, Robert Frost, T. S. Eliot
Writing About the Big Question

How does communication change us?

Big Question Vocabulary

aware	communication	comprehension	discuss	empathy
exchange	illuminate	informed	interpretation	meaning
react	relationship	resolution	respond	understanding

A. *Use one or more words from the list above to complete each sentence.*

1. Although the Martinez family spent a year away in Spain, we stayed in regular
_____ with them by e-mail.

2. In order to _____ ideas effectively, you need to listen carefully to
the other group members.

3. The twin sisters' _____ is so close that one can usually tell what
the other is thinking, even without speaking.

4. In an oral presentation, graphic aids like charts can help you
_____ your _____ for the audience.

B. *Follow the directions in responding to each of the items below.*

1. List two different times when good **communication** with another person helped you
solve a problem or overcome a challenge.

_____

_____

2. Write two sentences to explain one of these experiences, and describe how it made
you feel. Use at least two of the Big Question vocabulary words.

_____

_____

C. *Complete the sentence below. Then, write a short paragraph in which you connect the
sentence to the Big Question.*

Other people can make someone **aware** of his or her potential by _____

_____

_____

_____

_____

_____

All-in-One Workbook
215

Poetry Collection: Robert Frost, Emily Dickinson, and T. S. Eliot
Literary Analysis: Rhyme and Meter

Rhyme is the repetition of sounds at the ends of words. There are several types of rhyme:

- **Exact rhyme:** the repetition of words that end with the same vowel and consonant sounds, as in *end* and *mend*
- **Slant rhyme:** the repetition of words that end with similar sounds but do not rhyme perfectly, as in *end* and *stand*
- **End rhyme:** the rhyming sounds of words at the ends of lines
- **Internal rhyme:** the rhyming of words within a line

A **rhyme scheme** is a regular pattern of end rhymes in a poem or stanza. A rhyme scheme is described by assigning one letter of the alphabet to each rhyming sound. For example, in "Uphill" by Christina Rossetti, the rhyme scheme is *abab*:

Does the road wind uphill all the <u>way</u>?	*a*
Yes, to the very <u>end</u>.	*b*
Will the day's journey take the whole long <u>day</u>?	*a*
From morn to night, my <u>friend</u>.	*b*

Meter is the rhythmical pattern in a line of poetry. Meter results from the arrangement of stressed (´) and unstressed (˘) syllables. When you read aloud a line with a regular meter, you can hear the steady, rhythmic pulse of the stressed syllables:

"and maggie discovered a shell that sang"
"Let not Ambition mock their useful toil"

Not all poems include rhyme, a rhyme scheme, or a regular meter. However, poets often use one or more of these techniques to create musical effects and achieve a sense of unity.

DIRECTIONS: *Read this stanza from "Dream Variations," a poem by Langston Hughes. Identify the rhyme scheme and think about how it emphasizes the speaker's meaning. Also think about Hughes's use of meter in these lines. Then, answer the questions on the lines provided.*

> To fling my arms wide
> In some place of the sun,
> To whirl and to dance
> Till the white day is done.
> 5   Then rest at cool evening
> Beneath a tall tree
> While night comes on gently,
>   Dark like me—
> That is my dream!

1. What is the rhyme scheme of this stanza?

_____

2. How does the rhyme scheme help to set off the last line in the stanza?

_____

3. Is the meter in these lines regular or irregular? Explain your answer.

_____

Poetry Collection: Robert Frost, Emily Dickinson, and T. S. Eliot
Reading: Paraphrasing

Paraphrasing is restating in your own words what someone else has written or said. A paraphrase should retain the essential meaning and ideas of the original but should be simpler to read. One way to simplify the text that you are paraphrasing is to **break down long sentences.** Divide long sentences into parts and paraphrase those parts.

- If a sentence contains multiple subjects or verbs, see if it can be separated into smaller sentences with a single subject and a single verb.
- If a sentence contains colons, semicolons, or dashes, create separate sentences by treating those punctuation marks as periods.
- If a sentence contains long phrases or long passages in parentheses, turn each phrase or parenthetical passage into a separate sentence.

Poets often write sentences that span several lines to give their poems fluidity. By breaking down long sentences and paraphrasing them, you can enjoy a poem's fluid quality without missing its meaning.

DIRECTIONS: *On the lines provided, paraphrase the following passages from the poems in this collection. Remember that a paraphrase is a restatement in your own words. In your paraphrases, use short sentences with simple structures.*

1. Then took the other, as just as fair,
   And having perhaps the better claim,
   Because it was grassy and wanted wear;
   Though as for that, the passing there
   Had worn them really about the same. ("The Road Not Taken")

   _____

   _____

   _____

2. The Heroism we recite
   Would be a normal thing
   Did not ourselves the Cubits warp
   For fear to be a King—("We never know how high we are")

   _____

   _____

   _____

3. And when the Foreign Office find a Treaty's gone astray,
   Or the Admiralty lose some plans and drawings by the way,
   There may be a scrap of paper in the hall or on the stair—
   But it's useless to investigate—*Macavity's not there!* ("Macavity: The Mystery Cat")

   _____

   _____

   _____

Poetry Collection: Robert Frost, Emily Dickinson, and T. S. Eliot
Vocabulary Builder

Word List

bafflement   depravity   disclosed   diverged
rifled   warp

A. DIRECTIONS: *Match each word in Column A with the correct definition in Column B.*

Column A	Column B
___ 1. diverged	A. twist
___ 2. warp	B. corruption
___ 3. bafflement	C. branched out
___ 4. depravity	D. puzzlement

B. DIRECTIONS: *In each of the following items, think about the meaning of the italicized word and then answer the question.*

1. The burglars *rifled* through their victim's belongings. Would the burglars have searched thoroughly or rapidly?

   _____

2. If someone *disclosed* a secret, would he or she keep it or not? Explain.

   _____

3. If a wooden cutting board was *warped*, would its surface be flat or uneven?

   _____

C. WORD STUDY: Use the context of the sentences and what you know about the Latin suffix *-ment* to explain your answer to each question.

1. If you experience *astonishment*, are you surprised or not?

   _____

   _____

2. Is an *amendment* to a document an addition or a subtraction?

   _____

   _____

3. Does a *postponement* mean that something will be done now or later?

   _____

   _____

Name ___Julieth Angarita_____ Date _____

Poetry Collection: Robert Frost, E. E. Cummings, William Shakespeare
Writing About the Big Question

How does communication change us?

Big Question Vocabulary

aware	communication	comprehension	discuss	empathy
exchange	illuminate	informed	interpretation	meaning
react	relationship	resolution	respond	understanding

A. *Use one or more words from the list above to complete each sentence.* ~~communication~~

1. Because he was so shy, Mark found __relationship__ with strangers difficult.

2. Many schools have started conflict management programs that help students find a(n) __resolution__ to their disputes.

3. Building your vocabulary helps improve your __comprehension__ of a reading passage.

4. The goal of a panel discussion is usually for the panelists to __exchange__ ideas.

5. __Communication__ with less fortunate people is one of Sue's most attractive character traits.

B. *Follow the directions in responding to each of the items below.*

1. Assume that you are about to make a documentary film or video. List two different topics that you might choose in order to make your audience better **informed.**

__weather and economy__

_____

2. Write two sentences to explain your reasons for choosing one of the topics. Use at least two of the Big Question vocabulary words.

__weather can help us to understanding the clime__
__economy exchange ideas to discuss__

C. *Complete the sentence below. Then, write a short paragraph in which you connect the sentence to the Big Question.*

Communication between two people can seem like action in a play when __The__
__interpretation and the topic is the same.__
__Also they can discuss about the action in the__
__play To exchange ideas for the topic__
_____

Name _____ Date _____

Poetry Collection: Robert Frost, E. E. Cummings, and William Shakespeare
Literary Analysis: Rhyme and Meter

Rhyme is the repetition of sounds at the ends of words. There are several types of rhyme:

- **Exact rhyme:** the repetition of words that end with the same vowel and consonant sounds, as in *end* and *mend*
- **Slant rhyme:** the repetition of words that end with similar sounds but do not rhyme perfectly, as in *end* and *stand*
- **End rhyme:** the rhyming sounds of words at the ends of lines
- **Internal rhyme:** the rhyming of words within a line

A **rhyme scheme** is a regular pattern of end rhymes in a poem or stanza. A rhyme scheme is described by assigning one letter of the alphabet to each rhyming sound. For example, in "Uphill" by Christina Rossetti, the rhyme scheme is *abab*:

Does the road wind uphill all the <u>way</u>?	*a*
Yes, to the very <u>end</u>.	*b*
Will the day's journey take the whole long <u>day</u>?	*a*
From morn to night, my <u>friend</u>.	*b*

Meter is the rhythmical pattern in a line of poetry. Meter results from the arrangement of stressed (´) and unstressed (˘) syllables. When you read aloud a line with a regular meter, you can hear the steady, rhythmic pulse of the stressed syllables:

"and maggie discovered a shell that sang"

"Let not Ambition mock their useful toil"

Not all poems include rhyme, a rhyme scheme, or a regular meter. However, poets often use one or more of these techniques to create musical effects and achieve a sense of unity.

DIRECTIONS: *Read this stanza from "The Day-Breakers," a poem by Arna Bontemps. Identify the rhyme scheme and think about how it emphasizes the speaker's meaning. Also, think about the poet's use of meter in these lines. Then, answer the questions on the lines provided.*

The Day-Breakers

1 We are not come to wage a strife a
2 with swords upon this hill: b
3 it is not wise to waste the life a
4 against a stubborn will. b

5   Yet would we die as some have done:
     beating a way for the rising sun.

1. What is the rhyme scheme of this poem?
   abab

2. How does the rhyme scheme help to set off the last two lines?
   because the line 2 rhyme with the line 4, And line 1 with 3

3. Is the meter in these lines regular or irregular? Explain your answer.
   The meter is irregular because the rhyme is different

Name _____ Date _____

Reading: Paraphrasing

Paraphrasing is restating in your own words what someone else has written or said. A paraphrase should retain the essential meaning and ideas of the original but should be simpler to read. One way to simplify the text that you are paraphrasing is to **break down long sentences.** Divide long sentences into parts and paraphrase those parts.

- If a sentence contains multiple subjects or verbs, see if it can be separated into smaller sentences with a single subject and a single verb.
- If a sentence contains colons, semicolons, or dashes, create separate sentences by treating those punctuation marks as periods.
- If a sentence contains long phrases or long passages in parentheses, turn each phrase or parenthetical passage into a separate sentence.

Poets often write sentences that span several lines to give their poems fluidity. By breaking down long sentences and paraphrasing them, you can enjoy a poem's fluid quality without missing its meaning.

DIRECTIONS: *On the lines provided, paraphrase the following passages from the poems in this collection. Remember that a paraphrase is a restatement in your own words. In your paraphrases, use short sentences with simple structures.*

1. But if it had to perish twice,
   I think I know enough of hate
   To say that for destruction ice
   Is also great
   And would suffice. ("Fire and Ice")

   BUT IF IT had to perish twice, I thing that I have
   enough to hate, to say that the ice is great.

   _____

2. molly befriended a stranded star
   whose rays five languid fingers were ("maggie and milly and molly and may")

   Molly befriended a whose rays five languid
   fingers.

3. All the world's a stage,
   And all the men and women merely players:
   They have their exits and their entrances;
   And one man in his time plays many parts,
   His acts being seven ages. ("The Seven Ages of Man")

   All the world's a stage, the men and woman
   have entrances, one man in his time act
   seven ages.

Poetry Collection: Robert Frost, E. E. Cummings, and William Shakespeare
Vocabulary Builder

Word List
languid   oblivion   stranded   suffice   treble   woeful

A. DIRECTIONS: *Match each word in Column A with the correct definition in Column B.*

Column A	Column B
___ 1. suffice	A. high-pitched voice
___ 2. languid	B. weak
___ 3. woeful	C. be enough
___ 4. treble	D. sorrowful

B. DIRECTIONS: *Revise each sentence so that the underlined vocabulary word is used logically. Be sure not to change the vocabulary word.*

1. The amount of lemonade in that pitcher will <u>suffice</u>, so we will need to make more.

_____

2. Their behavior was extremely <u>languid</u>, and we could not believe the amount of energy they displayed.

_____

3. We were <u>stranded</u> in the middle of nowhere, so we felt extremely happy.

_____

4. He dreamed of losing himself in <u>oblivion</u>, where he could happily mingle with the friends whose company he most enjoyed.

_____

C. WORD STUDY: Use the context of the sentences and what you know about the Latin suffix *-ion* to explain your answer to each question.

1. If a restaurant serves dishes from many different countries, could its menu be described as a *fusion*?

_____

_____

2. If someone at a trial pleads guilty, does the plea amount to an *admission* of guilt?

_____

_____

3. If a person suffers from *delusions* of grandeur, does he or she have a mental or emotional disorder?

_____

_____

Poetry Collection: Robert Frost, Emily Dickinson, and T. S. Eliot
Poetry Collection: Robert Frost, E. E. Cummings, and William Shakespeare
Integrated Language Skills: Grammar

Infinitives and Infinitive Phrases

An **infinitive** is a verb form preceded by the word *to* that acts as a noun, an adjective, or an adverb. An **infinitive phrase** is an infinitive with its modifiers or complements. Like infinitives, infinitive phrases can function as nouns, adjectives, or adverbs. Unlike a **prepositional phrase** that begins with *to* and ends with a noun or pronoun, an infinitive phrase always ends with a verb.

Infinitive:	The schoolboy liked *to complain*. (acts as a noun, functioning as the direct object of the sentence)
Infinitive Phrase:	During the storm, I was afraid *to go outdoors*. (acts as an adverb by modifying *afraid*)
Prepositional Phrase:	The girls traveled *to the beach*.

A. DIRECTIONS: *On the line provided, write the infinitive phrase in each sentence. Be sure to write the entire infinitive phrase: the infinitive with all of its modifiers or complements. Then, identify whether the infinitive phrase functions as a noun, an adjective, or an adverb.*

1. On the beach, the girls found plenty of shells to collect.

   _____

2. May wanted to keep the smooth round stone.

   _____

3. Maggie pointed out that iridescent shells are sometimes hard to find.

   _____

4. Molly was afraid to admit her fear of the little crab.

   _____

5. The beach was an ideal place to enjoy the warm, sunny afternoon.

   _____

B. Writing Application: *Write a brief paragraph describing one of your favorite hobbies. Use at least three infinitive phrases in your writing, and underline each infinitive phrase you use.*

   _____

   _____

   _____

   _____

   _____

   _____

Name _____ Date _____

Integrated Language Skills: Support for Writing a Poem

Make prewriting notes for your poem by thinking about the issues below.

Rhyme Scheme:

_____

_____

_____

Topic/Event/Experience/Emotion:

_____

_____

_____

_____

Images/Details/Phrases/Words:

_____

_____

_____

_____

_____

_____

_____

_____

Main Idea/Theme:

_____

_____

_____

_____

_____

Poetry by Alice Walker, Bashō, Chiyojo, Walt Whitman, William Shakespeare

Writing About the Big Question

How does communication change us?

Big Question Vocabulary

aware	communication	comprehension	discuss	empathy
exchange	illuminate	informed	interpretation	meaning
react	relationship	resolution	respond	understanding

A. *Use one or more words from the list above to complete each sentence.*

1. Good _____ often helps deepen a(n) _____ between two people.

2. Kyra was _____ that she would have to improve her reading _____ skills if she were to score well on that test.

3. We workers attended the meeting to _____ our grievances, but the management seemed to _____ with hostility.

4. The professor's _____ of that story helped _____ the _____ for us.

B. *Follow the directions in responding to each of the items below.*

1. List two poems from this unit that have changed your perception of a person, place, event, or situation.

_____

_____

2. Write two sentences to explain how the poem changed your perception, and describe how this experience made you feel. Use at least two of the Big Question vocabulary words.

_____

_____

C. *Complete the sentence below. Then, write a short paragraph in which you connect the sentence to the Big Question.*

A powerful poem makes us **aware** of _____

_____

_____

_____

Name _____ Date _____

Literary Analysis: Lyric Poetry

Lyric poetry is poetry with a musical quality that expresses the thoughts and feelings of a single speaker. Unlike a narrative poem, a lyric does not try to tell a complete story. Instead, it describes an emotion or a mood, often by using vivid imagery, or language that appeals to the senses. A lyric poem is relatively short and usually achieves a single, unified effect.

There are a variety of lyric forms that can create different effects:

- A **sonnet** is a fourteen-line poem that is written in iambic pentameter and that rhymes. Two common sonnet types are the Italian, or Petrarchan, and the English, or Shakespearean. The English, or Shakespearean, sonnet consists of three quatrains, or four-line stanzas, and a final rhyming couplet.
- A **haiku** is an unrhymed Japanese verse form arranged into three lines of five, seven, and five syllables. A haiku often uses a striking image from nature to convey a strong emotion.
- A **free verse** poem does not follow a regular pattern. Free verse employs sound and rhythmic devices, such as alliteration and repetition, and may even use rhyme—but not in a regular pattern, as in metered poetry.

DIRECTIONS: *Analyze each poem. On the chart, write the type of lyric in the first column. Then, in the remaining columns, briefly describe the speaker of the poem, identify the speaker's emotion, and quote an example of a striking image or sound device.*

Author	Type of Lyric	Speaker	Emotion	Image/Sound Device
Walker				
Bashō				
Chiyojo				
Whitman				
Shakespeare				

Poetry by Alice Walker, Bashō, Chiyojo, Walt Whitman, William Shakespeare
Vocabulary Builder

Word List

intermission   stout   wail   woes

A. DIRECTIONS: *Revise each sentence so that the underlined vocabulary word is used logically. Be sure not to change the vocabulary word.*

1. Because she is <u>stout</u> of heart, she faces her future with great fear.

   _____

2. The film was 3 hours long with no <u>intermission</u>; we were grateful for the break.

   _____

3. He was cheerful as he recounted to us his many <u>woes</u> of the past year.

   _____

4. So many misfortunes in a single day caused her to <u>wail</u> with happiness.

   _____

B. DIRECTIONS: *On the line, write the letter of the choice that is the best synonym, or word with a similar meaning, for each numbered word.*

___ 1. wail
   A. strike
   B. publish
   C. grieve
   D. crawl

___ 2. woes
   A. signals
   B. factories
   C. songs
   D. sorrows

___ 3. intermission
   A. analysis
   B. break
   C. communication
   D. alliance

___ 4. stout
   A. plentiful
   B. sturdy
   C. weary
   D. energetic

Poetry by Alice Walker, Bashō, Chiyojo, Walt Whitman, William Shakespeare
Support for Writing to Compare

Use a chart like the one shown to make prewriting notes for an essay comparing the relationship between lyric form and meaning in two poems from the selections.

Title of Poem 1: _____	
Lyric Form: _____	
Characteristics of Form: _____ _____ _____	
Relationship of Poem's Form to Its Meaning: _____ _____ _____ _____	
Title of Poem 2: _____	
Lyric Form: _____	
Characteristics of Form: _____ _____ _____	
Relationship of Poem's Form to Its Meaning: _____ _____ _____ _____	

Do Your Dance, performed by Hydra

Yeah . . . it's Blitzkrieg (Blitzkrieg) . . . We gonna have fun with this one! U-huh, u-huh, Y'all get ready! Yes . . . Go!

Now how much fun would things be if everyone were the same?

Same face, same voice, same look, same name?

I don't know about you but, to me that sounds lame

and I'd do everything in my power to make it change/

See me? I'm in a different lane I do things my way,/

You don't **accept** me? Oh, you don't approve? Hit the highway, but if you're different too, hey, that's cool with me/ I don't **discriminate** / no I don't hate you / cool with me/ just don't pretend just to fit in that's **conformity**/ and not being who you are is something wrong to be/

So I'll help you show us something that makes you **unique** yeah,/ what makes you one of a kind so to speak/ you might have to use your hands maybe move your feet/ now everybody rock along to the beat . . . and do your dance now.

Yeah, yeah, go ahead, do your dance now/

Yeah, yeah, go ahead, do your dance now/

Yeah, yeah, go ahead, do that dance now/

Yeah, yeah, go ahead, an' do your dance now/

See I've been around the world and seen a bunch of different dances

Some **cultures** wear special clothes some start with special stances/

So depending on your **background** or where you were born/ use some of that in

your dance next time the chorus comes on/ it's all about **understanding** what makes you who you are/our **differences** set us apart and make you a star /your popularity shouldn't be based on a **similarity** / shouldn't want to be alike /let's think with a little clarity/ embrace what makes us different, show some **individuality**/

Don't **assimilate** let your style stand out happily/ it's almost time to dance again actually/ I hope you've been practicing/ now everyone repeat these words after me/

Yeah, yeah, go ahead, do your dance now/

Yeah, yeah, go ahead, do your dance now/

Yeah, yeah, go ahead, do that dance now/

Yeah, yeah, go ahead, do your dance now/

Continued

By now I think we can **determine** / think we can decide/

Without our differences life would be a boring ride/ so whatever your culture **values defend** it with pride/don't let them criticize what makes you feel alive inside/never conform to the norm go head and **differentiate**/ this song helps you along now go ahead and demonstrate.

Yeah, yeah, go ahead, do your dance now/

Yeah, yeah, go ahead, do your dance now/

Yeah, yeah, go ahead, do that dance now/

Yeah, yeah, go ahead, do your dance now/

Song Title: **Do Your Dance**
Artist / Performed by Hydra
Vocals: Rodney "Blitz" Willie
Lyrics by Rodney "Blitz" Willie
Music composed by Keith "Wild Child" Middleton
Produced by Keith "Wild Child" Middleton
Technical Production: Mike Pandolfo, Wonderful
Executive Producer: Keith London, Defined Mind

Unit 5: Drama
Big Question Vocabulary—1

The Big Question: Do our differences define us?

When someone is new to a group, it is important to help him or her feel welcome and to understand that, even though people may act differently because of different experiences and culture, they normally experience the same feelings that you do.

accept: to regard as normal, suitable, or usual

defend: to support someone or something that is being hurt or criticized

differentiate: to recognize the differences between two or more things

discriminate: to treat someone differently and/or unfairly

understanding: knowledge that is based on understanding or experience

DIRECTION: *Use all the vocabulary words to fill in the callouts.*

Caroline said, "That new girl, Nubia, is really weird. She speaks funny and her clothing is so colorful and loose! I don't want her to sit with us at lunch anymore!"

Caroline's lunch buddies did not agree. They thought it was important to welcome Nubia as a newcomer to their community. They said the following in response to Caroline:

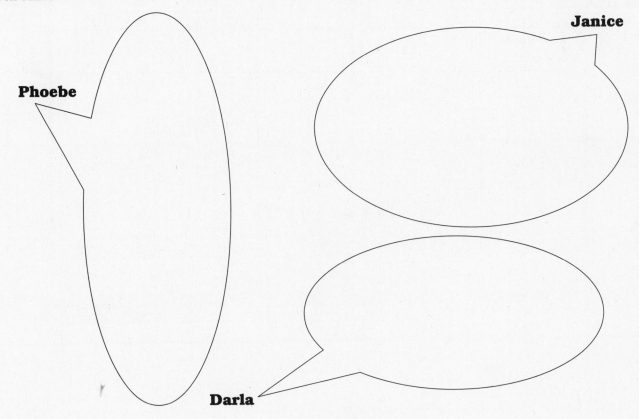

Unit 5: Drama
Big Question Vocabulary—2

The Big Question: Do our differences define us?

When you are in your own culture, you are similar to those around you, but if you take a trip to a foreign place you will quickly discover that you are suddenly the "different" one.

background: a person's family history, education, and social class

culture: ideas, beliefs, and customs that are shared by people in a society

determine: to conclude or ascertain after reasoning, observation, study, and so on

unique: having no like or equal; incomparable

values: one's principles concerning right and wrong and what is important in life

DIRECTIONS: *Use all the vocabulary words to complete the following exercise.*

You have just landed in a new country. Everybody is looking at you strangely. You are dressed differently from them, and your words sound like gibberish to them. There is only one person who speaks English, and he will be there for only twenty-four hours. He has offered to translate a short document that you write to introduce yourself and your culture to the people who live here.

Unit 5: Drama
Big Question Vocabulary—3

The Big Question: Do our differences define us?

Discrimination is often a result of people not having enough knowledge about others who appear different. Open dialogue can usually help people understand one another and can help people build tolerance and mutual respect.

assimilated: absorbed into the main cultural group

conformity: behavior that is within the accepted rules of a society or a group and is the same as that of most other people

differences: the quality or condition of being unlike or dissimilar

individuality: characteristics or qualities that distinguish one person from other people

similarity: having a likeness or a resemblance to something else or someone else

DIRECTIONS: *Newcomers to your school are feeling excluded. Write a proposed set of guidelines that tell your fellow students how newcomers should be treated at school. Use all of the vocabulary words.*

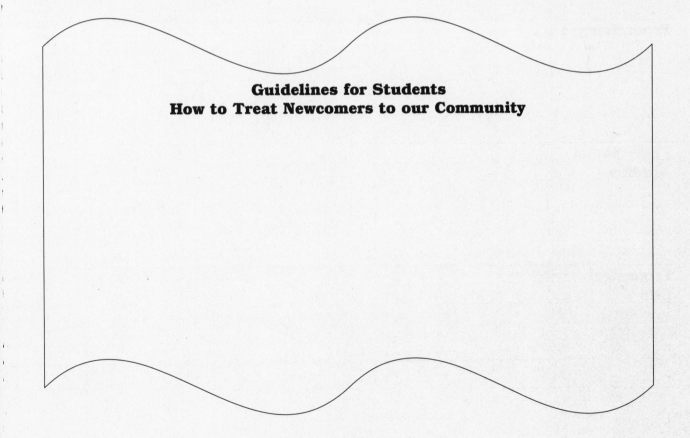

**Guidelines for Students
How to Treat Newcomers to our Community**

Name _____ Date _____

Unit 5: Drama
Applying the Big Question

The Big Question: Do our differences define us?

DIRECTIONS: *Complete the chart below to apply what you have learned about differences. One row has been completed for you.*

Example	Kinds of differences	The effect of the differences	What I Learned
From Literature	Differences in authority and position in "The Inspector-General"	The peasant outsmarts the powerful inspector-general.	Differences in authority and position don't define how clever someone is.
From Literature			
From Science			
From Social Studies			
From Real Life			

Gary L. Blackwood
Listening and Viewing

Segment 1: Meet Gary L. Blackwood
- What is *terra incognita*, and what does Gary L. Blackwood hope to accomplish by setting his stories there?
- What do you think you could learn by reading a story set in another place and time?

_____

_____

_____

_____

Segment 2: Drama
- What must Gary L. Blackwood do when transferring a story into a play?
- After listening to Gary L. Blackwood's reading of the book passage and a scene from the play, which do you prefer and why?

_____

_____

_____

_____

Segment 3: The Writing Process
- How do you think Gary L. Blackwood's acting experience has helped him as a playwright?
- How do you think this experience helps him write his sword-fighting scenes?

_____

_____

_____

_____

Segment 4: The Rewards of Writing
- What messages does Gary L. Blackwood hope to convey through his writing?
- What message do you think it would be important to convey through your writing? Why?

_____

_____

_____

_____

Name _____   Date _____

Unit 5
Learning About Drama

A drama or play is a story written to be performed by actors. It features **characters** facing a **conflict,** or struggle, that propels the sequence of events called the **plot.** The conflict reaches a **climax,** the point of greatest tension, and then is resolved. The **dialogue,** or speeches of the characters, tells the story, unlike fiction, in which the voice of a narrator tells the story.

The following chart shows some of the most important structural features and elements of drama.

Feature/Element	Function
acts and **scenes**	the basic units of drama
script	the play's text, containing dialogue and stage directions
stage directions	directions providing details about sets, lighting, sound effects, props, costumes, and acting
sets	constructions indicating where the drama takes place
props	movable objects that actors use onstage
theme	a drama's insight into life
dramatic effect	illusion of reality in a play's performance
dramatic speech	**monologue:** a long, uninterrupted speech delivered by a character to other characters who are on stage, but remain silent **soliloquy:** a speech in which a character alone on stage reveals private thoughts that the audience is allowed to overhear **aside:** a brief remark in which a character expresses private thoughts to the audience rather than to other characters

DIRECTIONS: *Circle the letter of the answer that best matches each numbered item.*

1. scenes
   A. directions to actors   B. props   C. subdivisions of acts

2. theme
   A. historical context   B. insight into life   C. dramatic speech

3. speech in which a character alone on stage reveals private thoughts and feelings
   A. dialogue   B. monologue   C. soliloquy

4. movable objects used on stage
   A. props   B. sets   C. asides

5. text of a play
   A. stage directions   B. dialogue   C. script

6. sequence of events in a drama
   A. climax   B. conflict   C. plot

Name _____ Date _____

from **The Shakespeare Stealer** by Gary L. Blackwood
Model Selection: Drama

In the script or text of a drama, playwrights combine **dialogue** with **stage directions** to tell the story, or plot, of the play. Stage directions are quickly recognizable because they are usually printed in italics and set off in brackets. When actors rehearse a play, they use the stage directions as a guide for delivering their lines, moving on stage, handling props, and using their posture and gestures to convey meaning.

DIRECTIONS: *Answer the following questions about* The Shakespeare Stealer *using the space provided.*

1. What specific information does the playwright provide in the stage directions at the beginning of Act I? Why would this information be helpful to the director and the actors?

_____

_____

_____

_____

2. Read the following excerpt from the play.

WIDGE:

Aye! It was a fortnight ago. 'A spotted me scribbling away, and afore I could make me escape, 'a collared me and snatched away me table-book!

BRIGHT:

Why did you not tell me this sooner?

WIDGE:

I was afeared. I kenned you'd be angry.

What conflict between Widge and Bright does this passage reveal?

_____

_____

3. When Falconer enters in the first scene, what kind of mood or atmosphere do the stage directions suggest should be established on stage?

_____

_____

4. How does Blackwood use stage directions in the fight between Falconer and the thieves?

_____

_____

5. Toward the end of the excerpt, what plan is revealed in the dialogue between Simon Bass and Widge?

_____

_____

Name _____ Date _____

The Tragedy of Romeo and Juliet, *Act I*, by William Shakespeare
Writing About the Big Question

Do our differences define us?

Big Question Vocabulary

accept	assimilated	background	conformity	culture
defend	determine	differences	differentiate	discriminate
individuality	similarity	understanding	unique	values

A. *Use one or more words from the list above to complete each sentence.*

1. The Big Question asks if our _____ define us.

2. Your _____ plays a role in making you who you are.

3. America has _____ people of many nations.

4. Although immigrants become part of the American way of life, many still cling to important aspects of their _____.

B. *Follow the directions in responding to each of the items below.*

1. In two sentences, name two ways that immigrant groups living in the United States might differ.

   _____

   _____

2. Write two sentences describing how one of the preceding differences is a positive thing. Use at least two of the Big Question vocabulary words.

   _____

   _____

C. *In* The Tragedy of Romeo and Juliet, *two young lovers come from families locked in a deadly feud. That difference defines their relationship and forces the plot toward tragic consequences. Complete the sentence below. Then, write a short paragraph in which you connect this idea to the Big Question.*

When family **differences** stand between lovers, they must _____

or _____

_____

_____

_____

Name _____ Date _____

The Tragedy of Romeo and Juliet, *Act I,* by William Shakespeare
Literary Analysis: Dialogue and Stage Directions

Dialogue is conversation between or among characters. In prose, dialogue is usually set off with quotation marks. In drama, the dialogue generally follows the name of the speaker, as in this example:

> BENVOLIO. I aimed so near when I supposed you loved.
>
> ROMEO. A right good markman. And she's fair I love.

Dialogue reveals the personalities and relationships of the characters and advances the action of a play.

Stage directions are notes in the text of a play that describe how the work should be performed, or staged. These instructions are usually printed in italics and sometimes set in brackets or parentheses. They describe scenes, lighting, sound effects, and the appearance and physical actions of the characters, as in this example:

> *Scene iii.* FRIAR LAWRENCE's cell.
>
> [*Enter.* FRIAR LAWRENCE *alone, with a basket.*]

As you read, notice how the dialogue and stage directions work together to help you "see" and "hear" the play in your mind.

DIRECTIONS: *Read the following passages from Act I and then use the lines provided to answer the questions.*

> TYBALT. Patience perforce with willful choler meeting
> Makes my flesh tremble in their different greeting.
> I will withdraw; but this intrusion shall,
> Now seeming sweet, convert to bitt'rest gall. (Act I, Scene v, ll. 88–91)

1. In the context of the scene, what does Tybalt mean by "this intrusion"?

   _____

2. What do the lines reveal about Tybalt's personality?

   _____

   _____

   _____

3. What do the lines foreshadow for the plot of the play?

   _____

   _____

   _____

Name _____   Date _____

The Tragedy of Romeo and Juliet, *Act I,* by William Shakespeare
Reading: Using Text Aids to Summarize

Summarizing is briefly stating the main points in a piece of writing. Stopping periodically to summarize what you have read helps you to check your comprehension before you read further.

To be sure that you understand Shakespeare's language before you summarize long passages, **use text aids**—the numbered explanations that appear alongside the text.

- If you are confused by a passage, check to see if there is a footnote or side note, and read the corresponding explanation.
- Reread the passage, using the information from the note to be sure you grasp the meaning of the passage.

DIRECTIONS: *Use the text aids to answer the following questions about what you read in Act I of the play.*

1. In your own words, summarize what is happening in Verona based on lines 1–4 of the Prologue.

   _____

   _____

   _____

2. In Scene i, as the two Montague Servingmen approach the two Capulet Servingmen, Sampson says, "Let us take the law of our sides; let them begin." What does he mean?

   _____

   _____

3. Later in Scene i, Benvolio and Montague talk about how unhappy Romeo has been. Then, they see Romeo. Benvolio tells Montague to leave so that he can talk to Romeo alone. Montague says, "I would thou wert so happy by thy stay / To hear true shrift." Put this wish into your own words.

   _____

   _____

4. In Scene iii, Juliet's mother tells her to "Read o'er the volume of young Paris's face." Refer to that passage (lines 81–92) and, with the help of text aids 9 and 10, restate the advice Lady Capulet gives to her daughter.

   _____

   _____

   _____

   _____

The Tragedy of Romeo and Juliet, *Act I,* by William Shakespeare
Vocabulary Builder

Word List

adversary   augmenting   grievance   oppression   pernicious   transgression

A. DIRECTIONS: *In each of the following items, think about the meaning of the italicized word and then answer the question.*

1. Would you be likely to praise an action that had *pernicious* consequences? Why or why not?

_____

2. In your opinion, does a *transgression* typically deserve punishment? Explain.

_____

3. Would a person expressing a *grievance* be likely to seem happy or sad? Explain.

_____

4. If your employer announces that she is *augmenting* your salary, how would you feel?

_____

5. Would you go out of your way to help an *adversary*? Explain.

_____

_____

6. Would a person experiencing *oppression* feel free or burdened? Explain.

_____

_____

B. WORD STUDY: The prefix *trans-* means "across" or "through." Answer each of the following questions using one of these words containing *trans-*: *transgression, transition, transitory, translucent, transport.*

1. What is one item that is *translucent*?

_____

2. What is one *transition* that people often make in life?

_____

3. What are two ways to *transport* goods?

_____

4. What kind of treatment does someone who has committed a *transgression* deserve?

_____

5. How would you feel if you found out that your troubles are *transitory*?

_____

The Tragedy of Romeo and Juliet, *Act II,* by William Shakespeare
Writing About the Big Question

Do our differences define us?

Big Question Vocabulary

accept	assimilated	background	conformity	culture
defend	determine	differences	differentiate	discriminate
individuality	similarity	understanding	unique	values

A. *Use one or more words from the list above to complete each sentence.*

1. My friend Steve wears _____ outfits to school, like bright orange shirts paired with purple pants.

2. He is quick to _____ his clothing by saying that he dresses to suit his mood.

3. You can certainly _____ between him and all the other boys in our class.

4. I have to admit that I admire his _____.

B. *Follow the directions in responding to each of the items below.*

1. In two sentences, describe a time when you stood out from others in your school.

   _____

   _____

2. Write two sentences explaining what the above experience revealed about you. Use at least two of the Big Question vocabulary words.

   _____

   _____

C. *In* The Tragedy of Romeo and Juliet, *two young lovers come from families locked in a deadly feud. That difference defines their relationship and forces the plot toward tragic consequences. Complete the sentence below. Then, write a short paragraph in which you connect this idea to the Big Question.*

   It is important to embrace our differences because _____

   _____

   _____

   _____

   _____

The Tragedy of Romeo and Juliet, *Act II,* by William Shakespeare
Literary Analysis: Blank Verse

Blank verse is unrhymed poetry written in a meter called iambic pentameter. A line written in iambic pentameter includes five stressed syllables, each preceded by an unstressed syllable, as in the following example:

'Tĭs bút thy̆ name that ĭs my̆ énĕmý.

Thŏu art thy̆sélf thŏugh nót ă Móntăgué.

Much of *The Tragedy of Romeo and Juliet* is written in blank verse. Shakespeare uses its formal meter to reinforce character rank. Important or aristocratic characters typically speak in blank verse. Minor or comic characters often do not speak in verse.

DIRECTIONS: *Mark the stressed and unstressed syllables in these lines from Act II, Scene v. Put a check mark next to any line that has one extra syllable or any line* not *written in iambic pentameter. The first line has been marked for you.*

JULIET. Thĕ clóck strŭck nine whĕn Í dĭd sénd thĕ núrse,
In half an hour she promised to return.
Perchance she cannot meet him. That's not so.
O, she is lame! Love's heralds should be thoughts,
5 Which ten times faster glide than the sun's beams
Driving back shadows over low'ring hills.
Therefore do nimble-pinioned doves draw Love,
And therefore hath the wind-swift Cupid wings.
Now is the sun upon the highmost hill
10 Of this day's journey, and from nine till twelve
Is three long hours, yet she is not come.
Had she affections and warm youthful blood,
She would be as swift in motion as a ball;
My words would bandy her to my sweet love,
15 And his to me.
But old folks, many feign as they were dead—
Unwieldy, slow, heavy and pale as lead.

Name _____ Date _____

Reading: Reading in Sentences to Summarize

Summarizing is briefly stating the main points of a piece of writing. Stopping periodically to summarize what you have read helps you to check your comprehension before you read further.

Summarizing is especially useful when reading a play that has long passages of blank verse. When you encounter one of these passages, **read in sentences,** just as if you were reading a poem. Pause according to punctuation and not necessarily at the end of each line.

Once you have grasped the meanings of individual sentences in blank verse, you can more easily and more accurately summarize long passages.

DIRECTIONS: *Read the following passage, and then answer the items on the lines provided.*

1 Two of the fairest stars in all the heaven,
2 Having some business, do entreat her eyes
3 To twinkle in their spheres till they return.
4 What if her eyes were there, they in her head?
5 The brightness of her cheek would shame those stars
6 As daylight doth a lamp; her eyes in heaven
7 Would through the airy region stream so bright
8 That birds would sing and think it were not night.

1. At the end of which line(s) should you make no pause at all?

_____

2. At the end of which line(s) should you make a major pause?

_____

3. At the end of which line(s) should you make a minor pause?

_____

4. Write a brief summary of the main points in this passage.

_____

_____

_____

_____

_____

_____

The Tragedy of Romeo and Juliet, *Act II,* by William Shakespeare
Vocabulary Builder

Word List

intercession   lamentable   predominant   procure   sallow   unwieldy

A. DIRECTIONS: *For each of the following items, think about the meaning of the italicized word and then answer the question.*

1. Would an *unwieldy* burden be easy or difficult to carry? Why?

   _____

2. If you received *lamentable* news, how would you feel?

   _____

3. Is *intercession* typically something you undertake on your own behalf or for the sake of someone else?

   _____

4. If a species of tree is *predominant* in your neighborhood, are there many or few of that species?

   _____

5. What might cause a person with a normally rosy complexion to suddenly look *sallow*?

   _____

6. If you need film for your camera, where might you try to *procure* it?

   _____

B. WORD STUDY: The Latin prefix *pro-* means "before," "forth," or "forward." Answer each of the following questions using one of these words containing *pro-*: *procure, profound, profuse, protrude, provoke.*

1. What would be difficult to *procure* in the desert?

   _____

2. What can you do to fix teeth that *protrude*?

   _____

3. How might someone react if you *provoke* that person?

   _____

4. What might be the subject of a *profound* discussion?

   _____

5. If a critic is *profuse* in her praise of a movie, how well did she like the movie?

   _____

Name _____ Date _____

The Tragedy of Romeo and Juliet, *Act III,* by William Shakespeare
Writing About the Big Question

Do our differences define us?

Big Question Vocabulary

accept	assimilated	background	conformity	culture
defend	determine	differences	differentiate	discriminate
individuality	similarity	understanding	unique	values

A. *Use one or more words from the list above to complete each sentence.*

1. Rosa Parks did not think that others should _____ against her because of her race.

2. In the South in 1955, there was an _____ that African Americans sit in a section in the back of the bus.

3. Parks refused to _____ this practice.

4. Her act of defiance helped _____ the course of the civil rights movement in America.

B. *Follow the directions in responding to each of the items below.*

1. In two sentences, tell why you think people are discriminated against because they are different. Use at least two of the Big Question vocabulary words.

   _____

   _____

2. Write two sentences explaining two things you might do to fight discrimination.

   _____

   _____

C. *In* The Tragedy of Romeo and Juliet, *two young lovers come from families locked in a deadly feud. That difference defines their relationship and forces the plot toward tragic consequences. Complete the sentence below. Then, write a short paragraph in which you connect this idea to the Big Question.*

Family differences are especially hard to overcome because _____

_____

_____

_____

The Tragedy of Romeo and Juliet, *Act III,* by William Shakespeare
Literary Analysis: Dramatic Speeches

Characters in plays often deliver these types of **dramatic speeches:**

- **Soliloquy:** a lengthy speech in which a character—usually alone on stage—expresses his or her true thoughts or feelings. Soliloquies are unheard by other characters.
- **Aside:** a brief remark by a character revealing his or her true thoughts or feelings, unheard by other characters.
- **Monologue:** a lengthy speech by one person. Unlike a soliloquy, a monologue is addressed to other characters.

Characters often add meaning to speeches by making **allusions**—references to well-known people, places, or events from mythology or literature. For example, in Act II, Mercutio insultingly calls Tybalt "Prince of Cats," alluding to a cat named Tybalt in French fables.

DIRECTIONS: *Answer the questions that follow about an aside, a soliloquy, a monologue, and an allusion.*

1. In Scene v, Juliet's mother refers to Romeo as a villain. In an aside, Juliet says, "Villain and he be many miles asunder." What is the effect of this aside? Why do you think Shakespeare wrote just the one remark as an aside?

_____

_____

2. In Scene v, Capulet delivers a monologue when he discovers that Juliet has rejected the match with Paris. Reread lines 177–197. What makes this speech a monologue?

_____

_____

3. Why is it important for Juliet and the others to hear Capulet's monologue?

_____

_____

4. At the close of Scene v, Juliet delivers a soliloquy. Reread lines 237–244. What makes these last eight lines a soliloquy?

_____

_____

5. Explain Juliet's allusion to Greek mythology in the opening lines of Scene ii.

    Gallop apace, you fiery-footed steeds,

    Toward Phoebus' lodging!

_____

_____

Name _____ Date _____

The Tragedy of Romeo and Juliet, *Act III,* by William Shakespeare
Reading: Using Paraphrases to Summarize

Summarizing is briefly stating the main points of a piece of writing. Before you summarize a long passage in a Shakespearean play, you should **paraphrase** it by restating the lines in your own words. For example, compare these two versions of a speech by Romeo:

Shakespeare's version: This gentleman, the prince's near ally, / My very friend, hath got his mortal hurt / In my behalf.

Paraphrase: My good friend, a close relative of the prince, has been fatally wounded in defending me.

Once you have paraphrased small portions of text, you can more easily and accurately summarize the entire passage.

DIRECTIONS: *Paraphrase the following passages from Act III. Remember that a paraphrase is a restatement in your own words for clarity. It is not a summary.*

1. **TYBALT.** Romeo, the love I bear thee can afford
   No better term than this: thou art a villain. (Scene i, ll. 57–58)

   _____

   _____

2. **PRINCE.** My blood for your rude brawls doth lie a-bleeding;
   But I'll amerce you with so strong a fine
   That you shall all repent the loss of mine. (Scene i, ll. 188–190)

   _____

   _____

   _____

3. **JULIET.** So tedious is this day
   As is the night before some festival
   To an impatient child that hath new robes
   And may not wear them. (Scene ii, ll. 28–31)

   _____

   _____

   _____

   _____

The Tragedy of Romeo and Juliet, *Act III,* by William Shakespeare
Vocabulary Builder

Word List

eloquence   exile   fickle   fray   gallant   martial

A. DIRECTIONS: *For each of the following items, think about the meaning of the italicized word and then answer the question.*

1. Would you describe the people participating on both sides of a *fray* as hostile or friendly? Explain.

   _____

2. Can a romance in which one or both partners are *fickle* be described as stable and happy? Why or why not?

   _____

3. Would the sound of *martial* music evoke war or peace? Explain.

   _____

4. If you call someone *gallant,* is that a compliment or an insult? Explain.

   _____

5. What might be one of the main sorrows or complaints of a person who is *exiled*?

   _____

6. If a candidate delivers a speech with *eloquence,* is it likely to be persuasive? Why or why not?

   _____

B. WORD STUDY: The Latin root *-loque-* means "to speak." Answer each of the following questions using one of these words containing *-loque-*: *colloquial, eloquence, loquacious, soliloquy, ventriloquist.*

1. Who gives a *soliloquy*?

   _____

2. With whom does a *ventriloquist* usually converse?

   _____

3. What is an example of when it is appropriate to use *colloquial* language?

   _____

4. What difficulty might you have conversing with someone who is *loquacious*?

   _____

5. How might you be affected by the *eloquence* of a speech?

   _____

The Tragedy of Romeo and Juliet, *Act IV,* by William Shakespeare
Writing About the Big Question

Do our differences define us?

Big Question Vocabulary

accept	assimilated	background	conformity	culture
defend	determine	differences	differentiate	discriminate
individuality	similarity	understanding	unique	values

A. *Use one or more words from the list above to complete each sentence.*

1. Some people believe that extreme _____ prevents original thought.

2. Galileo was an original thinker with a great _____ of science.

3. He got into trouble when he dared to _____ the idea that the earth revolved around the sun.

4. The religious _____ of the time held fast to the idea that the earth was the center of the universe.

B. *Follow the directions in responding to each of the items below.*

1. In two sentences, describe a time when your thinking did not conform with the thinking of your classmates.

   _____

   _____

2. Write two sentences defending your preceding position. Use at least two of the Big Question vocabulary words.

   _____

   _____

C. In The Tragedy of Romeo and Juliet, *two young lovers come from families locked in a deadly feud. That difference defines their relationship and forces the plot toward tragic consequences. Complete the sentence below. Then, write a short paragraph in which you connect this idea to the Big Question.*

Differences between families can result in tragedy if _____

_____

_____

_____

_____

Name _____ Date _____

The Tragedy of Romeo and Juliet, *Act IV,* by William Shakespeare
Literary Analysis: Dramatic Irony

Dramatic irony is a contradiction between what a character thinks and says and what the audience or reader knows is true. For example, in Act III, Capulet plans Juliet's wedding to Paris. He does not know what you know: that Juliet is already married to Romeo. Dramatic irony involves the audience emotionally in the story.

Shakespeare knew his audience could become *too* involved in the intense emotion of *Romeo and Juliet.* Therefore, he made sure to include the following elements to lighten the play's mood:

- **Comic relief:** a technique used to interrupt a serious scene by introducing a humorous character or situation
- **Puns:** plays on words involving a word with multiple meanings or two words that sound alike but have different meanings. For example, the dying Mercutio makes a pun involving two meanings of the word *grave:* "Ask for me tomorrow, and you shall find me a grave man."

DIRECTIONS: *Use the lines provided to answer the following questions.*

1. Explain the dramatic irony in this passage from Scene i, when Friar Lawrence asks Paris to leave.

   FRIAR. My lord, we must entreat the time alone.
   PARIS. God shield I should disturb devotion!
       Juliet, on Thursday early will I rouse ye.

   _____

   _____

2. In Scene ii, Juliet tells her father she will go through with the wedding, and he begins to make preparations for the celebration. How do Capulet's words create dramatic irony?

   CAPULET. My heart is wondrous light,
       Since this same wayward girl is so reclaimed.

   _____

   _____

3. Juliet prepares for bed in Scene iii. Why is this exchange dramatically ironic?

   LADY CAPULET. What, are you busy, ho? Need you my help?
   JULIET. No, madam; we have culled such necessaries
       As are behoveful for our state tomorrow. . . .
   LADY CAPULET. Good night.
       Get thee to bed, and rest: for thou hast need.

   _____

   _____

Name _____ Date _____

The Tragedy of Romeo and Juliet, *Act IV,* by William Shakespeare
Reading: Breaking Down Long Sentences to Summarize

Summarizing is briefly stating the main points of a piece of writing. Stopping periodically to summarize what you have read helps you to check your comprehension before you read further.

Before you summarize a long passage of Shakespearean dialogue, you should **break down long sentences.**

- If a sentence contains multiple subjects or verbs, separate it into smaller sentences with one subject and one verb.
- If a sentence contains colons, semicolons, or dashes, treat those punctuation marks as periods in order to make smaller sentences.

DIRECTIONS: *Read the following passages. Practice breaking down the sentences by reading them in meaningful sections according to the punctuation. Rewrite the sentences in your own words, using smaller sentences.*

1. **PARIS.** Immoderately she weeps for Tybalt's death,
   And therefore have I little talked of love;
   For Venus smiles not in a house of tears. (Act IV, Scene i)

   _____

   _____

   _____

2. **JULIET.** 'Twixt my extremes and me this bloody knife
   Shall play the umpire, arbitrating that
   Which the commission of thy years and art
   Could to no issue of true honor bring. (Act IV, Scene i)

   _____

   _____

   _____

3. **FRIAR.** Hold, daughter. I do spy a kind of hope,
   Which craves as desperate an execution
   As that is desperate which we would prevent.

   _____

   _____

   _____

The Tragedy of Romeo and Juliet, *Act IV*, by William Shakespeare
Vocabulary Builder

Word List

dismal   enjoined   loathsome   pensive   vial   wayward

A. DIRECTIONS: *In each of the following items, think about the meaning of the italicized word and then answer the question.*

1. Would most of the people at a lively party be likely to be in a *pensive* mood? Why or why not?

   _____

2. If a good friend's behavior was *wayward*, would you be pleased or concerned? Explain.

   _____

3. "That place is *dismal*," he remarked. Would you want to go there? Why or why not?

   _____

4. If you were *enjoined* to do something, would the action be ordered or recommended?

   _____

5. If a swampland you were visiting had a *loathsome* smell, would you be tempted to return?

   _____

6. Would a sick person or a well person be more likely to carry a *vial*? Explain.

   _____

B. WORD STUDY: The prefix *en-* means "in" or "cause to be." Answer each of the following questions using one of these words containing *en-*: *endanger, enjoined, enlighten, enlarge, entice.*

1. What might you be *enjoined* to do in a library?

   _____

2. What might a person *enlarge*?

   _____

3. How might you *entice* your dog to do a trick?

   _____

4. What might *enlighten* you about the subject of medicine?

   _____

5. What might *endanger* swimmers?

   _____

The Tragedy of Romeo and Juliet, *Act V,* by William Shakespeare

Writing About the Big Question

Do our differences define us?

Big Question Vocabulary

accept	assimilated	background	conformity	culture
defend	determine	differences	differentiate	discriminate
individuality	similarity	understanding	unique	values

A. *Use one or more words from the list above to complete each sentence.*

1. There is often a _____ among superheroes.

2. Many have _____ powers that set them apart from others.

3. They stand up for _____ such as truth, justice, and the American way.

4. They use their powers to _____ good people from evildoers.

B. *Follow the directions in responding to each of the items below.*

1. In two sentences, describe two superpowers you would most like to have to set you apart from others.

   _____

   _____

2. Write two sentences explaining why you would want to have one of the preceding powers. Use at least two of the Big Question vocabulary words.

   _____

   _____

C. In The Tragedy of Romeo and Juliet, *two young lovers come from families locked in a deadly feud. That difference defines their relationship and forces the plot toward tragic consequences. Complete the sentence below. Then, write a short paragraph in which you connect this idea to the Big Question.*

One thing that we can learn from the differences we see in others is _____

_____

_____

_____

_____

Name _____ Date _____

The Tragedy of Romeo and Juliet, *Act V,* by William Shakespeare
Literary Analysis: Tragedy and Motive

A **tragedy** is a drama in which the central character, who is of noble stature, meets with disaster or great misfortune. The tragic hero's downfall is usually the result of one of the following:

- fate
- a serious character flaw
- some combination of both

Motive is an important element of a tragic hero's character. A character's motive is the reason behind an individual's thoughts or actions. In many of Shakespeare's tragedies, the hero's motives are basically good, but sometimes misguided. As a result, the hero suffers a tragic fate that may seem undeserved.

Although tragedies typically have unhappy endings, they can also be uplifting. They often show the greatness of which the human spirit is capable when faced with grave challenges.

DIRECTIONS: *Use the lines provided to answer the questions about tragedy and motive in* Romeo and Juliet.

1. In what ways does Romeo fit the characteristics of a tragic hero? How does he *not* fit these characteristics? In your answer, include a consideration of his tragic flaw.

_____

_____

_____

_____

_____

_____

2. The ancient Greek philosopher Aristotle, in his treatise on tragedy entitled *Poetics,* identified another element that is common to most tragedies: the hero's recognition of the whole tragic situation. This recognition always comes too late for the hero to avoid disaster or death. However, Shakespeare departs from Aristotle's idea about the hero's recognition. In *Romeo and Juliet,* it is not Romeo who experiences recognition, but other characters in the play. Who are these characters, and when does the recognition occur?

_____

_____

_____

_____

_____

_____

Name _____ Date _____

Reading: Identifying Causes and Effects to Summarize

Summarizing is briefly stating the main points of a piece of writing. In summarizing the action in a tragedy, it is useful to first **identify causes and effects.**

- A *cause* is an event, an action, or a feeling that produces a result.
- An *effect* is the result produced by the cause.

Tragedies often involve a chain of causes and effects that advances the plot and leads to the final tragic outcome. Understanding how one event leads to another will help you to summarize complicated plots like the one in *Romeo and Juliet*.

DIRECTIONS: *As you read Act V, fill in the boxes in this chain-of-events graphic organizer. Note that Scene iii has two chains of events. When your chain-of-events graphic is complete, notice how the events in one scene have produced events in later scenes.*

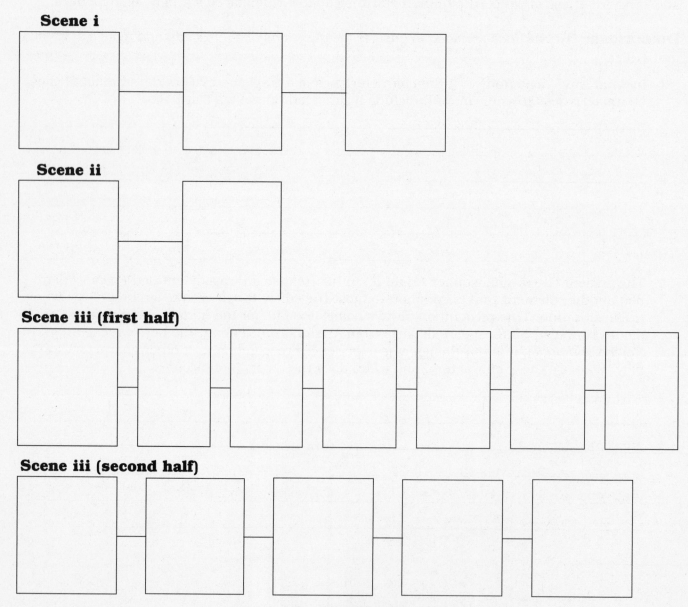

Scene i

Scene ii

Scene iii (first half)

Scene iii (second half)

The Tragedy of Romeo and Juliet, *Act V,* by William Shakespeare
Vocabulary Builder

Word List

  ambiguities   disperse   haughty   penury   remnants   scourge

A. DIRECTIONS: *In each of the following items, think about the meaning of the italicized word and then answer the question.*

1. Would someone living in *penury* be likely to purchase an expensive new home? Why or why not?

   _____

2. If a statement contains *ambiguities*, can you be sure of its meaning? Explain.

   _____

3. Would the sight of a *scourge* inspire happiness or fear?

   _____

4. If an area is pounded by the *remnants* of a hurricane, does it experience winds in advance of the storm or after the storm?

   _____

5. Would you praise or criticize someone for *haughty* behavior? Explain.

   _____

6. If you see a crowd at a concert *disperse*, are they coming or going? Explain.

   _____

B. WORD STUDY: The prefix *ambi-* means "both" or "around." Answer each of the following questions using one of these words containing *ambi-*: *ambiance, ambidextrous, ambient, ambiguities, ambivalent.*

1. Why might you have trouble understanding a speech that is full of *ambiguities*?

   _____

2. What are some things that help set the *ambiance* of a restaurant?

   _____

3. Why can someone who is *ambidextrous* write with either hand?

   _____

4. What might make you *ambivalent* about taking a course?

   _____

5. If a room has *ambient* lighting, where is the light coming from in the room?

   _____

The Tragedy of Romeo and Juliet, *Acts I–V,* by William Shakespeare
Integrated Language Skills: Grammar

Participles and Participial Phrases

A **participle** is a verb form that acts as an adjective.

There are two kinds of participles: present participles and past participles. **Present participles** end in *-ing.* The **past participles** of regular verbs end in *-ed.*

A **participial phrase** is a group of words that functions as an adjective in a sentence and contains a participle.

Participle:	She glimpsed a *soaring* eagle. (modifies *eagle*)
Participial Phrase:	She glimpsed a bird *soaring high in the sky.* (modifies *bird*)

A. DIRECTIONS: *In the following sentences, identify each participle or participial phrase. Indicate the word each one modifies.*

1. Frightened by the prospect of a brawl, Benvolio urges Mercutio to go indoors.

   _____

2. Trying to protect Mercutio, Romeo actually causes Mercutio's death.

   _____

3. The feuding families are punished by the Prince.

   _____

Gerunds and Gerund Phrases

A **gerund** is a form of a verb that acts as a noun. It can function as a subject, an object, a predicate noun, or the object of a preposition. A **gerund phrase** is a gerund and its modifiers; it also acts as a noun.

Look at the following examples:

Gerund:	*Singing* was a delight. (subject)
Gerund Phrase:	*Singing with the community chorus* was a way to make new friends. (subject)
	We always took pleasure in *attending the rehearsals on Friday nights.* (object of preposition)

B. DIRECTIONS: *In the following sentences, identify each gerund or gerund phrase, and identify its function.*

1. Rehearsing weekly was a necessity.

   _____

2. For weeks, we worked toward the goal of presenting a special Thanksgiving concert.

   _____

3. Maria practices playing the piano for several hours each day.

   _____

Name _____ Date _____

"Pyramus and Thisbe" by Ovid
from **A Midsummer Night's Dream** by William Shakespeare

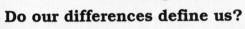

Writing About the Big Question

Do our differences define us?

Big Question Vocabulary

accept	assimilated	background	conformity	culture
defend	determine	differences	differentiate	discriminate
individuality	similarity	understanding	unique	values

A. *Use one or more words from the list above to complete each sentence.*

1. Sometimes it is up to the individual to _____ what is right and what is wrong.

2. During World War II, some people would not _____ the Nazi persecution of the Jews.

3. While many did as they were told, a few courageous people refused to act in _____ with oppressive German laws.

4. They showed a true _____ of what it means to be a human being by hiding Jewish people and helping them escape.

B. *Follow the directions in responding to each of the items below.*

1. Write two sentences explaining why it is not always popular to do the right thing.

   _____

   _____

2. Write two sentences explaining how standing up for your beliefs can be considered "courageous." Use at least two of the Big Question vocabulary words.

   _____

   _____

C. *In these selections, the main characters fall victim to love, which is ill-fated due to the differences in characters. Complete the sentence below. Then, write a short paragraph in which you connect this idea to the Big Question.*

When people have major **differences**, love _____

_____

_____

_____

Name _____ Date _____

"Pyramus and Thisbe" by Ovid
from A Midsummer Night's Dream by William Shakespeare
Literary Analysis: Archetypal Theme—Ill-fated Love

An **archetype** is a plot, a character, an image, or a setting that appears in literature from around the world and throughout history. Archetypes represent truths about life and are said to mirror the working of the human mind. Common archetypes include the following:

- *Characters:* the hero; the outcast
- *Plot types:* the quest, or search; the task
- *Symbol:* water as a symbol for life; fire as a symbol of power

A **theme** is the central idea, message, or insight of a literary work. **Archetypal themes** are those that develop or explore foundational, archetypal ideas. One example of an archetypal theme is ill-fated love, which appears in folklore, mythology, and literature from all over the world.

Works of literature may differ in their presentations of the same archetypal theme for a variety of reasons, including the following:

- the values of the author and the audience at the time the literary work was written
- the author's purpose for writing the literary work
- the culture and language of the author, including any literary styles and expectations

DIRECTIONS: *Write your answers to the following questions on the lines provided.*

1. In what sense are all three of these works stories of ill-fated love: *Romeo and Juliet*, "Pyramus and Thisbe," and the tale of Titania and Bottom's love in *A Midsummer Night's Dream?*

   _____

   _____

   _____

2. Why do you think Shakespeare added Romeo and Juliet's marriage to his story?

   _____

   _____

   _____

3. What message about love does Titania's love for Bottom suggest?

   _____

   _____

   _____

4. Which version of the archetypal theme of ill-fated love do you think best reflects the nature of love? Explain.

   _____

   _____

   _____

"Pyramus and Thisbe" by Ovid
from **A Midsummer Night's Dream** by William Shakespeare
Vocabulary Builder

Word List

enamored   enthralled   inevitable   lament

A. DIRECTIONS: *Revise each sentence so that the underlined vocabulary word is used logically. Be sure not to change the vocabulary word.*

1. We heard the mourners' <u>lament</u> and saw them smiling.

   _____

2. Since the defeat of our team in the big game was <u>inevitable</u>, we planned a victory celebration.

   _____

3. Mr. Schuyler nodded his agreement and said he was not <u>enamored</u> of our plan.

   _____

4. We sat <u>enthralled</u> as the lecturer droned on, endlessly repeating himself.

   _____

B. DIRECTIONS: *On the line, write the letter of the choice that is the best antonym, or opposite, for each word.*

___ 1. inevitable
   A. available
   B. presentable
   C. avoidable
   D. grotesque

___ 2. enamored
   A. charmed
   B. gratified
   C. assumed
   D. disgusted

___ 3. enthralled
   A. bored
   B. attracted
   C. captured
   D. amused

___ 4. lament
   A. predict
   B. celebrate
   C. protest
   D. despise

C. DIRECTIONS: *Choose the pair of words that expresses the same relationship as the pair in capital letters. Write the letter of your choice on the line.*

___ 1. MOURN : LAMENT
   A. delay: accelerate
   B. attempted: failed
   C. convince: discourage
   D. compliment: flatter

___ 2. INEVITABLE : DEATH
   A. feline: cow
   B. luscious: peach
   C. fantastic: table
   D. dangerous: perilous

"Pyramus and Thisbe" by Ovid
from **A Midsummer Night's Dream** by William Shakespeare
Support for Writing to Compare Literary Works

Use a chart like the one shown to make prewriting notes for an essay comparing and contrasting Shakespeare's treatment of the characters and events from "Pyramus and Thisbe" in *Romeo and Juliet* and in *A Midsummer Night's Dream.*

	Romeo and Juliet	*A Midsummer Night's Dream*
How Characters Affect Archetypal Theme		
How Settings Affect Archetypal Theme		
How Shakespeare Wanted Audience to Feel About Ill-fated Love		

Possible Reasons for Exploring the Same Story in a Tragedy and in a Comedy:

_____

_____

_____

_____

_____

"**The Inspector-General**" by Anton Chekhov
Writing About the Big Question

Do our differences define us?

Big Question Vocabulary

accept	assimilated	background	conformity	culture
defend	determine	differences	differentiate	discriminate
individuality	similarity	understanding	unique	values

A. *Use one or more words from the list above to complete each sentence.*

1. In the late nineteenth century, reformers decided that American Indians should be _____ rather than be put on reservations.

2. As a result, native children were sent to boarding schools where they were forced to abandon their _____.

3. The experience was traumatic for the children, since they were losing a sense of their _____.

4. The reformers did not realize how important our _____ are to our identity.

B. *Follow the directions in responding to each of the items below.*

1. In two sentences, give two important aspects of your **culture** that help you define yourself.

   _____

   _____

2. Write two sentences explaining how you would feel if the preceding aspects were taken from you. Use at least two of the Big Question vocabulary words.

   _____

   _____

C. *In* The Inspector-General, *the Inspector-General dresses in disguise so people will not know he is on official business. He is different from those around him, though, and the truth is hard to conceal. Complete the sentence below. Then, write a short paragraph in which you connect this idea to the Big Question.*

No matter how hard someone tries, his or her **background** _____.

_____

_____

_____

_____

Name _____ Date _____

Comedy is a form of drama that ends happily, and aims primarily to amuse. The humor in comic plays may arise from one or more of the following elements: funny names, witty dialogue, and comic situations, such as deception by a character, misunderstandings, or mistaken identities.

The humor of comic situations often relies on **dramatic irony,** which is a contradiction between what a character thinks and says and what the audience knows is true. In comedies, the audience often knows the truth about a situation while the characters remain unaware. As a result, the characters' statements and behavior may seem funny to the audience.

DIRECTIONS: *Read each passage. Then, briefly explain why it is humorous or comic.*

1. **STORYTELLER.** And when he'd thought to himself for long enough, he fell into conversation with the driver of the cart. What did he talk about? About himself, of course. [*Exit the* STORYTELLER.]

   TRAVELER. I gather you've got a new Inspector-General in these parts.

   _____

   _____

   _____

2. **DRIVER.** Oh, no, the new one goes everywhere on the quiet, like. Creeps around like a cat. Don't want no one to see him, don't want no one to know who he is.

   _____

   _____

   _____

3. **DRIVER.** He hops on a train just like anyone else, just like you or me. Then when he gets off, he don't go jumping into a cab or nothing fancy. Oh, no. He wraps himself up from head to toe so you can't see his face, and he wheezes away like an old dog so no one can recognize his voice.

   TRAVELER. Wheezes? That's not wheezing! That's the way he talks! So I gather.

   _____

   _____

   _____

4. **DRIVER.** Fixed himself up a tube behind his desk, he has. Leans down, takes a pull on it, no one the wiser.

   TRAVELER [*offended*]. How do you know all this, may I ask?

   _____

   _____

   _____

"The Inspector-General" by Anton Chekhov
Reading: Drawing Conclusions

A **conclusion** is a decision or an opinion that you reach based on details in a text. In drawing conclusions, you consider both stated and implied information. To draw conclusions about characters in a play, **use both dialogue and stage directions** to find meaningful information.

- Consider what characters' words suggest about their personalities and circumstances.
- Read stage directions closely for details about the scene, characters' appearances, and characters' behavior. Take note of other information that could prove essential to the plot or ideas expressed in the play.

DIRECTIONS: *As you read* The Inspector-General, *use the following chart to gather information and draw conclusions about the traveler's identity. Then, use the evidence you have gathered to answer the questions that follow the chart.*

Evidence of the Traveler's Appearance and of What He Says and Does:	Conclusions From the Evidence:
Example: The Traveler wears dark glasses and a long overcoat with its collar turned up.	He is traveling incognito and does not want his identity to be known.
1. _____	1. _____
2. _____	2. _____
3. _____	3. _____
4. _____	4. _____

5. Who is the traveler? _____

6. What is his reason for traveling incognito?

   _____

7. What conclusion can you draw about the traveler's attitude toward his work?

   _____

8. What does the evidence suggest about the traveler's expectations?

   _____

9. What conclusions can you draw about the traveler's character?

   _____

Name _____ Date _____

"The Inspector-General" by Anton Chekhov
Vocabulary Builder

Word List

anonymous   cunning   discreetly   incognito   telegraph   trundle

A. DIRECTIONS: *In each of the following items, think about the meaning of the italicized word and then answer the question.*

1. Why might a famous person travel *incognito*?

   _____

2. Which would be more likely to *trundle*, a cart or a horse? Why?

   _____

3. Is it easy or difficult to reply directly to the writer of an *anonymous* letter? Why?

   _____

4. If you perform a task *discreetly*, do you usually attract the notice of other people? Why or why not?

   _____

5. Is a *cunning* person likely to be candid or deceptive?

   _____

6. If you send a message via *telegraph*, how are you sending it?

   _____

B. WORD STUDY: The Latin root -*nym*- or -*nom*- means "name." Answer each of the following questions using one of these words containing -*nym*- or -*nom*- : *anonymous, antonym, misnomer, nominal, pseudonym.*

1. What is an *antonym* for the word *fortunate*?

   _____

2. Why is it impossible to know who wrote an *anonymous* poem?

   _____

3. Who was one author who used a *pseudonym*, and what was it?

   _____

4. Why is "fish" a *misnomer* for a whale?

   _____

5. Why would a king who is a *nominal* ruler not have much power?

   _____

"The Inspector-General" by Anton Chekhov
Integrated Language Skills: Grammar

Main and Subordinate Clauses

A **clause** is a group of words with a subject and a verb. A **main,** or **independent, clause** is a complete sentence. A **subordinate clause** has a subject and a verb but is not a complete thought.

A clause, a group of words that contains a subject and a verb, can be a main (independent) clause or a subordinate (dependent) clause. If the group of words needs additional information to make sense, it is a subordinate clause. Subordinate clauses can function as noun, adjective, or adverbial clauses. In the following examples, the main clause is underlined and the subordinate clause is italicized.

Main Clause:	The Internet is expanding.
Main Clause, Subordinate Clause:	It offers more and more *as time passes.*
Subordinate Clause, Main Clause:	*If we let it,* the Internet can change our lives.

A. DIRECTIONS: *Identify the subordinate clause in each sentence. Then, tell whether the subordinate clause functions as an adjective clause, an adverb clause, or a noun clause.*

1. Anton Chekhov began to write humorous sketches and short stories while he was studying medicine in Moscow.

   _____

2. His best-known plays, which include *The Seagull* and *The Cherry Orchard,* are notable for their wistful, bittersweet irony.

   _____

3. That Chekhov regarded others with tenderness and compassion is clearly evident in his stories and plays.

   _____

4. In *The Inspector-General,* much of the humor springs from the traveler's ignorance that he has already been recognized.

   _____

B. Writing Application: *Write a paragraph describing why you might like to undertake a journey incognito. Use at least three subordinate clauses in your writing, and underline each subordinate clause you use. Be prepared to tell whether each clause functions as an adjective, as an adverb, or as a noun.*

_____

_____

_____

_____

Name _____ Date _____

"The Inspector-General" by Anton Chekhov
Integrated Language Skills: Support for Writing a Play

As you prepare to write a **play** about students outwitting a bully, think about how you can make the school setting seem real. Make sure that the dialogue sounds like words and phrases that could be used by actual students.

In your play, use *dramatic irony*—that is, include information that is clear to the audience but not known by the character of the bully. Make your play entertaining and educational. Teach the lesson that it is always important to be kind, even to a bully. Use the chart below to help you organize your ideas.

Setting of the play: _____

Major characters (describe the main traits of each): _____
_____
_____
_____
_____

Basic plot of the play:
How the bully behaves toward others: _____
_____
_____
_____

How other students plan to outwit the bully: _____
_____
_____

Dramatic irony (what the audience knows that is not known to the bully): _____
_____

How the problem is resolved: _____

What you want the audience to learn from your play: _____
_____

Use additional sheets of paper to write the first scene of your play. Remember that you should include exciting action and dialogue that could be performed on stage.

All-in-One Workbook
268

Name _____ Date _____

from **The Importance of Being Earnest** by Oscar Wilde
from **"Big Kiss"** by Henry Alford

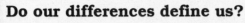

Writing About the Big Question

Do our differences define us?

Big Question Vocabulary

accept	assimilated	background	conformity	culture
defend	determine	differences	differentiate	discriminate
individuality	similarity	understanding	unique	values

A. *Use one or more words from the list above to complete each sentence.*

1. Most people cannot _____ between identical twins who dress alike.

2. My cousins are identical twins, but I can always _____ which twin is standing in front of me.

3. There are great _____ in their personalities.

4. Each girl is _____ in her own way.

B. *Follow the directions in responding to each of the items below.*

1. In two sentences, tell two ways that you might be able to tell identical twins apart.

   _____

   _____

2. Write two sentences explaining how you imagine someone would be able to tell you apart from an identical twin. Use at least two of the Big Question vocabulary words.

   _____

   _____

C. *Both these selections use people's differences to satirize an element of life or society. Complete the sentence below. Then, write a short paragraph in which you connect this idea to the Big Question.*

In some situations, our **differences** can be used to _____

   _____

   _____

   _____

   _____

from **The Importance of Being Earnest** by Oscar Wilde
from **Big Kiss** by Henry Alford
Literary Analysis: Satire

Satire is writing that exposes and makes fun of the foolishness and faults of an individual, an institution, a society, or a situation. Although a satire often makes readers laugh, it may also aim to correct the flaws that it criticizes. Some satires address serious social problems, while others address less important issues. Satirical writings vary in style and tone.

- A satire may be gentle and sympathetic or angry and bitter in tone. The tone will reflect the writer's attitude toward the subject.
- A satire may use **sarcasm** or **irony**—language that is "tongue-in-cheek" and means the opposite of what it says on the surface.
- A satire may **exaggerate** faults in order to make them both funny and obvious.

In addition, some satirists write as outside onlookers, while others include themselves as targets of the satire.

DIRECTIONS: *The following passages are from* The Importance of Being Earnest *and* Big Kiss. *Read each passage and think about it in the context of the selection as a whole. Then, write a brief phrase or statement that explains what the target of satire is in the passage. Add a comment on the satire's tone, and indicate whether the author includes himself as an object of satire.*

1. **GWENDOLEN.** We live, as I hope you know, Mr. Worthing, in an age of ideals. The fact is constantly mentioned in the more expensive monthly magazines, and has reached the provincial pulpits, I am told; and my ideal has always been to love someone of the name of Ernest. There is something in that name that inspires absolute confidence. The moment Algernon first mentioned to me that he had a friend called Ernest, I knew I was destined to love you. (*The Importance of Being Earnest*)

_____

_____

_____

_____

2. But five minutes later an assistant director who had assembled about a hundred of us in front of Federal Hall took away my camera.

   "I based my character interpretation on that!" I exclaimed, hoping that this would translate to him as "Serious actor. Could handle a line of dialogue."

   "I need it for up front," he reported tersely, then walked to the front of the crowd.

   One of my fellow colleagues . . . witnessed my loss of camera and counseled, "You were probably overpropped anyway."

   "Yes," I responded. "My work was getting proppy." (*Big Kiss*)

_____

_____

_____

_____

Name _____ Date _____

from **The Importance of Being Earnest** by Oscar Wilde
from **Big Kiss** by Henry Alford
Vocabulary Builder

Word List

allotment   assiduous   demonstrative   ignorance

A. DIRECTIONS: *Revise each sentence so that the underlined vocabulary word is used logically. Be sure not to change the vocabulary word.*

1. She is not especially <u>demonstrative</u>, so it is easy to know what she is feeling.

   _____

2. <u>Ignorance</u> of addition is a requirement for taking algebra.

   _____

3. The huge <u>allotment</u> of books from a generous donor required the library to reduce the number of shelves.

   _____

4. Teresa was so <u>assiduous</u> that she studied for about two minutes for the final exam.

   _____

B. DIRECTIONS: *On the line, write the letter of the choice that is the best definition for each word.*

___ 1. assiduous
   A. transient
   B. glossy
   C. diligent
   D. slapdash

___ 2. demonstrative
   A. childishly demanding
   B. naively taking risks
   C. showing feelings openly
   D. acting playfully

___ 3. allotment
   A. chance
   B. share
   C. majority
   D. minority

___ 4. ignorance
   A. lack of time
   B. lack of knowledge
   C. bad luck
   D. hunger

C. DIRECTIONS: *Choose the pair of words that expresses the same relationship as the pair in capital letters. Write the letter of your choice on the line.*

___ 1. IGNORANCE : INTELLIGENCE
   A. squalor: luxury
   B. insult: offense
   C. remainder: residue
   D. destiny: action

___ 2. HARD-WORKER : ASSIDUOUS
   A. elaborate: simple
   B. slacker: lazy
   C. hermit: sociable
   D. speech: noisy

from **The Importance of Being Earnest** by Oscar Wilde
from **Big Kiss** by Henry Alford
Support for Writing to Compare

Use a chart like the one shown to make prewriting notes for an essay discussing the effect of point of view in each of the satires.

Writer's Purpose and Perspective

	Wilde, *The Importance of Being Earnest*	Alford, *Big Kiss*
Target of Satire		
Purpose of Satire		
Writer: Participant/ Nonparticipant		
Attitude Toward Characters		

Ways in Which Writer's Perspective Shapes the Satire

How does each writer create humor and present insights? _____

_____

_____

_____

How does the writer's participation or lack of participation in the action affect the audience's sympathy for characters? _____

_____

_____

_____

My Evaluation of the Satires _____

_____

_____

_____

Role Model, performed by The Dave Pittenger Band

We've read the papers and watched the news
A role model, the cameras are focused on you
The **standards** that we're used to are being abused

Your **character** – all the flaws and strengths
Is reflected in your decisions, all the **choices** that you make
If you're never brought to **justice** when you're **involved** in something wrong
How are we to learn?

Oooo, everyone wants to **identify** with you
The **hero,** the **hero** we look up to
The **hero** that we love

You know you're held responsible
An **obligation** lies with you
Responsibility never carried so much weight
As when we **imitate** you

Oooo, everyone wants to **identify** with you
The **hero,** the **hero** we look up to
The **hero** that we love

All we are asking is for truth and **honesty**
Consider the consequences to which a lack of **wisdom** leads

You **serve** the people by the example you set
The **morality** of your actions are judged by how much good you do
Your goals and **intentions** may be noble
But we can't read your mind

Continued

All-in-One Workbook
273

Oooo, everyone wants to **identify** with you

The **hero,** the **hero** we look up to

The **hero** that we love

Ahhh . . .

Song Title: **Role Model**

Artist / Performed by The Dave Pittenger Band

Vocals & Guitar: Dave Pittenger

Bass Guitar: Jon Price

Drums: Josh Dion

Lyrics by Dave Pittenger

Music composed by Dave Pittenger

Produced by Mike Pandolfo, Wonderful

Executive Producer: Keith London, Defined Mind

Name _____ Date _____

Unit 6: Themes in Literature
Big Question Vocabulary—1

The Big Question: Do heroes have responsibilities?

Small children who watch a superhero on television will often pattern their behavior after the superhero's behavior.

honesty: truthfulness, sincerity

justice: fairness

morality: conformity to the rules of proper conduct

responsibility: reliability or dependability

wisdom: good sense and judgment, especially based on life experience

DIRECTIONS: *Create a superhero that little children could respect and admire. For each of the vocabulary words, give an example of how your superhero would demonstrate this quality. Use each vocabulary word in each description.*

HONESTY: _____

_____

_____

JUSTICE: _____

_____

_____

MORALITY: _____

_____

_____

RESPONSIBILITY: _____

_____

_____

WISDOM: _____

_____

_____

Unit 6: Themes in Literature
Big Question Vocabulary—2

The Big Question: Do heroes have responsibilities?

Often an athlete, a movie star, or a politician will be regarded as a hero. With that hero status comes a responsibility to act in a way that is consistent with good values.

character: a combination of valued qualities, such as honesty and integrity

hero: a person of great courage who is admired for his actions

imitate: to copy the way someone else behaves and/or speaks

intention: purpose or plan

serve: to be useful or helpful

DIRECTIONS: *Think of a public figure whom you consider a hero. Answer the following questions using the vocabulary words that are in parentheses.*

1. Who is the public figure you selected? (*hero*)

   _____

2. What qualities does this person have that make him or her admirable? (*character*)

   _____

   _____

3. How is this person useful or helpful to the world or to a particular community? (*serve*)

   _____

   _____

4. What do you suppose this person's purpose is with regard to the world or his or her community? (*intention*)

   _____

   _____

5. In what ways have you and others learned from this person? (*imitate*)

   _____

   _____

All-in-One Workbook
276

Unit 6: Themes in Literature
Big Question Vocabulary—3

The Big Question: Do heroes have responsibilities?

If we look around our communities, we will often discover that there are "unsung heroes," or people who do not get recognition for their exceptional actions.

choices: decisions

identify: to recognize and name something

involvement: taking part in an activity or event

obligation: moral or legal duty

standard: level of quality, skill, or ability that is acceptable in a particular situation

DIRECTIONS: *Recognize someone in your community who is an "unsung hero" by creating a plaque to award him or her. In the plaque, describe your hero's achievements using all the vocabulary words. Your hero can be real or imagined.*

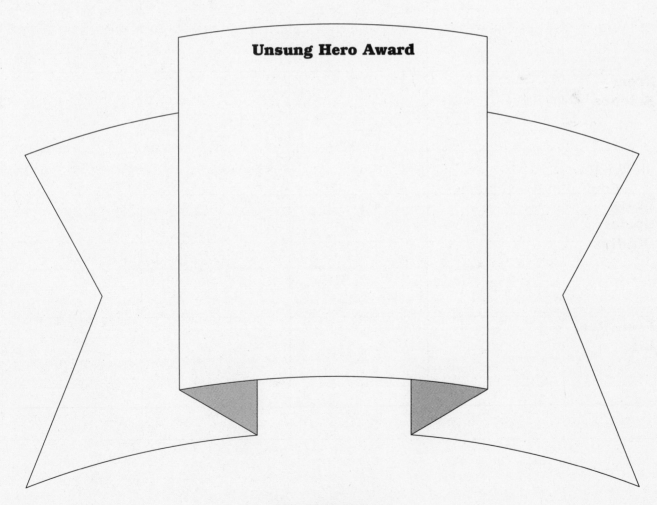

Unsung Hero Award

Name _____   Date _____

Unit 6: Themes in Literature
Applying the Big Question

The Big Question: Do heroes have responsibilities?

DIRECTIONS: *Complete the chart below to apply what you have learned about heroes and their responsibilities. One row has been completed for you.*

Example	The heroic act	Motivation for the act	The hero's responsibilities	What I learned
From Literature	In "Odysseus' Revenge" in the *Odyssey*, Odysseus kills his wife's suitors.	His sense of outrage and vengeance	To protect his wife, son, and the people of Ithaca	Heroes may have divided responsibilities and may give in to their emotions.
From Literature				
From Science				
From Social Studies				
From Real Life				

Name _____ Date _____

Dean Smith
Listening and Viewing

Segment 1: Meet Dean Smith
- What is the meaning of "the Carolina way"?
- How do you think Dean Smith's philosophy of "play hard, play smart, play together" also applies to life off of the basketball court?

_____

_____

_____

_____

Segment 2: Themes in Literature
- Why do you think sports writing is an important form of literature?
- What can Dean Smith and John Kilgo's book *The Carolina Way* teach its readers?

_____

_____

_____

_____

Segment 3: The Writing Process
- How did Dean Smith and John Kilgo work together to write books?
- What benefits and challenges exist when writing a book with a coauthor?

_____

_____

_____

_____

Segment 4: The Rewards of Writing
- How has writing been personally rewarding for both Dean Smith and John Kilgo?
- Have you ever read a piece of sports literature that has had a memorable impact on you as a reader? Explain.

_____

_____

_____

_____

All-in-One Workbook
279

Learning About Themes in Literature

Before there was written literature, stories and poems were passed down by **oral** tradition— from generation to generation by word of mouth. Many tales expressed basic human emotions and explored **universal themes,** or insights into life that are true for many different times and cultures. Among such themes are the importance of heroism, the power of love, the strength of loyalty, and the dangers of greed.

Storytellers explored such themes by means of **archetypes.** An archetype is a situation, a character, an image, or a symbol that appears in the tales of various cultures. For example, the hero's quest, the struggle between good and evil, and tricksters appear in the stories of many different cultures and times. The circle is another archetype, a symbol of loyalty, protection, and completion, as in Odysseus' return to his homeland, Ithaca. The **historical context** (the social and cultural background of a particular tale) influences the presentation of archetypes.

The following are important narrative forms that express universal themes. A **myth** is a tale explaining the actions of gods and the humans who interact with them. Myths explain the causes of a natural phenomenon. **Folk tales** are brief stories focusing on human or animal heroes and are not primarily concerned with gods or the creation of the world. A **legend** recounts the adventures of a human hero and may be based on historical fact. **Tall tales** are legends told in an exaggerated way, intended for entertainment. An **epic** is a long narrative poem about a larger-than-life hero who goes on a dangerous journey or quest that is important to the history of a group or culture.

DIRECTIONS: *Circle the letter of the answer that best matches each numbered item.*

1. historical context
   A. author's biography
   B. story's cultural background
   C. story's theme

2. archetype
   A. story element in many cultures
   B. universal theme
   C. hero

3. tall tale
   A. epic   B. exaggerated folk tale   C. story featuring monsters

4. epic
   A. factual narrative   B. legend   C. long narrative poem

5. the power of love
   A. universal theme   B. oral tradition   C. historical context

6. quest
   A. hero's journey   B. story that explains C. opposing person or force

7. main character in a folk tale
   A. historical figure   B. human or animal hero C. god or goddess

Name _____ Date _____

Model Selection: Themes in Literature

Stories, poems, and essays often offer **themes,** or central insights into human life or behavior. The theme of a work may be directly stated by the author. More often, however, it is implied or suggested indirectly. The reader must use clues from the writer's choice of details, as well as from the style and tone of the work, to infer the theme.

Narratives, poems, and essays usually express the **values,** ideals, and behaviors cherished by the society in which they are produced. **Shared values** are held in common by people across cultures, and literary works give voice to them by exploring **universal themes**. In contrast, **culturally distinct values** are specific to a group. In a literary work, **cultural details** are the beliefs, traditions, and customs that reflect a particular society. Modern fiction and nonfiction, though written by individuals rather than fashioned by a group, can also express universal themes.

DIRECTIONS: *Use the space provided to answer the following questions about "Play Hard; Play Together; Play Smart."*

1. What are three cultural values stressed by Dean Smith in the essay?

   _____

   _____

   _____

   _____

2. Dean Smith coached American college basketball in the second half of the twentieth century. Do you think the values he emphasizes in his essay are culturally distinct, or are they shared values found in cultures around the world, in the past and present? Explain your answer in a few sentences.

   _____

   _____

   _____

   _____

   _____

   _____

3. Do Smith's main ideas in the essay suggest one or more universal themes? Write a paragraph in which you give your opinion about whether or not his essay contains universal themes. Use reasons and examples to support your position.

   _____

   _____

   _____

   _____

   _____

Name _____ Date _____

from **the Odyssey, Part I** by Homer
Writing About the Big Question

 Do heroes have responsibilities?

Big Question Vocabulary

character	choices	hero	honesty	identify
imitate	intentions	involvement	justice	morality
obligation	responsibility	serve	standard	wisdom

A. *Use one or more words from the list above to complete each sentence.*

1. The _____ made by a(n) _____ in a literary work often determine the outcome of the plot.

2. A(n) _____ is usually someone who embodies the values of an entire culture or society.

3. _____ and _____ are two values that a(n) _____ typically upholds.

4. By any measure, Odysseus in Homer's *Odyssey* lives up to a heroic _____.

5. It is usually easy to _____ the hero of an epic poem.

B. *Follow the directions in responding to each of the items below.*

1. List two different times when you became aware of a **responsibility.**

   _____

   _____

2. Write two sentences to explain one of these experiences, and describe how it made you feel. Use at least two of the Big Question vocabulary words.

   _____

   _____

C. *Complete the sentences below. Then, write a short paragraph in which you connect the sentences to the Big Question.*

A **hero** has an **obligation** to _____. The **choices** he or she makes

must _____.

_____

_____

_____

_____

from **the Odyssey,** *Part 1* by Homer
Literary Analysis: Epic Hero

An **epic hero** is the larger-than-life central character in an epic—a long narrative poem about important events in the history or folklore of a nation or culture. Through adventurous deeds, the epic hero demonstrates traits—such as loyalty, honor, and resourcefulness—that are valued by the society in which the epic originates.

Many epics begin *in medias res* ("in the middle of things"), meaning that much of the important action in the story occurred before the point at which the poem begins. Therefore, an epic hero's adventures are often recounted in a **flashback,** a scene that interrupts the sequence of events in a narrative to relate earlier events. Flashbacks also allow the poet to provide a more complete portrait of the epic hero's character.

DIRECTIONS: *Consider the adventures shown in the left column of the following chart. Then, determine what evidence is contained in each adventure to support the position that Odysseus has the superior physical and mental prowess to be an epic hero. Write your answers in the chart.*

Adventure	Evidence of Mental Prowess	Evidence of Physical Prowess
1. The Lotus-Eaters		
2. The Cyclops		
3. The Sirens		
4. Scylla and Charybdis		

Name _____ Date _____

from **the Odyssey, *Part 1*** by Homer
Reading: Analyze the Influence of Historical and Cultural Context

The **historical and cultural context** of a work is the backdrop of details of the time and place in which the work is set or in which it was written. These details include the events, beliefs, and customs of a specific culture and time. When you read a work from another time and culture, **use background and prior knowledge** to analyze the influence of the historical and cultural context.

- Read the author biography, footnotes, and other textual aids to understand the work's historical and cultural context.
- Note how characters' behavior and attitudes reflect that context.

DIRECTIONS: *Answer the following questions on the lines provided.*

1. What does the common noun *odyssey* mean? Use a dictionary, if necessary, to look up this word and identify its meaning. How does this word relate to Homer's epic and the hero Odysseus?

_____

_____

_____

2. What does the word *Homeric* mean? How does this word relate to the ancient Greek epics the *Iliad* and the *Odyssey*?

_____

_____

_____

3. About when were the Homeric epics composed, or when did they assume their final form after centuries of development in the oral tradition?

_____

4. Reread Odysseus' description of the Cyclopes in Part 1, lines 109–120. What does this passage imply about ancient Greek values and beliefs? Explain your answer in a brief paragraph.

_____

_____

_____

_____

_____

_____

_____

Name _____ Date _____

from the Odyssey, *Part 1* by Homer
Vocabulary Builder

Word List

ardor   assuage   bereft   dispatched   insidious   plundered

A. DIRECTIONS: *In each of the following items, think about the meaning of the italicized word and then answer the question.*

1. If you regard someone as *insidious,* do you like or dislike that person? Why?

   _____

2. Historically, when do people tend to *plunder*—during wartime or peacetime?

   _____

3. If Maria *dispatched* her assignment, did it take her a long time or a short time to finish?

   _____

4. Would you use gentle words or provocative words to *assuage* someone's anger or demands? Explain.

   _____

5. If you were *bereft* of sleep, would you feel fatigued or well-rested?

   _____

B. WORD STUDY: *The Old English prefix* be-, *meaning "around," "make," or "covered with," can sometimes be added to a noun or an adjective to create a transitive verb. Examples include* beheld *and* begone. *Match the word in Column A with its meaning in Column B by writing the correct letter on the line provided.*

___ 1. bemoan   A. be on one's guard

___ 2. bewilder   B. lament

___ 3. beware   C. signify

___ 4. betoken   D. confuse

___ 5. bereft   E. deprived

Name _____ Date _____

from the Odyssey, *Part 1* by Homer
Integrated Language Skills: Grammar

Simple and Compound Sentences

A **simple sentence** consists of a single independent clause. Although a simple sentence is just one independent clause with one subject and verb, the subject, verb, or both may be compound. A simple sentence may have modifying phrases and complements. However, it cannot have a subordinate clause.

> **Example:** Odysseus returned to Ithaca and took his revenge on the suitors. (simple sentence with compound verb)

A **compound sentence** consists of two or more independent clauses. The clauses can be joined by a comma and a coordinating conjunction or by a semicolon. Like a simple sentence, a compound sentence contains no subordinate clauses.

> **Example:** The suitors reveled in the hall; in the meantime, Penelope questioned the disguised Odysseus.

A. DIRECTIONS: *Identify each sentence as simple or compound.*

1. In his monumental epic, the *Odyssey,* Homer recounts the wanderings of Odysseus on his journey home to Ithaca after the Trojan War. _____

2. Odysseus enjoys the favor of the goddess Athena, but his safe return is jeopardized by the hostility of Poseidon, the sea god. _____

3. Odysseus foolishly leads his men into the cave of the Cyclops; there, several of them meet a ghastly fate. _____

4. Odysseus tricks the Cyclops by telling him a false name: "Nohbdy." _____

5. At the end of this adventure, however, Odysseus boastfully reveals his true name, thereby making himself vulnerable to the Cyclops' curse. _____

B. WRITING APPLICATION: *On the following lines, write a paragraph in which you describe what you would wish for if you had three wishes. In your writing, use both simple and compound sentences. Be prepared to identify each type of sentence.*

_____

_____

_____

_____

_____

_____

_____

_____

_____

_____

Name _____ Date _____

from the Odyssey, *Part 1* by Homer
Integrated Language Skills:
Support for Writing an Everyday Epic

Use a chart like the one below to jot down notes for your everyday epic.

Everyday Event:
_____

Epic Dimensions (adventure, bravery, life-and-death challenges): _____
_____
_____
_____
_____
_____

Multiple Points of View: _____
_____
_____

Supernatural/Fantastic Elements: _____
_____
_____
_____
_____

Ideas for Performance/Recitation: _____
_____
_____
_____
_____
_____

Name _____ Date _____

from **the Odyssey, Part II** by Homer
Writing About the Big Question

 Do heroes have responsibilities?

Big Question Vocabulary

character	choices	hero	honesty	identify
imitate	intentions	involvement	justice	morality
obligation	responsibility	serve	standard	wisdom

A. *Use one or more words from the list above to complete each sentence.*

1. One definition of a(n) _____ is that he or she is someone whom large numbers of people would like to _____.

2. Many epics focus on a hero's _____ in a journey or quest.

3. Our _____ were good, but we could not steer the project to a successful outcome.

4. In epic narratives, heroes often profit from the _____ of a god, sage, or prophet.

5. Responsible politicians usually feel a(n) _____ to the voters who elected them.

B. *Follow the directions in responding to each of the items below.*

1. List two different times when you had to decide between two very different **choices.**

   _____

   _____

2. Write two sentences to explain one of these experiences, and describe how it made you feel. Use at least two of the Big Question vocabulary words.

   _____

   _____

C. *Complete the sentence below. Then, write a short paragraph in which you connect the sentences to the Big Question.*

The true **character** of a **hero** can be seen in _____

_____

_____

_____

_____

Name _____ Date _____

from **the Odyssey,** *Part 2* by Homer
Literary Analysis: Epic Simile

An **epic simile** is an elaborate comparison that may extend for several lines. Epic similes may use the words *like, as, just as,* or *so* to make the comparison. Unlike a normal simile, which draws a comparison to a single, distinct image, an epic simile is longer and more involved. It might recall an entire place or story. Epic similes are sometimes called Homeric similes.

DIRECTIONS: *Read the epic similes that follow. Then, circle the letter of the answer that best completes each sentence.*

A. But the man skilled in all ways of contending,
satisfied by the great bow's look and heft,
like a musician, like a harper, when
with quiet hand upon his instrument
he draws between his thumb and forefinger
a sweet new string upon a peg: so effortlessly
Odysseus in one motion strung the bow.

1. In the passage, what extended comparison does Homer use to complete this analogy:
   archer : bow ::
   A. composer : instrument.   C. musician : harp.
   B. peg : string.   D. hand : forefinger.

2. The comparison suggests that, like the musician, Odysseus
   A. is nervous before he begins.
   B. works with a stringed instrument.
   C. is proficient in music.
   D. knows his instrument and where to get good strings.

B. Think of a catch that fishermen haul in to a half-moon bay
in a fine-meshed net from the whitecaps of the sea:
how all are poured out on the sand, in throes for the salt sea,
twitching their cold lives away in Helios' fiery air:
so lay the suitors heaped on one another.

1. In the passage, what comparison does Homer use to complete this analogy: *Odysseus : suitors* ::
   A. big fish : little fish.   C. Odysseus : enemies.
   B. hunter : catch.   D. fisherman : fish.

2. The comparison suggests that
   A. Odysseus was also a good fisherman.
   B. the suitors had as much chance against Odysseus as fish have when they are caught in a net.
   C. something fishy was going on in Ithaca, and Odysseus had to correct it.
   D. the setting of much of the epic is the Greek isles, where fishing is an important industry.

Name _____ Date _____

from the Odyssey, *Part 2* by Homer
Reading: Analyze the Influence of Historical and Cultural Context

The **historical and cultural context** of a work is the backdrop of details of the time and place in which the work is set or in which it was written. These details include the events, beliefs, and customs of a specific culture and time. When you **identify influences on your own reading and responses,** the historical and cultural context reflected in a work becomes more apparent.

- As you read a work from another time and culture, keep your own beliefs and customs in mind.
- Notice the ways in which your reactions to ideas and situations in the work differ from the reactions of the characters.
- Consider whether your reactions reflect your own cultural values.

DIRECTIONS: *For each of the following events or elements in Part 2 of the* Odyssey, *write a few notes on the historical and cultural context. Pay special attention to whether the event or element seems to reflect a universal value or belief or whether it seems specifically rooted in the cultural context of ancient Greece.*

1. Odysseus' reunion with Telemachus

   _____

   _____

   _____

2. the episode focusing on Odysseus' dog, Argus

   _____

   _____

   _____

3. the laziness and arrogance of the suitors

   _____

   _____

   _____

4. Odysseus' and Penelope's testing of each other

   _____

   _____

   _____

5. Odysseus' slaughter of the suitors

   _____

   _____

   _____

Name _____ Date _____

from **the Odyssey,** *Part 2* by Homer
Vocabulary Builder

Word List

bemusing   contempt   dissemble   equity   incredulity   maudlin

A. DIRECTIONS: *In each of the following items, think about the meaning of the italicized word and then answer the question.*

1. From whom would you reasonably expect *equity*—a judge or a thief?

   _____

2. Would you treat someone whom you admire with *contempt*? Why or why not?

   _____

3. Does being *maudlin* involve your intelligence or your emotions? Explain your answer.

   _____

4. Are the intentions of people who *dissemble* likely to be good or bad?

   _____

5. What kind of story or report would inspire *incredulity* in you? Explain.

   _____

6. Would you react to a long, *bemusing* lecture with enthusiasm or with annoyance?

   _____

B. DIRECTIONS: *Use the context of the sentences and what you know about the Latin prefix dis- to explain your answer to each question.*

1. If one high school football team *displaces* another in the league rankings, what happens?

   _____

   _____

2. If you *disentangle* a complex problem, what have you done: solved it, or made it worse?

   _____

   _____

3. If two plays or novels are *dissimilar*, are they more notable for their likenesses or their differences?

   _____

   _____

from the Odyssey, *Part 2* by Homer
Integrated Language Skills: Grammar

Complex and Compound-Complex Sentences

A **complex sentence** consists of one independent clause, which can stand by itself as a sentence, and at least one subordinate clause, which cannot stand by itself as a sentence. A **compound-complex sentence** consists of two or more independent clauses and one or more subordinate clauses.

Complex sentence:	After Odysseus gave Telemachus the signal, Telemachus removed the weapons from the hall.
Compound-complex sentence:	Scholars, who live throughout the world, disagree about whether the epics were composed by the same person, and they also wonder about Homer's historical existence.

A. DIRECTIONS: *Identify each sentence as complex or compound-complex.*

1. Although Odysseus is in disguise, his old dog Argus recognizes him instinctively.

   _____

2. The suitors, who have competed to marry Penelope, behave arrogantly, and they conspire to murder Odysseus' son and heir, Telemachus.

   _____

3. Odysseus becomes anxious when Penelope questions him about the marriage bed.

   _____

4. The *Odyssey*, which has entertained audiences for thousands of years, contains many universal themes; its broad appeal can be explained by Homer's profound understanding of human nature.

   _____

B. WRITING APPLICATION: *On the following lines, write a paragraph in which you describe a gift that you would like to present to a loved one. In your writing, use all four types of sentences that have been mentioned: simple, compound, complex, and compound-complex. Be prepared to identify each type of sentence.*

_____

_____

_____

_____

_____

_____

_____

_____

Name _____ Date _____

Integrated Language Skills: Support for Writing a Biography

Use a chart like the one shown to make notes for your biography of Odysseus.

Events That Reveal Odysseus' Character

1. _____
   _____
   _____
2. _____
   _____
   _____
3. _____
   _____
   _____
4. _____
   _____
   _____
5. _____
   _____
   _____

Quotations From the Epic

1. _____
   _____
   _____
2. _____
   _____
   _____
3. _____
   _____
   _____

All-in-One Workbook
293

Poetry by Edna St. Vincent Millay, Margaret Atwood,
Derek Walcott, and Constantine Cavafy
Writing About the Big Question

Do heroes have responsibilities?

Big Question Vocabulary

character	choices	hero	honesty	identify
imitate	intentions	involvement	justice	morality
obligation	responsibility	serve	standard	wisdom

A. *Use one or more words from the list above to complete each sentence.*

1. A person's individual _____, or code of ethics, is often apparent in the _____ that he or she makes at moments of decision.

2. During the civil rights movement of the 1950s and 1960s, Dr. Martin Luther King, Jr., was one of our nation's most stirring spokesmen for social _____.

3. Since heroes usually embody values we all admire, most of us would like to _____ them.

4. In the legends of King Arthur, Merlin was an elderly sage whose good advice made him famous for his _____.

B. *Follow the directions in responding to each of the items below.*

1. List two occasions on which you felt that you, or someone you know, failed to receive **justice.**

   _____

   _____

2. Write two sentences to explain one of these experiences. Use at least two of the Big Question vocabulary words.

   _____

   _____

C. *Complete the sentences below. Then, write a short paragraph in which you connect the experience to the Big Question.*

In my own life, I know I am responsible for _____. If I do not live up to this **obligation,** one consequence might be _____. When I make responsible **choices,** one positive result is _____.

_____

_____

_____

Poetry by Edna St. Vincent Millay, Margaret Atwood, Derek Walcott, and Constantine Cavafy

Literary Analysis: Contemporary Interpretations

The characters and events of Homer's *Odyssey* are timeless and universal in their appeal and meaning and have inspired many contemporary interpretations. A **contemporary interpretation** of a literary work is a new piece of writing, such as a poem, story, or play, that a modern-day author bases on an ancient work. An **allusion** is a reference to a well-known person, place, event, literary work, or work of art. By reinventing Homer's tales or by making allusions to them, modern-day writers shed new light on Homer's ancient words. Contemporary interpretations may allude to any aspects of Homer's epic, including plot, characters, settings, imagery and language, and theme.

Even when they are based on the same work, contemporary interpretations can differ widely in purpose and theme. The cultural and historical backgrounds, ideas, attitudes, and beliefs of the contemporary writers profoundly affect their perceptions of the ancient work and the new writings that result.

DIRECTIONS: *Circle the letter of the answer that best completes the sentence.*

1. In Edna St. Vincent Millay's "An Ancient Gesture," the speaker focuses most closely on
   A. Odysseus' travels and the hero's relationships to the gods.
   B. the anguish of Odysseus' son Telemachus.
   C. Penelope's inner grief and frustration at Odysseus' long absence.
   D. the devastation wrought by the Trojan War.

2. In "Siren Song," Margaret Atwood's interpretation of the Sirens suggests that
   A. women are much more complex than they have been given credit for.
   B. the poet herself is not very clever.
   C. men are more clever than they think they are.
   D. women enjoy the roles they play.

3. In "Prologue" and "Epilogue" to the *Odyssey*, Derek Walcott suggests that Billy Blue
   A. has confused the chronological sequence of Odysseus' adventures.
   B. is a modern-day version of Homer, singing the adventures of a "main-man" hero.
   C. believes that we are all capable of behaving as heroically as Odysseus did.
   D. has misinterpreted the character of Penelope.

4. In "Ithaca," Constantine Cavafy sees the wanderings of Odysseus as representing
   A. a grand vacation to exotic places.
   B. the journey through life itself.
   C. a voyage of discovery made possible by such modern conveniences as a credit card.
   D. a trip without a real purpose.

5. In "Ithaca," the lines "Always keep Ithaca fixed in your mind, / . . . But do not hurry the voyage at all" suggest that
   A. the journey is more important than the destination.
   B. we need to know where we are going in life.
   C. everyone should have a home.
   D. some places always remain the same, no matter how other places may change.

Name _____ Date _____

Poetry by Edna St. Vincent Millay, Margaret Atwood, Derek Walcott, and Constantine Cavafy
Vocabulary Builder

Word List

  authentic   defrauded   lofty   picturesque   siege

A. DIRECTIONS: *Revise each sentence so that the underlined vocabulary word is used logically. Be sure not to change the vocabulary word.*

1. They refused to buy the old silver coin because they believe it is <u>authentic</u>.

   _____

2. Because the landscape was so <u>picturesque</u>, we did not bother to take any photographs.

   _____

3. The <u>siege</u> of the city was successful, so the soldiers outside the walls retreated.

   _____

4. Because he is a person of <u>lofty</u> ideals, we criticize him harshly.

   _____

5. As a merchant with great integrity, he always <u>defrauds</u> his customers.

   _____

B. DIRECTIONS: *On the line, write the letter of the choice that is the best synonym for each numbered word.*

___ 1. defrauded
    A. rejected
    B. praised
    C. cheated
    D. promoted

___ 2. lofty
    A. illusory
    B. pretentious
    C. drafty
    D. noble

___ 3. authentic
    A. genuine
    B. antique
    C. practical
    D. sentimental

___ 4. siege
    A. strong grip
    B. armed blockade
    C. military alliance
    D. crisis intervention

___ 5. picturesque
    A. grotesque
    B. paradoxical
    C. prevalent
    D. charming

All-in-One Workbook
296

Poetry by Edna St. Vincent Millay, Margaret Atwood, Derek Walcott, and Constantine Cavafy

Support for Writing to Compare Literary Works

For each poem in this section, use a chart like the one shown to make prewriting notes for an essay focusing on ways in which Homer's epic poem the *Odyssey* provides worthwhile material for a modern-day writer.

Title of Work: _____   _____
Author's purpose: _____   _____   _____   _____   _____
Contemporary conflict/situation addressed: _____   _____   _____   _____   _____
Additions by contemporary writer: _____   _____   _____   _____   _____
My personal response: _____   _____   _____   _____   _____

Name _Julieth Angarita_ Date _____

Writing About the Big Question

Do heroes have responsibilities?

Big Question Vocabulary

character	choices	hero	honesty	identify
imitate	intentions	involvement	justice	morality
obligation	responsibility	serve	standard	wisdom

A. *Use one or more words from the list above to complete each sentence.*

1. In epic tales, heroes often struggle against opponents who lack a sense of
   justice.

2. In our office, Raymond has the _obligation_ for purchasing supplies.

3. In a dramatic announcement, the president declared that he would not
   serve a second term.

4. During the debate, the panel of journalists quizzed the candidates about their
   intentions if they were elected.

5. Confucius was an ancient Chinese statesman and philosopher, much respected for
   his _wisdom_.

B. *Follow the directions in responding to each of the items below.*

1. List two of your personal heroes.
   ★ Jesus   ★ My dad

2. Write two sentences to explain your choice of one of these heroes. Use at least two
   of the Big Question vocabulary words.
   I chose my dad because its my hero and have respons
   I choose Jesus because he has wisdom, honesty in my life

C. *Complete the sentence below. Then, write a short paragraph in which you connect the
experience to the Big Question.*

A **hero** may not choose _the destiny_, but he or she must make **choices**
to change how the things can be solved. It's always
important to have a person to trust or in the
other

"Three Skeleton Key" by George Toudouze
Literary Analysis: Protagonist and Antagonist

The **protagonist** is the chief character in a literary work—the character whose fortunes are of greatest interest to the reader. Some literary works also have an **antagonist**—a character or force that fights the protagonist. The antagonist may be another character or an external force, such as nature, that acts as a character.

Although the protagonist is not always an admirable or even likeable character, readers are interested in what happens to him or her.

- The protagonist's motives may be commonly understood feelings and goals, such as curiosity, the search for love, or the desire to win.
- The protagonist's conflict with the antagonist may represent a larger struggle, such as the conflict between good and evil, success and failure, or life and death.

DIRECTIONS: *Answer the following questions on the lines provided.*

1. Who or what is the protagonist in "Three Skeleton Key"? What is the occupation of the protagonist?

   The Narrator, work at Lighthouses

2. What qualities or characteristics make the protagonist a bit unusual and attract our interest?

3. Who or what is the antagonist in the story?

   The Rats

4. How does the author use the technique of personification to make the antagonist seem like a difficult and even dangerous opponent?

   because the rats are discusting

5. What parts of the conflict between the protagonist and the antagonist in "Three Skeleton Key" can you identify?

   The Rats want to eat the narrator and Friends.

All-in-One Workbook
299

Name _____ Date _____

"Three Skeleton Key" by George Toudouze
Reading: Compare and Contrast Characters

Comparing and contrasting characters is recognizing and thinking about their similarities and differences. You can compare different characters within a work, characters from different works, or a single character at different points in a particular work. To make a valid, productive comparison, you must examine each character (or the same character at different points in the narrative) in the same way. As you read, ask questions about each character you are comparing in the following general categories. Then, **generate questions after reading** that are specific to the characters and situations in the story.

- What are the character's actions?
- What are the character's reasons for his or her actions?
- What qualities does the character demonstrate?

DIRECTIONS: *Use the space provided to answer these questions about the characters in "Three Skeleton Key."*

1. How does Itchoua contrast with Le Gleo and the narrator?

   _____

2. In the struggle with the rats, how does Le Gleo react differently from the other characters? What does this difference suggest about the ways in which human beings react to extreme pressure or danger?

   _____

   _____

   _____

   _____

3. How successful is Toudouze in personifying the ship's rats, making them seem like characters rather than rats?

   _____

   _____

   _____

4. What attitudes does the narrator display about his profession and Three Skeleton Key at the beginning of the story? What attitudes does he display at the end? What does a comparison of his before-and-after outlooks suggest about the narrator's personality?

   _____

   _____

   _____

   _____

   _____

Name _____ Date _____

"Three Skeleton Key" by George Toudouze

Vocabulary Builder

Word List

derisive   diminution   incessantly   lurched   monotonous   provisions

A. DIRECTIONS: *Circle the letter of the best answer to each of the following questions.*

1. Which of the following answers is the best synonym for *lurched*?
   A. moved jerkily   B. launched   C. subsided

2. Which of the following answers most nearly means the OPPOSITE of *diminution*?
   A. delay   B. memory   C. increase

3. If you answered someone in a *derisive* fashion, which of the following answers would best describe your tone of voice?
   A. soothing   B. mocking   C. loud

B. DIRECTIONS: *For each of the following items, think about the meaning of the underlined word and then answer the question.*

1. If you wrote a derisive review of a film, would your review be admiring or critical?

   _____

2. If the company for which you worked reported a sharp diminution in sales, would the company's owners feel pleased or concerned?

   _____

3. Would you feel comfortable on a bus that lurched during most of a five-hour journey? Why or why not?

   _____

4. If your kitchen was stocked with provisions, would you likely go hungry in the near future?

   _____

5. If a lecturer's voice is monotonous, would the audience find it easy to pay attention?

   _____

6. If children complain incessantly, would they likely feel satisfied?

   _____

C. WORD STUDY: *The Latin root -min- means "small." Use the context of the sentences and what you know about the Latin root -min- to explain your answer to each question.*

1. If an event has a *minimal* impact on you, has it affected you greatly? Why or why not?

   _____

   _____

2. If there are *minuscule* traces of an element in a chemical compound, can they be described as significant? Why or why not?

   _____

   _____

Name _____ Date _____

"The Red-headed League" by Sir Arthur Conan Doyle

Writing About the Big Question

Do heroes have responsibilities?

Big Question Vocabulary

character	choices	hero	honesty	identify
imitate	intentions	involvement	justice	morality
obligation	responsibility	serve	standard	wisdom

A. *Use one or more words from the list above to complete each sentence.*

1. In Massachusetts during the 1600s, laws passed by the Puritans were evidence of their stern _____.

2. When you take out a bank loan for a house, your mortgage is a formal document stating your _____ to repay the money.

3. Can you _____ the rhyme scheme of this brief lyric poem?

4. Merchants known for their _____ will never knowingly sell a defective product.

5. Patricia promised that, if she were elected to the student council, she would _____ the sophomore class with dedication.

B. *Follow the directions in responding to each of the items below.*

1. List two ways in which you might like to **serve** your community.

_____

_____

2. Write two sentences to explain one of your **choices** of community service. Use at least two of the Big Question vocabulary words.

_____

_____

C. *Complete the sentences below. Then, write a short paragraph in which you connect the experience to the Big Question.*

When a crime is being committed, a **hero** will _____. The hero's **involvement** may _____

_____

_____

_____

"The Red-headed League" by Sir Arthur Conan Doyle
Literary Analysis: Protagonist and Antagonist

The **protagonist** is the chief character in a literary work—the character whose fortunes are of greatest interest to the reader. Some literary works also have an **antagonist**—a character or force that fights the protagonist. The antagonist may be another character or an external force, such as nature, that acts as a character.

Although the protagonist is not always an admirable or even likeable character, readers are interested in what happens to him or her.

- The protagonist's motives may be commonly understood feelings and goals, such as curiosity, the search for love, or the desire to win.
- The protagonist's conflict with the antagonist may represent a larger struggle, such as the conflict between good and evil, success and failure, or life and death.

DIRECTIONS: *Answer the following questions on the lines provided.*

1. Who or what is the protagonist in "The Red-headed League"? What is the occupation of the protagonist?

   _____

2. What qualities or characteristics make the protagonist somewhat unusual and attract our interest?

   _____

   _____

   _____

3. Who or what is the antagonist in the story?

   _____

   _____

4. What parts of the conflict between the protagonist and the antagonist in "The Red-headed League" can you identify?

   _____

   _____

   _____

   _____

   _____

   _____

   _____

Name _____ Date _____

Reading: Compare and Contrast Characters

Comparing and contrasting characters is recognizing and thinking about their similarities and differences. You can compare different characters within a work, characters from different works, or a single character at different points in a particular work. To make a valid, productive comparison, you must examine each character (or the same character at different points in the narrative) in the same way. As you read, ask questions about each character you are comparing in the following general categories. Then, **generate questions after reading** that are specific to the characters and situations in the story.

- What are the character's actions?
- What are the character's reasons for his or her actions?
- What qualities does the character demonstrate?

DIRECTIONS: *Use the space provided to answer these questions about the characters in* "The Red-headed League."

1. How does Sherlock Holmes compare and contrast with Dr. Watson?

   _____

   _____

   _____

2. How does Sherlock Holmes contrast with Peter Jones, the police agent from Scotland Yard?

   _____

   _____

   _____

3. How would you compare Sherlock Holmes with his antagonist, the murderer and thief John Clay?

   _____

   _____

   _____

4. How does Holmes's outlook on life at the beginning of "The Red-headed League" compare or contrast with his outlook at the end of the story?

   _____

   _____

   _____

Name _____ Date _____

Vocabulary Builder

Word List

embellish   endeavored   formidable   introspective   tenacious   vex

A. DIRECTIONS: *Circle the letter of the best answer to each question.*

—— 1. Which of the following answers is the best synonym for *vex*?
    A. predict   **B.** annoy   **C.** promise

—— 2. Which of the following answers most nearly means the OPPOSITE of *introspective*?
    A. outgoing   **B.** exhausted   **C.** optimistic

—— 3. Which of the following answers is the best synonym for *formidable*?
    A. bashful   **B.** lively   **C.** awe-inspiring

—— 4. Which of the following answers is the best synonym for *embellish*?
    A. demand   **B.** encourage   **C.** decorate   **D.** replace

—— 5. Which of the following answers is the best synonym for *endeavored*?
    A. attempted   **B.** analyzed   **C.** suspected   **D.** traversed

—— 6. Which of the following answers is the best synonym for *tenacious*?
    A. realistic   **B.** gallant   **C.** translucent   **D.** persistent

B. DIRECTIONS: *In each of the following items, think about the meaning of the underlined word and then answer the question.*

1. If you faced a <u>formidable</u> enemy, would you face an easy or a difficult challenge?

_____

2. If you found a situation <u>vexing</u>, would you be pleased or annoyed?

_____

3. Would a person in an <u>introspective</u> mood be feeling thoughtful, bored, or excited?

_____

C. WORD STUDY: *The Latin root -spec(t)- means "see" or "look." For example, a retrospective looks back at past events; a spectator is a person who views an event. Using what you know about the root -spec(t)-, match the word in Column A with its meaning in Column B by writing the correct letter on the line provided.*

____ 1. introspective   **A.** general view or survey

____ 2. respective   **B.** point of view

____ 3. perspective   **C.** looking inward; reflective

____ 4. conspectus   **D.** as relates individually to each of two persons

"Three Skeleton Key" by George Toudouze
"The Red-headed League" by Sir Arthur Conan Doyle
Integrated Language Skills: Grammar

Using Commas Correctly

Study the following list, which contains helpful suggestions on correct comma usage.

- Use a comma before the coordinating conjunction to separate two independent clauses in a compound sentence.

  We wanted to attend the concert, but our friends wanted to stay home.

- Use commas to separate three or more words, phrases, or clauses in a series.

  She bought onions, tomatoes, and peas.

- Use a comma after an introductory word, phrase, or clause.

  At the end of our day at the beach, we returned home.

- Use commas to set off parenthetical and nonessential expressions.

  His painting, which I saw yesterday, is difficult to understand.

- Use commas with places, dates, and titles.

  Edgar Allan Poe was raised in Richmond, Virginia.

- Use a comma to set off a direct quotation.

  Teresa asked, "Has everyone had enough salad?"

A. DIRECTIONS: *Rewrite the following sentences, adding commas where they are needed.*

1. Sir Arthur Conan Doyle the creator of Sherlock Holmes first studied to be an eye doctor.

   _____

2. When Doyle was in medical school he became aware of a certain professor.

   _____

3. This doctor who could diagnose illnesses that puzzled his colleagues may have been the model for the great Sherlock Holmes.

   _____

B. WRITING APPLICATION: *On the following lines, write a paragraph in which you tell what you like or dislike about detective stories. Use a variety of sentence structures, and be sure you use commas correctly.*

_____

_____

_____

_____

_____

"Three Skeleton Key" by George Toudouze
"The Red-headed League" by Sir Arthur Conan Doyle

Integrated Language Skills: Support for Writing Journal Entries

For your journal entries, use the following chart to jot down notes.

Timeline: (1) _____
_____
(2) _____
_____
(3) _____
_____
(4) _____
_____
(5) _____
_____
(6) _____
_____

Choice of Days for Journal Entries: (1) _____
_____
(2) _____
_____
(3) _____
_____

As you write, remember to stay in character and make sure that your journal entries reflect any changes that the character experiences in the course of the story.

"There Is a Longing" by Chief Dan George

Writing About the Big Question

Do heroes have responsibilities?

Big Question Vocabulary

character	choices	hero	honesty	identify
imitate	intentions	involvement	justice	morality
obligation	responsibility	serve	standard	wisdom

A. *Use one or more words from the list above to complete each sentence.*

1. Our guidance counselor, Mr. Palumbo, helps students make _____ about their college applications.

2. Mayor Selfridge is highly respected for her _____ and her sense of fair play.

3. Because the Internet research returned hundreds of Web sites, it was hard to _____ which sites would be most helpful.

4. We admire the Penningtons because of their _____ in raising money for charitable causes.

5. In a democracy, every citizen has a(n) _____ to vote in elections.

B. *Follow the directions in responding to each of the items below.*

1. List the top two personality traits that a **hero** should have.

   _____

   _____

2. Write two sentences to explain your choice of these two traits. Use at least two of the Big Question vocabulary words.

   _____

   _____

C. *Complete the sentences below. Then, write a short paragraph in which you connect the sentences to the Big Question.*

All heroes do not have to _____. A leader can be a true hero when

_____

_____

_____

_____

_____

Name _____ Date _____

Literary Analysis: Author's Philosophical Assumptions

An author's **purpose,** or goal, is shaped by his or her **philosophical assumptions,** or basic beliefs. These philosophical assumptions may be political, moral, or ethical beliefs. They may be assumptions about human nature. The author may use basic beliefs as support for an argument. The response of the **audience,** or readers, to the author's work will depend on whether the audience shares the author's beliefs.

To read with understanding, find the basic beliefs and assumptions in the author's work. Decide whether you accept them and whether others would be likely to accept them. Then, evaluate whether these assumptions support the author's purpose.

DIRECTIONS: *Consider the philosophical assumption, or basic belief, underlying each of the following passages from "There Is a Longing." Then, write a brief note on the chart to identify and comment on the philosophical assumption.*

Passage	Philosophical Assumption
1. There is a longing in the heart of my people to reach out and grasp that which is needed for our survival.	
2. But they will emerge with their hand held forward, not to receive welfare, but to grasp the place in society that is rightly ours.	
3. Oh, Great Spirit! Give me back the courage of the olden Chiefs. Let me wrestle with my surroundings. Let me once again, live in harmony with my environment.	
4. Like the thunderbird of old, I shall rise again out of the sea; I shall grab the instruments of the white man's success—his education, his skills.	
5. I shall see our young braves and our chiefs sitting in the houses of law and government, ruling and being ruled by the knowledge and freedoms of our great land.	

"There Is a Longing" by Chief Dan George
Reading: Recognize Compare-and-Contrast Organization

Comparing and contrasting means recognizing similarities and differences. In persuasive writing, authors often compare and contrast one point of view with another. As you read, use **self-monitoring** techniques like the ones shown to make sure you understand the comparisons.

- Find the things or ideas being compared.
- Restate the similarities and differences in your own words.
- Explain the significance of the similarities and differences.

If you cannot find, restate, or explain the author's points, reread words or phrases that were unclear, and make sure you understand them.

DIRECTIONS: *Answer the following questions to self-monitor your reading of "There Is a Longing."*

1. According to Chief Dan George, how would the "new warriors" contrast with those of "olden days"?

   _____

   _____

   _____

2. Once the "new warriors" accepted and mastered the challenge, how would Native American society of the future contrast with the conditions that existed in Chief Dan George's time?

   _____

   _____

   _____

3. How does Chief Dan George say that he differed from past chiefs?

   _____

   _____

4. In what ways does the chief hope that he might be like past chiefs?

   _____

   _____

"There Is a Longing" by Chief Dan George
Vocabulary Builder

Word List

determination   emerge   endurance   humbly   longing   segment

A. DIRECTIONS: *In each of the following items, think about the meaning of the underlined word and then answer the question.*

1. Would running 26 miles require <u>endurance</u>? Why or why not?

   _____

2. If you faced a challenge or task with <u>determination</u>, would your mind be made up to master or complete it? Explain.

   _____

3. If you were accepting an award <u>humbly</u>, would you make a long speech describing your achievement? Why or why not?

   _____

4. Would a <u>longing</u> for your homeland be a pleasant feeling? Why or why not?

   _____

5. If a <u>segment</u> of the population wanted free college tuition, would everyone be in agreement? Explain.

   _____

B. DIRECTIONS: *The Latin root -merg- means "dip" or "plunge." Use the context of each sentence to correct the sentence so that it makes sense. Be careful not to change the word in italics.*

1. Kevin *emerged* from the shower covered in dust and filth.

   _____

   _____

2. The submarine was easily detectable as it was *submerged* in deep waters.

   _____

   _____

3. Celia was so *immersed* in her reading that she turned on the television for some distraction.

   _____

   _____

"Glory and Hope" by Nelson Mandela
Writing About the Big Question

Do heroes have responsibilities?

Big Question Vocabulary

character	choices	hero	honesty	identify
imitate	intentions	involvement	justice	morality
obligation	responsibility	serve	standard	wisdom

A. *Use one or more words from the list above to complete each sentence.*

1. In ancient times, a _____ was often a warrior or a statesman, but today in the United States he or she may just as likely be a sports star or a movie idol.

2. People should not be judged by the color of their skin, said Martin Luther King, Jr., but by the content of their _____.

3. Heroes set a high _____ for all of us, and we would do well to _____ them.

4. If you baby-sit a small child, you have a(n) _____ to look after the child's welfare while you are on duty.

B. *Follow the directions in responding to each of the items below.*

1. List two different times when you read about someone who was admired as a hero and then behaved badly.

   _____

   _____

2. Write two sentences to explain one of these situations. Use at least two of the Big Question vocabulary words.

   _____

   _____

C. *Complete the sentences below. Then, write a short paragraph in which you connect the sentences to the Big Question.*

When a leader promises to **serve** his or her nation, he or she must _____.
The leader has an **obligation** to _____

   _____

   _____

   _____

Name _____ Date _____

"Glory and Hope" by Nelson Mandela
Literary Analysis: Author's Philosophical Assumptions

An author's **purpose,** or goal, is shaped by his or her **philosophical assumptions,** or basic beliefs. These philosophical assumptions may be political, moral, or ethical beliefs. They may be assumptions about human nature. The author may use basic beliefs as support for an argument. The response of the **audience,** or readers, to the author's work will depend on whether the audience shares the author's beliefs.

To read with understanding, find the basic beliefs and assumptions in the author's work. Decide whether you accept them and whether others would be likely to accept them. Then, evaluate whether these assumptions support the author's purpose.

DIRECTIONS: *Consider the philosophical assumption, or basic belief, underlying each of the following passages from "Glory and Hope." Then, write a brief note on the chart to identify and comment on the philosophical assumption.*

Passage	Philosophical Assumption
1. Out of an experience of an extraordinary human disaster that lasted too long must be born a society of which all humanity will be proud.	
2. Each time one of us touches the soil of this land, we feel a sense of personal renewal.	
3. The time for the healing of the wounds has come. The moment to bridge the chasms that divide us has come. The time to build is upon us.	
4. We enter into a covenant that we shall build a society in which all South Africans, both black and white, will be able to walk tall, without any fear in their hearts, assured of their inalienable right to human dignity—a rainbow nation at peace with itself and the world.	
5. Never, never, and never again shall it be that this beautiful land will again experience the oppression of one by another. . . .	

"**Glory and Hope**" by Nelson Mandela
Reading: Recognize Compare-and-Contrast Organization

Comparing and contrasting means recognizing similarities and differences. In persuasive writing, authors often compare and contrast one point of view with another. As you read, use **self-monitoring** techniques like the ones shown to make sure you understand the comparisons.

- Find the things or ideas being compared.
- Restate the similarities and differences in your own words.
- Explain the significance of the similarities and differences.

If you cannot find, restate, or explain the author's points, reread words or phrases that were unclear and make sure you understand them.

DIRECTIONS: *Answer the following questions to self-monitor your reading of "Glory and Hope."*

1. According to Nelson Mandela, how does the present in South Africa contrast with the past?

_____

_____

_____

2. How does South Africa's international standing now contrast with its position in the past?

_____

_____

_____

3. How does Nelson Mandela's portrait of a future society in South Africa strengthen the contrasts he has drawn between the present and the past?

_____

_____

_____

_____

"Glory and Hope" by Nelson Mandela
Vocabulary Builder

Word List

confer   covenant   distinguished   intimately   pernicious   reconciliation

A. DIRECTIONS: *Circle the letter of the best answer to each question.*

1. Which of the following is the best synonym for *confer*?
   A. divide   B. respect   C. give

2. Which of the following most nearly means the OPPOSITE of *pernicious*?
   A. negative   B. harmless   C. courageous

3. If you have made a *covenant* with someone, what did you probably exchange?
   A. information   B. directions   C. solemn promises

B. DIRECTIONS: *For each item, think about the meaning of the underlined word and then answer the question.*

1. Would a <u>covenant</u> typically involve an advertisement or a promise? Explain.
   _____

2. If you regarded a person as <u>pernicious</u>, would you recommend him or her for a job? Explain.
   _____

3. If you <u>confer</u> an award on someone, do you give it or do you take it away?
   _____

4. Would you expect a candidate for mayor to look <u>distinguished</u>? Why or why not?
   _____

5. If you know a novel or a play <u>intimately</u>, have you read it carefully? Explain.
   _____

6. Does <u>reconciliation</u> bring people closer together or drive them apart? Explain.
   _____

C. WORD STUDY: *The Latin root -fer- means to bring or carry. For example, a ferry is a boat that carries passangers. To transfer is to move to another place. Use the context of the sentences and what you know about the Latin root -fer- to explain your answer to each question. Use the italicized vocabulary word in each answer.*

1. If you *defer* your decision on an issue, do you decide now or later?
   _____
   _____

2. When you *refer* to a dictionary, do you use it or ignore it?
   _____
   _____

3. When you make an *inference*, do you draw a conclusion about something?
   _____
   _____

"There Is a Longing" by Chief Dan George
"Glory and Hope" by Nelson Mandela

Integrated Language Skills: Grammar

Using Colons, Semicolons, and Ellipsis Points Correctly

Use a **colon** in order to introduce a list of items following an independent clause, to introduce a formal quotation, or to follow the salutation in a business letter.

- He bought materials for the salad: lettuce, tomatoes, onions, and radishes.

- Nelson Mandela evokes his fellow South Africans' love for their land in these words: "Each time one of us touches the soil of this land, we feel a sense of personal renewal."

- Dear Sir:

Use a **semicolon** to join independent clauses that are not already joined by a conjunction. Also, use a semicolon to avoid confusion when independent clauses or items in a series already contain commas.

- The government of South Africa finally rejected apartheid; in 1994, the first free elections were held.

- We visited Boston, Philadelphia, and Washington, D.C.; altogether, our tour of the eastern seaboard was a great success.

Ellipsis points (. . .) are punctuation marks that are used to show that something has not been expressed. Usually, ellipsis points indicate one of the following situations:
Words have been left out of a quotation.
A series continues beyond the items mentioned.
Time passes or action occurs in a narrative.

- Nelson Mandela says, "We are moved . . . when the grass turns green and the flowers bloom."

- We thought wistfully about the cats' curiosity, agility, and grace. . . .

- They keep their discontent to themselves . . . but will they do so forever?

A. DIRECTIONS: *Rewrite each sentence on the lines provided, correcting errors in the use of colons, semicolons, and ellipsis points. There is only one error in each sentence.*

1. Julius Caesar described his victory as follows . . . "I came, I saw, I conquered."
   _____

2. Statesmanship is a rare gift, few heads of government in the modern world, in fact, have risen to its challenges.
   _____

   _____

B. WRITING APPLICATION: *On the lines, write a paragraph in which you describe a favorite animal or bird. In your paragraph, use at least one example of each of the following: a colon, a semicolon, and ellipsis points.*

_____

_____

_____

_____

"There Is a Longing" by Chief Dan George
"Glory and Hope" by Nelson Mandela

Integrated Language Skills: Support for Writing a Letter

Use the following chart to make prewriting notes for your letter to Nelson Mandela or Chief Dan George about his speech.

Words That Show Your Reactions
_____
_____
Support for Your Reactions
_____
_____
Reason(s) for Writing Your Letter
_____
_____
What People Can Learn From the Message
_____
_____
_____
_____

On a separate page, write a letter using your notes. Make sure that you maintain a respectful tone.

Name _____ Date _____

Writing About the Big Question

Do heroes have responsibilities?

Big Question Vocabulary

character	choices	hero	honesty	identify
imitate	intentions	involvement	justice	morality
obligation	responsibility	serve	standard	wisdom

A. *Use one or more words from the list above to complete each sentence.*

1. Mayor Jarowski will be sorely missed because he set a high _____ for _____ and civic _____ in the community.

2. In Shakespeare's play *Julius Caesar*, Brutus is a heroic _____, even though his _____ do not turn out the way he planned them.

3. Engraved on the Supreme Court building in Washington, D.C., are the famous words, "Equal _____ Under Law."

4. According to a Constitutional Amendment, the President may not _____ more than two consecutive four-year terms.

5. Grandfather was a living example of the truth that _____ goes deeper than mere knowledge.

B. *Follow the directions in responding to each of the items below.*

1. List two situations in which you think a person's **honesty** might be tested.

   _____

   _____

2. Write two sentences to explain one of these situations. Use at least two of the Big Question vocabulary words.

   _____

   _____

C. *Complete the sentence below. Then, write a short paragraph in which you connect the sentence to the Big Question.*

   In some situations, heroes have a responsibility to _____

   _____

   _____

   _____

   _____

Name _____ Date _____

"Pecos Bill: The Cyclone" by Harold W. Felton
"Perseus" by Edith Hamilton
Literary Analysis: Tall Tale and Myth

A **tall tale** is a type of folk tale that contains some or all of the following features:

- a larger-than-life central hero
- far-fetched situations and amazing feats
- humor
- *hyperbole*, or exaggeration

Tall tales are a particularly American form of story. Many tall tales originated during the American frontier period and reflect the challenges and values of that place and time.

A **myth** is an anonymous story that explains the actions of gods or human heroes, the reasons for certain traditions, or the causes of natural features. Every culture has its own *mythology*, or collection of myths, which express the central values of the people who created them. **Mythic heroes** often share three characteristics: they have at least one divine parent, they gain special knowledge or weapons, and they face seemingly impossible tasks. In general, myths tell how gods shape human life while tall tales tell how humans make things happen.

DIRECTIONS: *Write your answers to the following questions on the lines provided.*

1. How would you compare and contrast Pecos Bill and Perseus as **heroes**?
   Pecos Bill is an mythic hero and perseus as am
   Mythic heroes

2. What elements of **exaggeration** or **fantasy** can you identify in each tale?
   "Pecos Bill: The Cyclone": The fantasy was riding the
   cyclone
   "Perseus": The exaggeration was fighting the
   monster

3. **Mood** is the overall atmosphere or feeling created by a literary work. **Tone** is the author's attitude toward the subject, the characters, or the audience. How would you compare and contrast "Pecos Bill: The Cyclone" with "Perseus" in mood and tone?
   Mood: Pecos Bill was a happier person
   Perseus was more agressive.
   Tone: The tone or pecous was more dramatic

4. In their original versions, many tall tales and myths were **oral literature**—or works that were passed down by word of mouth from one generation to the next. What qualities in "The Cyclone" and "Perseus" would lend themselves especially well to oral storytelling?
   that people should be brave

Name _____ Date _____

"Pecos Bill: The Cyclone" by Harold W. Felton

"Perseus" by Edith Hamilton

Vocabulary Builder

Word List

mortified   revelry   skeptics   usurped

A. DIRECTIONS: *Revise each sentence so that the underlined vocabulary word is used logically. Be sure not to change the vocabulary word.*

1. After the tyrant <u>usurped</u> the king's throne, most people acclaimed him as the legitimate ruler.

   _____

2. The professor's arguments were so convincing that many <u>skeptics</u> questioned her conclusions.

   _____

3. When Eugene made such diplomatic comments to our hosts, we felt <u>mortified</u>.

   _____

4. The sounds of <u>revelry</u> from the party next door were low and soothing.

   _____

B. DIRECTIONS: *On the line, write the letter of the choice that is the best synonym for each numbered word.*

___ 1. revelry
   A. slow improvement
   B. agile maneuver
   C. early departure
   D. noisy merrymaking

___ 2. usurped
   A. researched
   B. incorporated
   C. seized power
   D. reorganized

___ 3. skeptics
   A. allies
   B. doubters
   C. forecasters
   D. inventors

___ 4. mortified
   A. buried
   B. embarrassed
   C. disguised
   D. deceived

Name _____ Date _____

"Pecos Bill: The Cyclone" by Harold W. Felton
"Perseus" by Edith Hamilton

Support for Writing to Compare Literary Works

Use a chart like the one shown to make prewriting notes for an essay comparing and contrasting the values that Pecos Bill and Perseus represent.

Values	Pecos Bill	Perseus
Respect		
Fears		
Goals		
Achievements		
Motivations		

Tips for Improving Your Reading Fluency

You've probably heard the expression "Practice makes perfect." Through your own experiences, you know that practice improves all types of skills. If you play a guitar, you know that practicing has made you a better player. The same is true for sports, for crafts, and for reading. The following tips will help you to practice skills that will lead to reading **fluency**—the ability to read easily, smoothly, and expressively.

Choose your practice materials carefully.

Make reading fun! Make a list of subjects that interest you. Then, search for reading materials—books, magazines, newspapers, reliable Web sites. As you learn more about your interests, you will also be practicing your reading skills.

Choose your practice space and time carefully.

Help your concentration skills. Find a quiet, comfortable place to read—away from the television and other distractions. Get in the habit of treating yourself to an hour of pleasure reading every day—apart from homework and other tasks. Reading about interesting topics in a quiet, comfortable place will provide both pleasure and relaxation.

Practice prereading strategies.

A movie preview gives viewers a good idea about what the movie will be about. Before you read, create your own preview of what you plan to read. Look at pictures and captions, subheads, and diagrams. As you scan, look for unfamiliar words. Find out what those words mean before you start reading.

Use punctuation marks.

Think of punctuation marks as stop signs. For example, the period at the end of a sentence signals the end of a complete thought. From time to time in your reading, stop at that stop sign. Reread the sentence. Summarize the complete thought in your own words.

Read aloud.

Use your voice and your ears as well as your eyes. Read phrases and sentences expressively. Pause at commas and periods. Show emphasis in your voice when you come to an exclamation point. Let your voice naturally rise at the end of a question. If possible, record your reading. Then listen to the recording, noting your pacing and expression.

Pause to ask questions.

Stop reading after a short amount of time (for example, five minutes) or at the end of a meaty paragraph. Look away from the text. Ask yourself questions—What are the main ideas? What message does the author want me to get? What might happen next? If the answers seem unclear, reread—either silently or aloud. Find the answers!

Use what you know.

As you read an informational article, think about what you already know about the topic. Use your knowledge and ideas as background information. Doing so will help you to understand new ideas. As you read fiction or a personal narrative, think about your own experiences. If you have been in a situation that is similar to that of a fictional character, you will be better able to understand his or her feelings, actions, and goals.

Talk about it.

Ask a friend or family member to read what you have read. Take turns reading aloud together, listening to both content and expression. Then discuss what you read. Share, compare, and contrast your ideas. Doing so will reinforce your knowledge of the content of what you read, and may provide new and interesting perspectives about the topic.

Reading Fluency Assessment Passage 1

When developers talk about homes of the future, they often use the term *smart homes*. In such homes, electronic devices are able to "communicate" with each other. This is accomplished by networking the electric circuits of different parts of the home so that the functions of certain devices and appliances[50] affect each other.

Imagine hearing your alarm clock ring. You wake up knowing that a frenzy of activity has begun. Your hot chocolate is brewing, your oatmeal is cooking in the microwave, and your cinnamon bun is browning in the toaster. Additionally, lights in the bathroom have switched on, and[100] water for your shower has warmed to the correct temperature.

In this "smart" world, the home's appliances, as well as the heating and cooling systems, work to save energy. For example, during the winter, the heat automatically readjusts to a cooler temperature when people leave the house. The closing door[150] automatically cues the system to reset itself.

The kitchen has become a particularly interesting place for designers and innovators. Someday most appliances will be able to perform multiple functions. The refrigerator will no longer merely store perishable foods. With a television screen in its door, it will also become an[200] entertainment center. Cookbooks will become unnecessary because the refrigerator will suggest recipes based on the food it has on hand. It might even help you decide which foods should be discarded, once it analyzes which ones are no longer fresh.

Another item that could change how we cook is the[250] smart oven mitt. When used to handle hot pots in the oven, it would be able to inform us whether or not the food has been adequately cooked.

Will tomorrow's consumers get advice and assistance from their "smart" homes? Only time will tell.[293]

1030L

Check Your Understanding

1. In "smart homes," refrigerators will be able to

   a. help with recipes.
   b. cook food.
   c. wake someone up.
   d. talk.

2. Name one way in which a "smart home" can work to save energy.

   _____

   _____

Reading Fluency Assessment Passage 2

The United States is often called a nation of immigrants. In fact, nearly the entire population of this country has ancestors who chose to leave their original homelands, make dramatic and often difficult journeys, and create new lives in a new place. People from all over the world have come[50] to the United States in search of a new beginning. Some of these immigrants redirected their lives due to wars or other dangers. Others came looking for a better life. The flow of immigrants to the United States has always come in waves. Heavy periods of immigration have usually been[100] followed by a backlash against newcomers.

For many immigrants, the idea of living in America had long hovered in their minds before their actual journeys began. They saw a golden, pastoral country of green fields and new chances. They saw a land in which opportunity was open and accessible to[150] anyone. This added to the joyful exhilaration that so many must have felt as they sailed past the Statue of Liberty or saw the San Francisco skyline for the first time.

These new arrivals were sometimes inspired by false claims of what they would find here, including streets paved with[200] gold. Therefore, their initial excitement upon arrival often became a fleeting emotion, once reality set in. In spite of these false claims, many immigrants have found that the reality they found in the United States was better than the reality of their homelands.

In both historic and modern times, many[250] newcomers have been able to build successful lives in their adopted country. But it is far from simple. Adapting to a new language and new customs is often extremely difficult. Even so, streams of hopeful people continue to make the journey to the United States.[295]

1040L

Check Your Understanding

1. Most of the people who live in the United States have ancestors who were immigrants.

   True / False? Explain:

   _____

2. What has caused many immigrants to feel their excitement about coming to America fade once they arrive here?

   _____

   _____

Reading Fluency Assessment Passage 3

When my uncle Roberto was a little boy, his grandfather was a railroad engineer. Uncle Roberto didn't really know what that meant, but he did know that he had to be very quiet after dinner so that his grandfather could sleep. This was very hard. He usually succeeded, though, thanks[50] to the large supply of bedtime stories that his grandmother would read to him as they cuddled together in her big armchair.

Uncle Roberto knew that his grandfather went to bed so early because he had to get up at 3:30 each morning to leave for his job at the[100] yard behind the railroad station. One morning when it was still dark, Uncle Roberto's grandmother woke him up and said, "Hurry and get dressed, little one. Grandpa is taking us for a ride on his train!" Uncle Roberto was so excited that he could hardly wriggle into his clothes.

First[150] they took a streetcar to the railroad yard. There were only a few other riders because it was still so early. Before he knew it, they arrived at the yard. Uncle Roberto watched as his grandfather climbed up into the locomotive. Then Uncle Roberto and his grandmother climbed up the[200] stairs into the first passenger car. It was an observation car with a glass ceiling.

They rode for about two hours in the observation car, which gave them a wonderful view of the glowing sunrise and the rural countryside. Uncle Roberto couldn't see his grandfather, but it gave him a[250] great feeling of pride to know that he was up front, driving the powerful locomotive. Now Uncle Roberto understood why it was so important to let his grandfather get to sleep so early each night![285]

1040L

Check Your Understanding

1. The grandfather went to bed very early every night because he

   a. had to get up early for work.

   b. was very tired after working all day.

   c. had to ride a streetcar to work.

   d. had to take care of Uncle Roberto.

2. Explain what gave Uncle Roberto a great feeling of pride.

   _____

   _____

Reading Fluency Assessment Passage 4

The so-called "Rebel Yell" became famous on the battlefields of the Civil War. The now-famous battle cry was conceived for the southern soldiers, created to delay their stress before a fight. A good yell could totally release their stress, not just slow it down. The reputation of such shouting earned[50] the "Rebel Yell" its establishment in our vocabulary, setting it up for use by future generations.

The yell was often used to scare northern forces, the Yankees. Often the Rebels would resolve to holler for the duration of their charge, deciding to yell for minutes at a time. Sometimes the[100] Yankees thought that they were outnumbered based solely on the amount of noise coming from their enemy.

The yell was also used a lot when fighting occurred under the cover of trees or the night sky. Out of nowhere, the northern soldiers would hear the eerie and frightening "Rebel Yell." [150] It was also effective on fields set for a large-scale battles. Cannons would be arrayed in long, neat lines in front of troops standing shoulder to shoulder. The generals, whom soldiers admired and thought of as virtuous leaders, were mounted on patient steeds, waiting calmly for the battle. However, the[200] yell could even spook them.

While the "Rebel Yell" became famous during the Civil War, its origins can be traced to an earlier time. Some people believe that the shout was used for hunting. Other research mentions the Southern Appalachian region, where there used to be quite some distance between[250] neighbors. People often climbed the hilltops and shouted in order to talk with one another. Today's greater prosperity and technical advances have changed that. Now most people can afford to use phones and computers to communicate across distances. They no longer need to yell![295]

1050L

Check Your Understanding

1. One reason that the Rebel soldiers used the "Rebel Yell" was to

   a. scare their horses.
   b. scare the Yankees.
   c. find each other after a battle.
   d. hunt for bear.

2. Identify two probable uses of the "Rebel Yell" prior to the Civil War.

   _____

   _____

Reading Fluency Assessment Passage 5

You might have heard the proverb *Variety is the spice of life*. This familiar saying suggests that making changes can make your life more interesting. Long ago, many farming communities made an important discovery. They learned that variety can be more than interesting. It can be necessary!

Early farmers noticed[50] that growing the same crop on the same field year after year exhausted the nutrients in the soil, gradually making the land infertile. Through experimentation, they discovered that changing the crops could help to restore lost nutrients. By so doing, they discovered the effectiveness of crop rotation.

During the Middle[100] Ages, farmers developed a three-year crop rotation cycle. They sowed rye or winter wheat during the first year. Then, in the second year, they planted oats or barley. During the third year, the land was left fallow, or unplanted. After that one year of rest, the land was planted afresh[150] with rye or winter wheat.

Problems with such agricultural pests as beetles, aphids, and worms have recurred repeatedly. When researchers tried to find ways to limit the damage caused by these pests, they discovered that crop rotation could provide a solution. Pests that feed on one crop often are not[200] able to feed on other kinds of crops. Therefore, crop rotation can be used successfully to limit the populations of certain pests through removal of their food source.

Modern farming technology has changed a great deal since the Middle Ages. However, crop rotation remains one of the most[250] effective ways to keep soil fertile and productive through the elimination of pests.[261]

1060L

Check Your Understanding

1. Crop rotation helps to eliminate agricultural pests by

   a. making the land fertile.

   b. producing more crops.

   c. making the land fallow.

   d. removing their food source.

2. Give an example of how farmers might accomplish a 3-year cycle of crop rotation.

   _____

   _____

Reading Fluency Assessment Passage 6

Christopher and his father hiked part of the way up Mt. Washington in New Hampshire's White Mountains to spend the night at Greenleaf Hut. The hut could accommodate forty-eight hikers every night, in two bunk rooms—one for male hikers and one for female hikers. Dinner was served family-style at[50] long harvest tables, which offered an opportunity for conversation among the hikers. Over hearty chicken stew and freshly baked cornbread, they could share their impressions, trail information, and general musings about their experiences on the mountain trails.

Christopher asked a woman sitting near him where to spot bald eagles up[100] here in the mountains. She replied that because eagles often nested near bodies of water, Christopher might be more likely to find them near lakes or rivers in the valleys, rather than up in the mountains. Christopher felt discouraged because he had looked forward to this mountain hike as an[150] opportunity to watch the eagles soar.

After dinner, Christopher and his father went outside for a quiet stroll in the deep pine forest. In a clearing, they sat on a boulder and watched shooting stars. "Dad, I really wanted to see those eagles," Christopher said.

"Well, Christopher, perhaps we'll be[200] lucky tomorrow. Let's wait and be hopeful."

Then they went back to the hut to sleep in the men's bunk room.

After breakfast the next morning, Christopher and his father strapped on their backpacks and set out for the summit of the mountain. It was a clear, crisp morning and,[250] once atop Mt. Washington, they had incredibly beautiful views of the hills and valleys below. A river wound through one valley like a long blue ribbon. Then Christopher saw them—two eagles, soaring on the winds above the river. "You were right, Dad," he said. "We did get lucky!"[297]

1070L

Check Your Understanding

1. The woman said that Christopher would be more likely to see eagles

   a. on the top of the mountain.

   b. in the deep pine forest.

   c. near Greeleaf Hut.

   d. down in the valleys.

2. Explain how Christopher's feelings at the end of the story were different from his feelings at dinner the night before.

   _____

   _____

Reading Fluency Assessment Passage 7

You have probably had many experiences that prove that two people can observe the same situation and have two very different opinions about it. That phenomenon is exemplified in this riddle: If a glass is filled with water to its midpoint, is the glass half full, or half empty? In other words, are you an optimist or a pessimist?

Optimists tend to answer the water-and-glass question by saying that the glass is half *full*. That is because optimists are habitually hopeful. They feel that life is basically fair, and people are generally fortunate because good things will happen.

By contrast, a pessimist will probably answer the question by saying that the glass is half *empty*. That is because pessimists tend to think that life is unhappy or unfair and that bad things will probably happen.

Fortunately, most people are able to think in a balanced way. They possess the ability to apply both positive and negative thinking as they face the challenges of daily life. Positive thoughts such as hope, appreciation, and gratitude foster a cheerful outlook on life. Negative thoughts such as concern, doubt, and even worry may be helpful too, if they allow the person to be guarded and cautious in potentially dangerous situations. Therefore, a combination of both positive and negative thinking seems to be the healthiest way to face reality. That's why people who are able to combine positive and negative thoughts are called "realists."

Realists are practical people. They focus on what actually seems possible. Perhaps, then, it is realists who could set aside the extremes of optimism and pessimism and simply pick up that glass of water, ignore how full or empty it is, and just enjoy a refreshing sip.[286]

1080L

Check Your Understanding

1. A pessimist will tend to answer the riddle by saying that the glass is half full.

   True / False? Explain:

   _____

2. Explain the differences between an optimist, a pessimist, and a realist.

   _____

   _____

Reading Fluency Assessment Passage 8

Every family has interesting and inspiring stories to tell, but many of them get forgotten over time. Creating an oral history will insure that you preserve your family's unique past and, in the process, create a priceless inheritance to be passed down from one generation to the next. All that[50] you need to get started is an audio or video recorder and one or more family members to interview.

Prepare carefully for that first interview. List topics to discuss, such as daily life in the 1950s or popular music of the 1940s. You might also ask questions about a memorable[100] family incident, such as a wedding or the birth of a child. Use your creativity to come up with interesting questions to get people talking. You might ask people to talk about their childhood heroes or their favorite vacations or holidays. You might ask about "firsts"—their first car, their[150] first day at school, their first job.

Decide if you will interview family members one at a time or as a group. Whichever method you use, begin with a clear introduction in which you ask each person to say their name, age, and relation to your family. This will help[200] future viewers or listeners to identify each participant.

Once you begin recording, encourage people to talk in clear, distinct voices. Ask follow-up questions to gather further details, but be careful not to interrupt. If you are using a video recorder, simply set it up and let it run.

You might[250] also record an oral history when a family member accomplishes something special, such as graduating from school, winning a contest, or running a marathon. Talking to achievers about how they met their goals can inspire other family members to work harder to meet their own goals and challenges.[297]

1090L

Check Your Understanding

1. An oral history of a family contains

   a. photographs and awards.

   b. recordings of interviews.

   c. letters and journals.

   d. goals and challenges.

2. Why might a family's oral history become a "priceless inheritance" to be passed down from generation to generation?

   _____

   _____

Reading Fluency Assessment Passage 9

Many people have ambitions to achieve the American dream of home ownership. Owning a home is an admirable goal. However, renting a home is also a desirable choice for many Americans.

Renting a home can be beneficial for several reasons. For example, renting usually costs less than buying. When you[50] rent, you are required to do only minor maintenance chores, such as cleaning the interior and taking care of the yard. However, you do not have to do major chores such as maintaining the heating system or repairing the roof. Those types of chores are the responsibility of your landlord,[100] the owner of the property.

Renters may be required to pay for utilities, including electricity, gas, and water service. All such conditions and rules should be clearly stated in the lease, a written contract that is signed by both the landlord and the tenant, or renter. Other important contents of[150] the lease include the amount of money the tenant will pay for rent each month, and the term—the number of months or years—that the tenant will stay in the home. At the end of the term of the lease, the landlord and the tenant decide whether or not[200] to renew it.

Most people rent a home at some point in their lives. Most young, single people living independently for the first time are renters. Other renters include families relocating to new areas and older citizens who may find renting a good choice once their children have grown up[250] and moved away.

The goal of home ownership is an excellent one. However, people who rent benefit from lower expenses and fewer time-consuming household chores. With that extra time and money, they have greater flexibility and opportunities to pursue a hobby, degree, profession, or some other important goal.[297]

Check Your Understanding

1. The contract between a tenant and a landlord is called the

   a. rent
   b. utility
   c. lease
   d. maintenance

2. Name two benefits of renting a home rather than buying a home.

   _____

   _____

1090L

Reading Fluency Assessment Passage 10

Serena sat in the cramped office of her high school newspaper, *The Tattler*, feeling melancholy. It all had started with an essay and a cartoon she had created for the paper. They were about the cross-country team, which had never won a single meet in the 40-year history of the[50] school. In a rage, the team's coach had gone to Mr. Ramirez, the school principal, and demanded that every copy of the newspaper be confiscated.

The next day, Mr. Ramirez told *The Tattler* staff he was sorry, but the ultimate responsibility for such matters in a school always resides with[100] its principal. Therefore, he would store all 2,000 copies of the paper in his office until a teacher advisory committee could meet and reach a peaceful agreement about how to proceed.

The Tattler's faculty advisor, Ms. Thistle, insisted that the coach had misunderstood Serena's work and misinterpreted her intent. She[150] brought Serena to testify before the faculty committee to explain that her writing and art were intended to poke fun at the school's tradition of losing and not meant to criticize the coach or any particular team member.

For a week, the embattled *Tattler* staff printed fliers protesting that their[200] rights to freedom of speech were being denied. Meanwhile, Serena and the newspaper staff felt clouded with despair.

Then it happened. As Serena sat in *The Tattler* office before school one day, word came from Mr. Ramirez. The advisory committee had made their final decision. They had sided with the[250] newspaper! Suddenly, despair was replaced by exhilaration. Cheers went up in the office. In the cafeteria at lunch that day, Serena was ecstatic to see students from every class, including members of the cross-country team, reading copies of *The Tattler* and laughing at her cartoon.[295]

1100L

Check Your Understanding

1. The person who did not want *The Tattler* to be distributed at school was

   a. the school principal.
   b. Serena.
   c. the cross-country coach.
   d. Ms. Thistle.

2. What was the purpose of Serena's essay and cartoon?

   _____

   _____

Reading Fluency Assessment Passage 11

World War I greatly influenced authors of the early twentieth century. For example, the stress of the difficult war left a lasting impression on Ernest Hemingway. Prior to his writing career, Hemingway served as a Red Cross ambulance driver on the World War I battlefields. He was wounded and spent[50] time as an invalid at a hospital in Milan, Italy. These experiences led him to write his short story, "In Another Country."

In Hemingway's story, we get only glimpses of the horrors of World War I. The story focuses on a few wounded soldiers. Hemingway's approach is different from that[100] taken by most writers of adventure stories. Such stories usually highlight the heroic aspects of battle. In contrast, what Hemingway shows us are quiet, skeptical men receiving treatment for their wounds and going through the motions of physical therapy. Each day, they participate in experimental treatments that may not work.[150] The machines designed to heal their injuries appear almost sinister. They are products of the same industrial world that led to the war in the first place.

Hemingway's characters have a fragile quality. They have been humbled by their wartime experiences and their wounds, and they seem more like children[200] or old men than rugged, patriotic soldiers. They are grateful for simple treats, such as warm chestnuts roasted over charcoal.

Hemingway went on to write many other books and stories after "In Another Country." Some of his major novels, including *For Whom the Bell Tolls* and *A Farewell to Arms*, take[250] place during wartime. They contain both tragic events and characters deeply affected by the chaos of war. There is no doubt that Hemingway's own experiences during World War I had a permanent impact on his life and work.[288]

1110L

Check Your Understanding

1. The author Ernest Hemingway served in World War I as a

   a. soldier.

   b. ambulance driver.

   c. war reporter.

   d. physical therapist.

2. In what ways were the soldiers in Hemingway's story different from most characters in adventure stories?

   _____

   _____

Reading Fluency Assessment Passage 12

Although she is most famous for her writing, the author Eudora Welty was also a photographer. During the Great Depression, she became a publicity agent for the Works Progress Administration. As part of this job, she traveled throughout the state of Mississippi, taking pictures of a wide variety of people[50] and events. Like her writing, Welty's photographs are characterized by fondness, respect, and admiration for ordinary people. Welty also displayed a talent for capturing the emotions of her subjects, the people she photographed.

She titled one of her photographs "Tomato-packers' Recess." It depicts a group of men and boys taking[100] a break from a taxing day of hard, physical labor. At the center, a man in rolled-up jeans and a cowboy hat plays a guitar. The others lean forward and smile in pleasure as they listen. Their relaxed poses, entirely without rigidity, suggest that they were extremely comfortable being photographed[150] by Welty. The only solemn face is that of a man who looks out of the frame, as if checking to see if it"s time to return to work already. More in tune with the happy ambiance, a young boy is positioned in front of the guitar player. He seems[200] to observe intently, as though absorbing every slight movement the musician makes while strumming his instrument. Perhaps it is the contrast between these two figures that captures the essence of the moment.

The Works Progress Administration was a government program that gave many artists and writers work during the Depression[250], and aided thousands of people at a time when work was extremely scarce. Thanks to the Works Progress Association, we have an accurate, visual record of ordinary people of the era, through the work of the many WPA photographers, including Eudora Welty.[292]

1120L

Check Your Understanding

1. The Works Progress Association gave work to artists and writers during World War II.

   True / False? Explain:

   _____

2. Why are the works of the Works Progress Association photographers so valuable to people today?

   _____
   _____

Screening Test

Directions: Read the following passages. Then answer the questions. On the answer sheet, fill in the bubble for the answer that you think is correct.

The report contained few remarkable facts. A factory in which satisfactory water tanks were manufactured was forced to close. One factor was the less than factual bookkeeping. The <u>dissatisfaction</u> of the company factotums also had to be factored into the failure.

---

1 The word root *-port-* in the word *report* can be found in words such as <u>import</u>, <u>export</u>, and <u>transport</u>. Which verb *best* defines the meaning of *-port-* in these words?

A to pour
B to carry
C to send
D to receive

2 Many words in the passage contain the word root *-fact-*. It comes from the Latin verb *facere*. Which verb below *best* defines the meaning of *-fact-*?

F to fake
G to fail
H to make or do
J to cheat

3 What does the prefix *dis-* mean in the word <u>dissatisfaction</u>?

A not
B before
C apart
D exclude

4 She saw the dark clouds gathering in the sky and closed the window as a <u>precaution</u>. What do you think the prefix *pre-* means in <u>precaution</u>?

F against
G knowing
H ending
J before

Directions: Read the following sentences. Then choose the meaning of the underlined word. On the answer sheet, fill in the bubble for the answer that you think is correct.

5 Arleen went to tell the neighbors that their goat had eaten most of the plants in her mother's garden, and the chilly greeting they gave her was not very <u>hospitable</u>.

A negative
B like a hospital
C welcoming
D hostile

6 The sixth challenger <u>transformed</u> Charlie's mood by cornering Charlie's king in ten minutes flat.

F carried
G changed
H shoved
J flipped

Directions: Read the following passages. Then answer the questions. On the answer sheet, fill in the bubble for the answer that you think is correct.

---

1   Utzel got a job as a water carrier. Poverty became a maid. For the first time in their lives, they worked diligently. They were kept so busy that they did not even think of the new shoes until one Sabbath morning Poverty decided she would try them on again. Lo and behold, her feet slipped easily into them. The new shoes fit.

2   At last Utzel and Poverty understood that all a man possesses he gains through work, and not by lying in bed and being idle. Even animals were industrious. Bees make honey, spiders spin webs, birds build nests, moles dig holes in the earth, squirrels store food for the winter.

---

7 Why did Utzel and Poverty forget about the shoes?
A They were too tired to think about them.
B They were too busy to think about them.
C They had learned that shoes were not so important.
D Poverty had tried on the shoes, and they didn't fit.

8 Which statement *best* expresses the main idea of the passage?
F By working hard, people can earn money for shoes.
G The more a person works, the more he or she can possess.
H It is only possible to profit by being late.
J Only through diligent work do people get what they want.

---

1   "This is a kind horse, a gentle and a faithful horse," Pierre said, "and I can see a beautiful spirit shining out of the eyes of the horse. I will name him after good St. Joseph, who was also kind and gentle and faithful and a beautiful spirit."

2   Within a year Joseph knew the milk route as well as Pierre. Pierre used to boast that he didn't need his reins—he never touched them. Each morning Pierre arrived at the stables of the Provençal Milk Company at five o'clock. The wagon would be loaded and Joseph hitched to it. Pierre would call "*Bonjour, vieux ami*,"[1] as he climbed into his seat and Joseph would turn his head. The other drivers would smile and say that the horse would smile at Pierre.

---

1 *Bonjour, vieux ami:* "Good morning, old friend."

---

9 According to the selection, what can be inferred about Pierre?
A Pierre dislikes the foreman.
B Pierre loves Joseph.
C Pierre dislikes Joseph.
D Pierre loves all horses.

10 According to the selection, why did Pierre name the horse Joseph?
F Pierre's favorite son's name was Joseph.
G The horse's beautiful spirit reminded Pierre of St. Joseph.
H St. Joseph is the patron saint of horses.
J A horse Pierre had owned before was called Joseph.

1   The ancients were familiar with five of the planets—Mercury, Venus, Mars, Jupiter, and Saturn—because they are visible to the naked eye. Mercury is quite difficult to see, but the others shine brilliantly.

2   There are great differences among the planets. Earth belongs to a group of inner planets, which circle relatively close to the Sun. They are as different from the outer planets as chalk from cheese.

3   The inner planets are relatively small rocky balls, like Earth, and they are often called the terrestrial (Earth-like) planets. They contrast markedly with the four giant outer planets—Jupiter, Saturn, Uranus, and Neptune. These planets are huge balls of gas. They probably do not have any solid surfaces.

4   Only Pluto, the tiny fifth outer planet, has not been visited by space probes. It is so distant that it is still as mysterious as ever.

11 How are the inner planets different from the four outer planets?
A They do not shine as brilliantly.
B They have not been visited by space probes.
C They are smaller, rocky balls, like Earth.
D They all have surface water, unlike the outer planets.

12 How are Jupiter, Saturn, Uranus, and Neptune all alike?
F They are all made of chalk.
G They are all the same distance from the Sun.
H They all shine brilliantly in the night sky.
J They are all giant balls of gas.

1   His room was as black as pitch with the thick darkness (for the shutters were close fastened, through fear of robbers), and so I knew that he could not see the opening of the door, and I kept pushing on it steadily, steadily.

2   I had my head in, and was about to open the lantern, when my thumb slipped upon the tin fastening, and the old man sprang up in bed, crying out—"Who's there?"

3   I kept quite still and said nothing. For a whole hour I did not move a muscle, and in the meantime I did not hear him lie down. He was still sitting up in the bed listening—just as I have done, night after night, hearkening to the death watches,[1] in the wall.

_____
1 death watches: Small beetles that live in wood and make a ticking sound.

13 When does the old man sit up in bed?
A before the narrator opens the door
B after the narrator's thumb slips on the lantern's tin fastening
C before the narrator's thumb slips on the lantern's tin fastening
D after the narrator keeps still for an hour

14 What does the narrator do just after he hears the old man cry out?
F He pushes the door open.
G He keeps still for an hour.
H He listens to the death watches in the wall.
J He opens the lantern.

Name _____ Date _____

Directions: Use the chart below to answer the following questions. On the answer sheet, fill in the bubble for the answer that you think is correct.

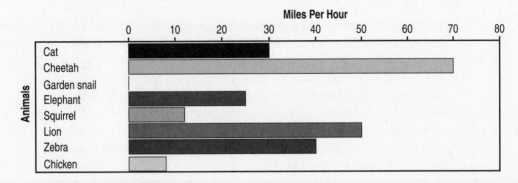

15 According to the chart, how fast does a squirrel move?
  A 50 miles per hour
  B 9 miles per hour
  C 12 miles per hour
  D 20 miles per hour

16 According to the chart, which animal moves the fastest?
  F Cheetah
  G Lion
  H Zebra
  J Cat

Directions: Read the following passages. Then answer the questions. On the answer sheet, fill in the bubble for the answer that you think is correct.

> My grandmother. My poor, poor grandmother. Old people aren't supposed to have those kinds of memories. You see their pictures in the family albums, and that's what they are: pictures. They're not supposed to come to life. You drive out in your father's Le Mans doing seventy-five on the pike and all you're doing is visiting an old lady in a nursing home. A duty call. And then you find that she's a person. She's *somebody*. She's my grandmother, all right, but she's also herself, like my own mother and father. They exist outside of their relationship to me. I was scared again. I wanted to get out of there.

17 Which of the following statements *best* summarizes the passage?
  A Visiting a grandmother in a nursing home is a duty.
  B It is boring to look at old pictures in a family album.
  C A grandmother is her own person.
  D Old people lose their memories.

1   It costs twenty-two cents for a regular stamp now. That's a terrible number, and you don't dare buy a roll of twenty-two cent stamps because you know it's going to change before you get used to it and certainly before you use up a roll.

2   I object to the fact that it costs me more to send a letter to a friend than it costs some fly-by-night real estate operator to send me a phony brochure in the mail telling me that I'm the provisional winner of a $10,000 sweepstakes. I don't like strangers knocking on my door trying to sell me something, and I don't want my mail clustered with advertising. If anyone wants to accuse me of feeling that way because I make a living from advertising found in newspapers and on television, go ahead and accuse me of it. It isn't true.

3   I don't get five good, genuine, personal letters a year. The time is coming when the letter written with pen and ink and sent as a personal message from one person to another will be as much of a rarity as the gold pocket watch carried on a chain. It's a shame.

18 Which of the following states an *opinion* about the author's views in the selection?

  F It costs more to mail a personal letter than it costs to mail an advertising brochure.

  G The narrator does not like strangers knocking on his door.

  H The narrator dislikes sweepstakes.

  J The narrator thinks that all advertising by mail is dishonest.

19 Which of the following states a *fact* about the narrator's views in the selection?

  A The narrator was probably robbed by a door-to-door salesman.

  B The narrator thinks that you have to throw out twenty-two-cent stamps if the postage rate goes up.

  C The narrator makes a living from newspaper and television advertising.

  D The narrator thinks that he or she will probably never again receive a handwritten letter.

Why does Kitty act not like the beast of prey she is but like a better-class human being? I don't know the answer. The point is, she does it—and it makes you her slave. After you have been presented with a mouse by your cat, you will never be the same again. She can use you for a doormat. And she will, too.

20 Which would be the *best* conclusion about how the author feels about cats?

  F A cat is better than a human being.

  G A cat rules its owner.

  H A dog is friendlier than a cat.

  J Cats give mice to their owners.

The first thing to understand about poetry is that it comes to you from outside you, in books or in words, but that for it to live, something from within you must come to it and meet it and complete it. Your response with your own mind, body, memory, and emotions gives the poem its ability to work its magic; if you give to it, it will give to you, and give plenty.

21 Which of the following statements *best* summarizes the passage?
   A Most poetry is not very rewarding.
   B Poetry lives only on the written page.
   C If you give to poetry, it will give to you.
   D Poetry comes to you from outside you.

Directions: Read the following sentences. Look for mistakes in grammar or usage. For each item on the answer sheet, fill in the bubble for the answer that has the mistake. If there is no mistake, fill in the last answer choice.

22 F A number of people
   G has offered suggestions about
   H which restaurant should be chosen.
   J *(No mistakes)*

23 A Not wanting to be late for school,
   B Sheila and her brother, Charlie,
   C asked her mom for a ride.
   D *(No mistakes)*

Practice Test 1

Answer the following questions.

1. Suppose that you have to present a literary selection to the class. When choosing a selection, what should you consider?
   A. the selection's length
   B. the selection's subject matter
   C. the selection's difficulty
   D. all of the above

2. You would ***most likely*** use props when presenting which literary form?
   A. short poem
   B. drama
   C. short story
   D. myth

3. Which of the following techniques would be ***inappropriate*** to use during an oral presentation?
   A. speaking clearly
   B. using slang
   C. speaking slowly
   D. using gestures

4. When evaluating the impact of an oral presentation, which of the following elements would be ***inappropriate*** to consider?
   A. the speaker's purpose
   B. the speaker's clothing
   C. the speaker's tone
   D. the speaker's volume

Read the following text of an oral presentation. Then answer the questions that follow.

Language in Hong Kong

Hong Kong poses a different problem to someone learning to speak Chinese. The native dialect of most residents of Hong Kong is Cantonese, a dialect that cannot be understood by native speakers of the Mandarin dialect. Mandarin has become more and more popular in Hong Kong with the return of Hong Kong to China by the British in 1997. But because English is a widely spoken second language in Hong Kong, an English-speaking visitor should be able to get by with little difficulty.

5. If you were presenting the information shown above, it would probably be ***most*** helpful to include a definition of which of the following terms?
   A. dialect
   B. visitor
   C. popular
   D. language

6. Which of the following details supports this main idea: "Hong Kong poses a different problem to someone learning to speak Chinese"?
   A. Native speakers of the Mandarin dialect cannot understand Cantonese.
   B. An English-speaking visitor to Hong Kong should be able to get by with little difficulty.
   C. In 1997 the British returned Hong Kong to China.
   D. Cantonese and English are the main languages spoken in Hong Kong.

7. Suppose that a member of the audience asks the following question about the presentation: "Why did the British return Hong Kong to China?" Which of the following would be the **best** response?
   A. How would I know the answer to that question?
   B. I don't have that information in my notes, but I can give you the titles of some sources that might tell you the answer.
   C. You really should find that information yourself.
   D. What a fascinating question!

Answer the following questions.

8. Which of the following examples illustrates this main idea: "Spiral galaxies—galaxies that have stars arranged on arms that curve out from the center bulge—are very common in the universe"?
   A. In some spiral galaxies, the arms are close together; in others, the arms are wide open.
   B. Some galaxies have no arms at all.
   C. A barred-spiral galaxy has spiral arms coming from a band of stars that passes through the center.
   D. Our galaxy, the Milky Way, is a spiral galaxy, and one of our neighbors in space, the Andromeda Galaxy, is another spiral.

9. Suppose that an oral presentation about heart disease includes statistics taken from a book. Which of the following information would you include in your citation of your source?
   A. the book's library due date   C. the book's title
   B. the book's price   D. the book's color

10. Suppose that you are giving an oral presentation to a group of fourth graders. The presentation is about ways to conserve energy. Which of the following sentences would be the **most** appropriate beginning for the presentation?
   A. Fellow students, today I will declare the benefits of conserving our most precious resources.
   B. Well, I guess I'll tell you about energy.
   C. Hey, pipe down, and listen to what I have to say.
   D. Conserving energy is a very important issue that we all must face.

Read the following passages. Then answer the questions that follow.

Narcissus and Echo

Deluded by his reflection, Narcissus fell in love with the beauty that was his own. Without thought of food or rest he lay beside the pool addressing cries and pleas to the image, whose lips moved as he spoke but whose reply he could never catch. Echo came by, the most constant of disdained lovers. She was a nymph who had once angered Hera, the wife of Zeus, by talking too much, and in consequence was deprived of the use of her tongue for ordinary conversation: all she could do was repeat the last words of others. Seeing Narcissus lying there, she pleaded with him in his own words. "I will die unless you pity me," cried Narcissus to his beloved. "Pity me," cried Echo as vainly to hers.

11. How is this passage formatted?
   A. as an outline
   B. as a stanza
   C. as a list
   D. as a paragraph

12. Which statement **best** expresses the main idea of the passage?
   A. Narcissus and Echo are in love with each other.
   B. Both Narcissus and Echo love in vain.
   C. It is important to love others more than oneself.
   D. Echo is committed to love Narcissus forever.

13. Which of the following features distinguishes the passage as part of a myth?
   A. the use of dialogue
   B. the mention of the god Zeus
   C. the establishment of setting
   D. the use of description

14. Which emotion does the second sentence of the passage evoke?
   A. sorrow
   B. joy
   C. anger
   D. jealousy

15. Which of the following words **best** describes the effect of the author's style?
   A. humorous
   B. tragic
   C. satirical
   D. suspenseful

from My Antonia by Willa Cather

I do not remember our arrival at my grandfather's farm sometime before daybreak, after a drive of nearly twenty miles with heavy work-horses. When I awoke, it was afternoon. I was lying in a little room, scarcely larger than the bed that held me, and the window-shade at my head was flapping softly in a warm wind. A tall woman, with wrinkled brown skin and black hair, stood looking down at me; I knew that she must be my grandmother. She had been crying, I could see, but when I opened my eyes she smiled, peered at me anxiously, and sat down on the foot of my bed.

"Had a good sleep, Jimmy?" she asked briskly. Then in a very different tone she said, as if to herself, "My, how you do look like your father!" I remembered that my father had been her little boy; she must often have come to wake him like this when he overslept. "Here are your clean clothes," she went on, stroking my coverlid with her brown hand as she talked. "But first you come down to the kitchen with me, and have a nice warm bath behind the stove. Bring your things; there's nobody about."

…"Can you do your ears, Jimmy? Are you sure? Well, now, I call you a right smart little boy."

It was pleasant there in the kitchen. The sun shone into my bath-water through the west half-window, and a big Maltese cat came up and rubbed himself against the tub, watching me curiously. While I scrubbed, my grandmother busied herself in the dining-room until I called anxiously, "Grandmother, I'm afraid the cakes are burning!" Then she came laughing, waving her apron before her as if she were shooing chickens.

16. Which of the following *best* describes how Jimmy's grandmother feels in this passage?

    A. sad   **C.** nostalgic

    B. happy   **D.** all of the above

17. What is the point of view of this passage?

    A. third person   **C.** second person

    B. first person   **D.** none of the above

from "The New Frontier" *by* John F. Kennedy

We set sail on this new sea because there is new knowledge to be gained, and new rights to be won, and they must be won and used for the progress of all people. For space science, like nuclear science and all technology, has no conscience of its own. Whether it will become a force for good or ill depends on man, and only if the United States occupies a position of pre-eminence can we help decide if the new ocean will be a sea of peace or a new terrifying theater of war. I do not say that we should or will go unprotected against the hostile misuse of space any more than we go unprotected against the hostile use of land or sea, but I do say that space can be explored and mastered without repeating the mistakes that man has made in extending his writ[1] around this globe of ours.

    [1]**writ** (rit): n. here, "claims or laws."

18. This excerpt from President Kennedy's 1962 speech discusses the topic of space exploration. Which of the following issues has Kennedy **omitted**?

    A. the latest developments in nuclear science

    B. the role of the United States in space exploration

    C. man's potential hostile misuse of space

    D. the reasons for engaging in space exploration

19. Which of the following literary devices does Kennedy use in the first sentence?

    A. simile   **C.** hyperbole

    B. metaphor   **D.** paradox

20. Which of the following *best* describes Kennedy's position?

    A. Space exploration is expensive.   **C.** Space exploration is dangerous.

    B. Space exploration is impossible.   **D.** Space exploration is important.

Creating a Table

To create a table using a word-processing program, first create a new document (or place the cursor where you want the table to appear in an existing document). Next, select Insert Table from the Table menu. A window will appear on your screen. Type in the number of columns and rows that you want your table to have. Then click on the OK button. The table will appear in your document. (Note: These instructions may not work with every word-processing program. Check your program's owner's manual for help.)

21. Which of the following questions is left unanswered by this passage?
    A. How do you create a new word-processing document?
    B. Which option do I select from the Table menu?
    C. What happens after I click on the OK button?
    D. How do I select the number of columns and rows for my table?

22. What is the first step in creating a table in an existing document?
    A. Select Insert Table from the Table menu.
    B. Create a new document.
    C. Click on the OK button.
    D. Put the cursor where the table is to appear.

Robert Frost

Like the title of his poem "Fire and Ice," Robert Frost seemed witty and warm to some, cold and bitter to others. All agreed, however, that poetry came first in his life. Frost produced a large body of work and became the most popular American poet of his time, winning four Pulitzer Prizes. He is known not only for his poetic skills, but also for his reading of two poems at the inauguration of President John F. Kennedy in 1961.

23. How could you evaluate the accuracy of this passage?
    A. by researching Frost's poem "Fire and Ice"
    B. by researching John F. Kennedy's life
    C. by researching Robert Frost's life
    D. by researching the Pulitzer Prize

Answer the following questions.

24. Suppose that you have to synthesize information from a variety of sources in order to write a presentation. What do you need to do in order to synthesize?
    A. combine the information
    B. question the information
    C. recall the information
    D. support the information

25. In which of the following materials would jargon, or specialized vocabulary, be **inappropriate**?
    A. poem
    B. technical manual
    C. textbook
    D. catalog

Read the following passage. Then answer the questions that follow.

from The Tragedy of Romeo and Juliet *by* William Shakespeare

Act I

Scene I. Verona. *A public place.*

[*Enter* SAMPSON *and* GREGORY, *with swords and bucklers[1], of the house of Capulet.*]

Sampson. Gregory, on my word, we'll not carry coals.[2]

Gregory. No, for then we should be colliers.[3]

Sampson. I mean, an we be in choler, we'll draw.[4]

Gregory. Ay, while you live, draw your neck out of collar.[5]

Sampson. I strike quickly, being moved.

[1] **bucklers** small shields

[2] **carry coals** endure insults

[3] **colliers** sellers of coal

[4] **an...draw** If we are angered, we'll draw our swords

[5] **collar** the hangman's noose

26. What part of the drama is indicated by the words *Verona. A public place* in the excerpt above?
    A. staging
    B. scripting
    C. dialogue
    D. characterization

27. What part of the drama is indicated by the exchange between Sampson and Gregory?
    A. scenery
    B. setting
    C. scripting
    D. staging

28. The stage directions "Enter SAMPSON and GREGORY, with swords and bucklers, of the house of Capulet" help the reader understand which of the following?
    A. mood
    B. characters
    C. plot
    D. all of the above

Answer the following questions.

29. Which of the following is true about one-act plays and full-length plays?
    A. Both have characters.
    B. Both have stage directions.
    C. Both have plots.
    D. all of the above

30. What literary device is used by Alfred, Lord Tennyson in the following lines from the poem "The Eagle"?

    He clasps the crag with crooked hands;
    close to the sun in lonely hands

    A. onomatopoeia
    B. alliteration
    C. hyperbole
    D. irony

Practice Test 2

Answer the following questions.

1. Which of the following would be the **least** effective way to generate and gather ideas for writing?
   A. brainstorming
   B. creating a word web
   C. consulting others
   D. playing video games

2. When planning a writing assignment, which of the following questions would be the **least** helpful to ask yourself?
   A. What is the goal of this paper?
   B. What is my topic?
   C. Who is my audience?
   D. What kind of grade do I want?

Read the following passage. Then answer the questions that follow.

The Earth also has another motion in relation to the sun. It orbits, or circles, around the sun once every 365 days, the period we call a year. It orbits in this way because it is a planet, held in its place by the sun's powerful gravity. The sun also holds captive eight other planets. They orbit the sun in the following durations: Mercury, 88 days; Venus, 225 days; Mars, 687 days; Jupiter, 11.9 years; Saturn, 29.5 years; Uranus, 84 years; Neptune, 165 years; Pluto, 248 years.

Compared with the other bodies, the sun is huge. It contains 750 times more mass than all of them put together. Its diameter, about 865,000 miles, is 100 times larger than Earth's.

3. Suppose that this passage is part of an essay you have written. Which of the following **best** states the purpose for your writing?
   A. to persuade the audience that Earth is an interesting planet
   B. to inform the audience about the relationship between the planets and the sun
   C. to persuade the audience that Earth and Mars are similar
   D. to inform the audience about the force of gravity

Answer the following questions.

4. Suppose that you must write an essay about basketball. Which of the following vocabulary terms would you most likely use?
   A. free throw
   B. goal
   C. batting average
   D. target

5. When writing, which of the following should you use?
   A. wordy expressions
   B. slang and profanity
   C. incorrect spelling
   D. clear and varied sentences

Read the following passage. Then answer the questions that follow.

Jupiter's "surface" is an ocean of liquid hydrogen that covers the entire planet. This ocean may be ten thousand or more miles deep—no one knows. Perhaps Jupiter has no solid surface at all but is entirely liquid down to its rocky center, almost nine thousand miles below the clouds.

The colors of the clouds change as you fly lower. The upper clouds are mainly white and blue. The lower clouds are orange, yellow, and brown, and the temperature is warmer here. It is dark outside your spaceship, as little or no sunlight filters down through the clouds. Below you, gigantic bolts of lightning flash across the sky and illuminate the darkness.

Imagine exploring Jupiter from a spaceship. As you look down at the tops of the clouds, the air has the same light blue color that Earth's sky has in the daytime. The temperature here is very cold—over 250 degrees (Fahrenheit) below freezing.

6. If you were revising the passage above, which of the following would be the **best** order for the paragraphs?
   A. 2, 3, 1
   B. 1, 3, 2
   C. 3, 1, 2
   D. 3, 2, 1

7. Which of the following is the **best** revision of "Jupiter has a very thick atmosphere. But it may have no solid surface"?
   A. Jupiter has a very thick atmosphere. It has no solid surfaces.
   B. The atmosphere of Jupiter is very thick but it may have no solid surface.
   C. Jupiter has a very thick atmosphere, but the planet may have no solid surface.
   D. Jupiter's atmosphere is very thick and has no solid surface.

The following passage contains several errors. Read the passage. Then answer the questions that follow.

The Epic

The Gilgamesh epics, which come from the anceint Middle East, are older even than the *Iliad* and the *Odyssey*. The european tradition of the epic, however, begins with these works by Homer. The Roman poet, Virgil used Homer's epics as a model when he wrote the *Aeneid*, which tells how the city of Rome was founded.

8. Suppose that you have to proofread this piece of writing. What revision, if any, is needed in the first sentence?
   A. Change *anceint* to *ancient*.
   B. Change *epics* to *Epics*.
   C. Change *Middle East* to *middle east*.
   D. No revision is needed.

9. What revision, if any, is needed in the second sentence?
   A. Change *works* to *work*.
   B. Delete the commas.
   C. Change *european* to *European*.
   D. No revision is needed.

10. What revision, if any, is needed in the third sentence?
   A. Change *model* to *modle*.
   B. Delete the comma after *poet*.
   C. Change *city* to *City*.
   D. No revision is needed.

Choose the sentence that is written correctly.

11. **A.** Marcus wrote the email address in his planner.
    B. Marcus wroted the email address in his planner.
    C. Marcus writed the email address in his planner.
    D. Marcus write the email address in his planner.

Answer the following questions.

12. In the sentence "The movie gave me chills," what are the direct object and the indirect object?
    A. movie; chills   **C.** chills; me
    B. movie; me   **D.** gave; me

13. In the sentence, "Lee is our best player," what is the predicate nominative?
    A. Lee   **C.** best
    B. is   **D.** player

14. Which of the following sentences reflects parallel sentence structure?
    A. Many authors are selling their books on the Internet and promotes their work on Web sites.
    B. Many authors sell their books on the Internet and promoting their work on Web sites.
    C. Many authors are selling their books on the Internet and promoting their work on Web sites.
    D. Many authors sell their books on the Internet and promotes their work on Web sites.

15. Suppose that you must rewrite the following sentence: "*The Courier* does not have a classifieds section." Your new sentence must contain the appositive, "a daily newspaper." Which of the following sentences is the ***best*** rewrite?
    A. *The Courier*, a daily newspaper, does not have a classifieds section.
    B. *The Courier*, does not have classifieds sections, a daily newspaper.
    C. *The Courier*, a classifieds section, does not have a daily newspaper.
    D. *The Courier* does not have a daily newspaper, a classifieds section.

16. Suppose that you must combine the independent clause "the letter was from Carl" with the subordinate clause "just as she suspected" to create one sentence. Which of the following would be the ***best*** combination?
    A. The letter was from Carl; just as she suspected.
    B. Just as she suspected: the letter was from Carl.
    C. Just as she suspected, the letter was from Carl.
    D. Just as she suspected the letter, was from Carl.

All-in-One Workbook: Standardized Test Practice
350

17. Suppose that you must combine the independent clause "the parade will draw thousands of spectators" and "therefore, parking will be an issue" to create one sentence. Which of the following would be the **best** combination?
    A. Therefore, parking will be an issue; the parade will draw thousands of spectators.
    B. The parade will draw thousands of spectators, therefore, parking will be an issue.
    C. Therefore, parking will be an issue, the parade will draw thousands of spectators.
    D. The parade will draw thousands of spectators; therefore, parking will be an issue.

18. What does it mean to **plagiarize** a writer's work?
    A. to critique the writer's ideas   C. to summarize the writer's ideas
    B. to copy the writer's language or ideas   D. to use the writer's ideas for research

19. When using sources to write an essay, you should distinguish your ideas from those contained in a source by doing which of the following?
    A. citing the sources of information
    B. putting quotes around the information taken directly from a source
    C. paraphrasing or summarizing information
    D. all of the above

Read the following passage. Then answer the question that follows.

Citing Sources

The Modern Language Association (MLA) system of citing sources requires a book used as a source to be documented in the following way: the author's name (last name first); the title, which should be underlined or italicized; the place of publication, the publisher; and the date.

20. On a works cited page, how would a writer document the following book?

    Desert Oasis, by Gordon Verde, published in 2001 by Hohokham Books, Phoenix

    A. *Desert Oasis*. Gordon Verde. Phoenix 2001.
    B. Verde, Gordon. *Desert Oasis*. Phoenix: Hohokham Books, 2001.
    C. 2001. Gordon Verde. Hohokham Books: Phoenix. *Desert Oasis*.
    D. Verde, Gordon. Phoenix: Hohokham Books, 2001. *Desert Oasis*.

Answer the following questions.

21. Suppose that you are conducting library research on wooly mammoths. Which type of library catalog search would be the **most** effective?
    A. title search   C. subject search
    B. author search   D. none of the above

22. Suppose that you are conducting Internet research on the ancient Egyptian god Osiris. Which of the following pairs of key words would **most** effectively narrow your search?
   A. god, Osiris
   B. ancient, god
   C. ancient, Egyptian
   D. Egyptian, god

23. Suppose that you have to write an essay on the history of ballet. Which of the following research tools would be **most** helpful?
   A. an atlas
   B. a thesaurus
   C. an encyclopedia
   D. an almanac

24. Which of the following factors is **least** important when determining whether a Web site is reliable?
   A. the content
   B. the date when the site was last updated
   C. the URL ending (.com, .edu, .gov, .org)
   D. the artwork

Read the following passage. Then answer the questions that follow.

from In My Place *by* Charlayne Hunter-Gault

On January 9, 1961, I walked onto the campus of the University of Georgia to begin registering for classes. Ordinarily, there would not have been anything unusual about such a routine exercise, except, in this instance, the officials at the university had been trying for two and a half years to keep me out. I was not socially, intellectually, or morally undesirable. I was Black. And no Black student had ever been admitted to the University of Georgia in its 176-year history. Until the landmark *Brown v. Board of Education* decision that in 1954 declared separate but equal schools unconstitutional, the university was protected by law in its exclusion of people like me. . . . It took us two and a half years of fighting our way through the system and the courts, but finally . . . we won the right that should have been ours all along. With the ink barely dry on the court order of three days before, Hamilton Holmes and I walked onto the campus and into history.

25. Which of the following is the implied main idea of the text?
   A. The author is working to make good grades in school.
   B. The author is applying to the university.
   C. The author is battling the racism that oppressed African Americans in the 1960s.
   D. The University of Georgia did not extend equal opportunities to all students.

26. Which of the following statements best summarizes the passage?
   A. The author begins her college career as a promising student.
   B. The author waits for two and a half years to begin classes.
   C. The author describes the routine exercises involved in starting college.
   D. The author challenges a university's policy of segregation.

27. What is the theme of the passage?
    A. Entering college is frightening.
    B. Resisting change is futile.
    C. A good education is vital.
    D. Courage and perseverance can overcome injustice.

28. Which of the following details is used in the passage to support the main idea?
    A. The University of Georgia did not admit black students for 176 years.
    B. The University of Georgia immediately changed its admission policy after *Brown v. Board of Education*.
    C. The University of Georgia thought the author was an intellectually desirable student.
    D. The University of Georgia admitted the author, but not Hamilton Holmes.

Writing Prompt #1

What is the most important thing about ninth-grade students that you would like older students to know? You might choose a characteristic that has to do with ninth-graders' interests, behavior, or abilities. Write an essay in which you identify and describe for one of the officers of the senior class some important quality of ninth graders. Be sure to tell why you believe it is the most important characteristic, and give examples and reasons to support your idea.

Writing Prompt #2

Suppose that each month, your local newspaper honors one person as a community hero. This person is usually an outstanding individual who serves or helps your community in a noticeable way. Think of someone you admire in your community. How has this person affected your community? What are some specific examples of ways that this person has made a contribution? Write a letter to the newspaper in which you describe your impressions of this person. Be sure to provide specific details that clarify why the person's actions and behavior demonstrate outstanding service or heroism.

Practice Test 3

Read the following narrative and then answer the questions that follow.

"Traveling With Lewis and Clark" *from* Bird Woman, *by* Sacajawea

1)   A Shoshone woman named Sacajawea, her husband, and her baby son Pomp accompanied Lewis and Clark on their expedition across the Louisiana Territory. As a child Sacajawea had been kidnapped from her Mandan village by the Minnetarees, a rival Native American group. She was adopted by a Minnetaree family and lived in their village. Sacajawea met Lewis and Clark when they camped at the Minnetaree village. Years later, Sacajawea told her life story to James Willard Schultz. This passage is from Sacajawea's autobiography, Bird Woman. In this passage, Sacajawea refers to Lewis and Clark as Long Knife and Red Hair.

2)   Upon my man's return to the fort the boats were all loaded. We had two large ones and six small ones, and we abandoned the fort and headed up river. At the same time that we started, Long Knife and Red Hair sent their very large boat down the river in charge of some of their men. It was loaded with many skins, bones, and other things, presents for the great chief of the whites. Counting in my son, we were thirty-three people in our eight boats.

3)   I was given a place in one of the two large ones. As we went on and on up the river, sometimes making a long distance between the rising and the setting of the sun, I was, at times, I believe, happier than I had ever been in my life, for each day's travel brought me so much nearer my people whom I so much longed to see. Then at other times, whenever I thought of what was before us, I would become very unhappy. I would say to myself that we could not possibly survive the dangers we should be sure to encounter along the way.

4)   I may as well say it: my good, kind white chiefs were not cautious; they were too brave, too sure of themselves. From the very start they and their men would foolishly risk their lives by attacking all the mankilling bears that came in sight of us. At night they would build great fires and would be sure to attract to us any wandering war party that might be in the country. After we passed the mouth of the Yellowstone and entered the country of the Blackfeet, I begged my chiefs to be more cautious. I asked them to stop always a short time before dark and build little cooking-fires, and then, after our meal, to put out the fires, and then go on until dark and make camp in the darkness. But they only laughed at me and answered: "We have good guns and know how to use them."

5)   I often said to myself, "Strange are these white men! Strange their ways! They have a certain thing to do, to make a trail to the west to the Everywhere-Salt-Water. Why, then, are we not on horseback and traveling fast and far each day? Here we are in boats, heavily loaded with all kinds of useless things, and when the wind is bad or the water swift, we make but little distance between sun and sun! We could have all got all the horses that we needed from the Earth House tribes, and had we done that, we should long since have arrived at the mountains.

6)   Yes, right now I should probably be talking with my own people!" And those medicine packages of theirs, packages big and little piled all around me in the boat in which I rode, how my chiefs valued them! One day a sudden hard wind struck our sail and the boat began to tip and fill with water. More and more it filled, and the men in

it and those on the shore went almost crazy with fear. But I was not afraid. Why should I be when I knew that I could cast off my robe and swim ashore with my little son? More and more water poured into the boat and the medicine packages began to float out of it. I seized them one by one as they were going, and kept seizing them and holding them, and when, at last, we reached the shore, my good white chiefs acted as though I had done a wonderful thing in saving their packages; it seemed as though they could not thank me enough for what I had done.

7) Thinking about it, after it was all over, and when the things had been spread out to dry, I said to myself, "Although I cannot understand them, these little instruments of shining steel and these writings on thin white paper must be powerful medicine. Here after, whenever we run into danger, I shall, after my son, have my first thought for their safety, and so please my kind white chiefs."

8) After leaving the mouth of Little River, or, as my white chiefs named it, Milk River, we went up through a part of the Big River Valley that I had not seen. When we arrived at the mouth of the stream, my white chiefs named the Musselshell, some of the men went up it during the afternoon, and, returning, told of a stream coming into it from the plain on the right. My chiefs then told me that it should have my name, as they called it, Sah-ka-já-we-ah. I asked my man to tell them that I wished they would give it my right name, Bo-í-naiv, Grass Woman.

1. Why **most likely** did Sacajawea refer to Lewis and Clark as Long Knife and, Red Hair?

A. She did not know their real names.

B. She called them by their Indian Names.

C. She was afraid of them.

D. She thought they were strange.

2. Why did Sacajawea want the Lewis and Clark party to be more careful?

A. She understood the dangers of the wilderness.

B. She was afraid of being kidnapped.

C. She wanted to keep her son safe.

D. She did not want to be attacked by a bear.

3. Why does Sacajawea have mixed feelings in Paragraph 3?

A. She is afraid of the Blackfoot Indians.

B. She is afraid her people will not want her to come home.

C. She is tired of the long days but wants to see her people.

D. She wants to see her people but is afraid of the danger.

4. Why **most likely** did Sacajawea want to make small cooking fires and then travel on until dark before making camp for the night?

A. She wanted to get to her people as soon as possible.

B. She knew that would make them safer at night.

C. She knew the bears were attracted to the fires.

D. She new the Yellowstone would be dangerous.

5. What **most likely** was "Everywhere-Salt-Water"?

A. the Yellowstone River

B. the Earth House tribes

C. the Pacific Ocean

D. the Mandan village

6. What **most likely** was in the containers that were carried in the boats?

A. letters to the Indian chiefs

B. treaties from the government

C. personal supplies and letters

D. maps and mapmaking materials

7. Why did Sacajawea refer to the containers as powerful medicine?

   A. They had medial supplies in them.

   B. They were very important to the White chiefs.

   C. They were the only things in the boat.

   D. They did not get wet when the boat filled with water.

8. Why was Sacajawea concerned for the safety of the packages?

   A. She wanted to help Lewis and Clark.

   B. She was afraid of the strong medicine.

   C. She wanted the medicine kept safe for her people.

   D. She wanted to save her child.

9. Why **most likely** did the men think the stream should be named for Sacajawea?

   A. because she was an Indian

   B. because she has people in the area

   C. because she was born there

   D. because she had been helpful

10. Why did Sacajawea want the stream called Grass Woman?

   A. It was the color of grass.

   B. Her real name was Grass Woman.

   C. Her husband called her Grass Woman.

   D. It was very small.

Name _____ Date _____

Read the following poem and then answer the questions that follow.

"El Dorado," *by* Edgar Allan Poe

When we are aiming for a goal, we may seek it at the expense of everything else. "El Dorado" is the name that Spanish explorers gave to the New World's Seven Cities of Gold—which they searched for but never found. Poets sometimes use mysterious narratives to represent deep human needs. Edgar Allan Poe was a great American writer whose short, tragic life was driven by the need for love and success. Perhaps this poem describes part of his struggle.

Gaily bedight,
A gallant knight
In sunshine and in shadow,
Had journeyed long,
(5) Singing a song,
In search of El Dorado.

But he grew old—
This knight so bold—
And o'er his heart a shadow
(10) Fell as he found
No spot of ground
That looked like El Dorado.

And as his strength
Failed him at length,
(15) He met a pilgrim shadow—
"Shadow," said he,
"Where can it be—
This land of El Dorado?"

"Over the Mountains
(20) Of the Moon,
Down the Valley of the Shadow,
Ride, boldly ride,"
The shade replied—
"If you seek for El Dorado."

11. Based on the context of stanza 1, what is the probable meaning of "bedight"?

   A. thinking

   B. starved

   C. silenced

   D. dressed

12. What *most likely* does "shadow" represent in stanza 2?

   A. age

   B. sadness

   C. trees of the forest

   D. death

13. Based on the context of the poem, which of the following is represented by the knight?

   A. the reader

   B. the poet

   C. a great ruler

   D. a misfit

14. What is the main idea of the poem?

   A. It is dangerous to ride too far alone.

   B. We can never reach our goals, but we should still pursue them.

   C. It is foolish to be optimistic because you are doomed to failure.

   D. Age brings wisdom and happiness that the young cannot appreciate.

15. Based on what you have read about Poe, how did he probably feel about a quest like that of the knight?

   A. He probably thought such a quest was ridiculous.

   B. He probably felt attracted to the danger of this quest.

   C. He could not understand a quest like that.

   D. He probably believed he had succeeded in reaching his own life goals whereas the knight had failed.

from A Journey to the Centre of the Earth, *by* Jules Verne

In this passage, the narrator has become separated from the explorers with whom he is traveling.

1)   No words in any human language can depict my utter despair. I was literally buried alive; with no other expectation before me but to die in all the slow horrible torture of hunger and thirst.

2)   Mechanically I crawled about, feeling the dry and arid rock. Never to my fancy had I ever felt anything so dry.

3)   But, I frantically asked myself, how had I lost the course of the flowing stream? There could be no doubt it had ceased to flow in the gallery in which I now was. Now I began to understand the cause of the strange silence which prevailed when last I tried if any appeal from my companions might perchance reach my ear.

4)   It so happened that when I first took an imprudent step in the wrong direction, I did not perceive the absence of the all-important stream.

5)   It was now quite evident that when we halted, another tunnel must have received the waters of the little torrent, and that I had unconsciously entered a different gallery. To what unknown depths had my companions gone? Where was I?

6)   How to get back! Clue or landmark there was absolutely none! My feet left no signs on the granite and shingle. My brain throbbed with agony as I tried to discover the solution of this terrible problem. My situation, after all sophistry and reflection, had finally to be summed up in three awful words—

7)   *Lost!* Lost!! LOST!!!

8)   Lost at a depth which, to my finite understanding, appeared to be immeasurable.

9)   These thirty leagues of the crust of the earth weighed upon my shoulders like the globe on the shoulders of Atlas. I felt myself crushed by the awful weight. It was indeed a position to drive the sanest man to madness!

10)   I tried to bring my thoughts back to the things of the world so long forgotten. It was with the greatest difficulty that I succeeded in doing so. Hamburg, the house on the Konigstrasse, my dear cousin Gretchen—all that world which had before vanished like a shadow floated before my now vivid imagination...

11)   "Oh, Uncle!" was my despairing cry.

12)   This was the only word of reproach which came to my lips; for I thoroughly understood how deeply and sorrowfully the worthy Professor would regret my loss, and how in his turn he would patiently seek for me.

13)   When I at last began to resign myself to the fact that no further aid was to be expected from man, and knowing that I was utterly powerless to do anything for my own salvation, I kneeled with earnest fervor and asked assistance from Heaven. The remembrance of my innocent childhood, the memory of my mother, known only in my infancy, came welling forth from my heart.

14)   This renewal of my youthful faith brought about a much greater amount of calm, and I was enabled to concentrate all my strength and intelligence on the terrible realities of my unprecedented situation.

15)   I had about me that which I had at first wholly forgotten—three days' provisions. Moreover, my water bottle was quite full. Nevertheless, the one thing which it was impossible to do was to remain alone. Try to find my companions I must, at any price. But which course should I take? Should I go upwards, or again descend? Doubtless it was right to retrace my steps in an upward direction.

16)   By doing this with care and coolness, I must reach the point where I had turned away from the rippling stream. I must find the fatal bifurcation or fork... Why had I not thought of this before? This, at last, was a reasonable hope of safety...

17)   After a slight meal and a draught of water, I rose like a giant refreshed. Leaning heavily on my pole, I began the ascent of the gallery. The slope was very rapid and rather difficult. But I advanced hopefully and carefully, like a man who at last is making his way out of a forest, and knows there is only one road to follow.

16.   Based on the context of paragraph 1, what is the meaning of the word *depict*?

   A. cry

   B. stop

   C. describe

   D. lessen

17.   Which of the following attributes does *not* describe the speaker?

   A. enthusiastic

   B. scared

   C. worried

   D. determined

18.   Based on the context of paragraph 4, what is the meaning of the word *imprudent*?

   A. unwise

   B. naïve

   C. careful

   D. uncertain

19.   Which of the following *best* describes what finally alerts the speaker to his situation?

   A. He realizes he no longer has contact with his companions.

   B. He realizes night has fallen, so it will be more difficult for his friends to find him.

   C. He realizes that he is no longer following the river.

   D. A and C

20.   Which of the following statements *best* describes the turning point in this passage?

   A. The speaker realizes he has three days of provisions and a full bottle of water.

   B. The speaker's prayer brings him reminders of his youth, which calms him so he can think clearly.

   C. The speaker has a meal and feels refreshed.

   D. all of the above

21.   Which of the following gave the speaker hope that he might find his companions?

   A. He realizes his footprints have left marks which he can follow.

   B. He makes a plan to go back and find the spot where the path had a fork.

   C. He finds his way out of the forest.

   D. A and B

Excerpts from an Interview of Colin Powell:
We Have a Dream

This passage is an excerpt from an interview with Secretary of State Colin Powell on November 26, 2003 in which he recalls that because he was serving in Vietnam in the U.S. Army during the early 1960s, he did not understand the importance of Dr. Martin Luther King, Jr.'s civil rights leadership until he returned to the United States.

Who challenged you? You're quoted as saying ... challenge young people by having high expectations of them, and I'm curious as to who challenged you when you were young.

1)   When I was a young kid growing up in the South Bronx section of New York City, I was principally challenged by my parents to do better than they had been able to do in life. Although they were very successful in life, they wanted their children to do better. It was that American immigrant dream. And so they had high standards for me and for my sister and all of the cousins in our very large extended family.

2)   I didn't meet the challenge as often as I should have as a kid, but when I got out of college and found ROTC and a military life, then I realized what high standards were all about and how you had to meet those high standards if you want to be successful. And then throughout my entire 35-year career as a soldier, high standards are essentially at the heart of the culture of being a soldier.

3)   And when I left the Army and went to work with young people in America's Promise, the organization that I founded, I would use my military experience to talk to youngsters all over America— white kids, black kids, Hispanic kids, you name them, at whatever age: have high standards for yourself, believe in yourself, meet those standards, exceed those standards, and you'll be surprised what this wonderful country can do for you.

What are your earliest—your first memories of Martin Luther King? What do you remember when you first heard about him?

4)   I'm so old I'm not sure I can remember when I first heard of Dr. King. It was in the late '50s, I'm quite sure when I was a young soldier. I entered

the Army in 1958, and he was beginning his great work then.

5)   When he became a powerful consciousness in my life was when I went to Vietnam in 1962, and I was there from '62 to '63, when he was really beginning his work, and we had the riots in Birmingham when he gave his famous speech. I was in Vietnam serving my country, but my wife and my infant son, they were in Birmingham, Alabama when those riots were taking place and the dogs were running up and down the street snapping at the Negroes, as we used to call ourselves. And my father-in-law was guarding my wife and my infant child in Birmingham while I was fighting for my country in Vietnam. So I didn't know about all of that. They kept that hidden from me because I didn't need to be bothered with that.

6)   When I came back home at the end of 1963 and realized the turmoil that was taking place in my country, and there was one individual who was going to lead this country through that turmoil, and that was Dr. Martin Luther King, and that's when I gained the greatest respect for him and for his work. And he is the one who finished the Civil War of a century earlier. Lincoln freed the slaves. Lincoln signed the Emancipation Proclamation. But it was Martin Luther King, through his efforts, who freed America.

He (Martin Luther King) is remembered for so many things, but obviously the most important thing is his speech. How did the speech affect you?

7)   It affected me long after, and unto this day. Not at the time, because I wasn't here. I was in Vietnam. But when I came back home, I could see

the impact that the speech had on all of America, and not just black America, but all of America.

8)   The speech was essentially a mirror placed in the face of the nation, and that speech said: Look at yourselves, look at us, look at who we are and what we are, and let's all have this dream. And with that speech he convinced all of America that what we had been doing was wrong and that things had to change. And I will never forget that after I came home from Vietnam in late 1963, and my wife and I and our infant son went to Fort Benning, Georgia, still in the deepest segregated South at that time, we had a hard time finding a place to live. When I was on the base at Fort Benning, everything was fine, but once I came off base it was a segregated Columbus, Georgia, and a segregated Phoenix City, Alabama, where we lived.

9)   Until July of 1964 when the Civil Rights Act was passed, and I was able to go to the drive-in hamburger stand that had denied me service just a few weeks earlier, that now had to serve me, and I'll never forget that particular day. And it was brought about by whites and blacks coming together to end a terrible period in the nation's history. And no one deserves greater credit for bringing about that day and that act than Dr. King.

Can you imagine how he (Martin Luther King) must be looking down, thinking, you know, you are Secretary of State?

10)   Well, I am where I am because of what he did and what so many others did at that time, whether it's Jesse Jackson or Ralph Abernathy and too many others to name, but also what a lot of people did before then as well. In my profession of soldiering, the Buffalo soldiers, other wonderful men, the Tuskegee Airmen, the Triple Nickel Parachute Regiment, the Montford Point Marines, the first black Marines—all of them went and served their nation over a period of close to 300 years of military service in this country when they were only asked to give blood for the nation but were not going to get the privileges of being citizens of this nation.

11)   But they did it anyway. They did it anyway in the certainty that sooner or later right would triumph and our Constitution would be made whole. And I'm sitting here because of what they did, as well as my own efforts, but I never fail to recognize what they did, and especially what Dr. Martin Luther King, Jr., did.

22. Based on the context of paragraph 6, what is the meaning of the word **turmoil**?

   A. improvement

   B. confusion

   C. boredom

   D. sadness

23. Which of the following statements **best** describes Powell's parents?

   A. They have high standards for all of their children.

   B. They want their children to do as well as they have.

   C. They were not as successful in their careers.

   D. They encouraged their children to leave the South Bronx.

24. Based on the context of paragraph 8, what is the meaning of the word **segregated**?

   A. revolutionary

   B. welcoming

   C. discriminating against

   D. riotous

25. In paragraph 11, Powell says he is "sitting here because of what they did." Which of the following **best** describes who Powell meant by "they"?

   A. Jesse Jackson and Ralph Abernathy

   B. Buffalo soldiers and all black soldiers and marines

   C. Lincoln and Martin Luther King, Jr.

   D. all of the above

26. Which of the following statements **best** described what happened in July of 1964?

   A. Whites and blacks came together to pass the Civil Rights Act.

   B. Some restaurants begin serving blacks.

   C. Colin Powell left Vietnam

   D. Dr. Martin Luther King, Jr., gave his famous speech.

27. In paragraph 5, Powell says that King "became a powerful consciousness in my life." What **most likely** does Powell mean by this?

   A. Powell became a supporter of Martin Luther King, Jr., and attended all of his speeches.

   B. Powell became very involved with the work of Martin Luther King, Jr.

   C. Powell became more aware of the need for America to change.

   D. Powell became interested in a career in politics.

Read the following advice on how to take an essay exam and then answer the questions that follow.

How to Study for an Essay Exam *and* How to Take an Essay Exam

Essay exams are tough to prepare for because you cannot always predict what you will need to know. One thing for sure, essay exams require more thinking than multiple choice. The best way to prepare is to study all your material as thoroughly as possible.

The following are a few tips that should make that job easier.

How to Study

1)   Get all of your materials together in one study location. Include your class notes, your reading notes and your textbook.

2)   Look through your notes quickly and highlight the major themes that were discussed/emphasized in class.

3)   Create an index card for each important theme. Look through all your notes and write important ideas about each theme on the index card. If your notes are not complete look back at your text to find the important elements.

4)   Study each card several times. Quiz yourself on each theme and write your answers in brief statements. Check your index cards to see if you remembered all the important details and ideas.

5)   Review your index cards several times before the test. The more you review the more you will remember on test day.

How to Take the Exam

6)   Look over the entire exam before you begin to write.

7)   Choose the questions that you know best to answer first and then answer the remaining questions according to how well prepared you feel about the topic.

8)   Set a time limit for each question and then stick to the time you allotted. Bring a watch: do not count on someone else to keep track of time for you.

9)   Some people find it helpful to write a brief outline for their response.

10)   Don't try to proofread your answer the minute you finish a question. Rather, complete the test and then go back to each question and proofread.

11)   Most often, your teacher will be more concerned with content than with writing style.

12)   Most people are concerned with the tight time constraints associated with essay exams. Don't panic! Allow your self to stop periodically and take a few deep breaths. That time you give yourself can help your memory and ultimately your final grade.

28. According to the selection, why are multiple choice tests easier than essay tests?

   A. Because they do not require writing.

   B. Because it is easier to guess on multiple choice.

   C. Because you do not need to reorganize your notes.

   D. Because you cannot always predict what will be on an essay test.

29. What is a major benefit or organizing your notes?

   A. It forces you to look for major ideas and concepts.

   B. It forces you to rewrite your notes.

   C. It helps you guess what the questions will be.

   D. It helps you look for notes that you lost.

30. Why *most likely* is it important to look over the entire test before you begin?

   A. You can figure out how difficult each question will be.

   B. You can start with the easiest questions.

   C. You can decide which questions to answer.

   D. You can answer the questions you know best, first.

31. Why should you set a time limit for each question?

   A. You won't panic if you know how much time you have.

   B. Your score will probably be better if you answer all the questions.

   C. You can spend all of your time on the questions you know best.

   D. Your score will be determined by the questions you get right.

32. Why *most likely* do some people make higher grades on essay test when they make an outline for each response?

   A. They spend less time on each question.

   B. They don't spend all their time on a few questions.

   C. They have a better chance of including important ideas in their answer.

   D. They don't get hung up on one question and fail to complete the test.

Name _____ Date _____

Read the following excerpt from* Hamlet *and then answer the questions that follow.

    Once you get past the difficulties of the language, you will probably enjoy Hamlet. The message of the play is that life is worth living even when we must live with imperfect people in an imperfect world. In the following scene, Hamlet speaks with his father's ghost and learns the circumstances of his father's death.

from Hamlet, *by* William Shakespeare

Hamlet: A young man whose father was the King of Denmark

Ghost: The ghost of Hamlet's father

King Claudius: The brother of Hamlet's father who has married Hamlet's mother and taken over the throne of Denmark.

Queen Gertrude: Hamlet's mother

    Setting:
    Elsinore. The Castle. Another part of the fortifications.
    Enter Ghost and Hamlet.

Hamlet: Whither wilt thou lead me? Speak! I'll go no further.

Ghost: Mark me.

Hamlet: I will.

Ghost: My hour is almost come, When I to sulph'rous and tormenting flames Must render up myself

Hamlet: Alas, poor ghost!

Ghost: Pity me not, but lend thy serious hearing To what I shall unfold.

Hamlet: Speak, I am bound to hear.

Ghost: So art thou to revenge, when thou shalt hear.

Hamlet: What?

Ghost: I am thy father's spirit,
Doom'd for a certain term to walk the night, And for the day confin'd to fast in fires, Till the foul crimes done in my days of nature Are burnt and purg'd away. But that I am forbid
To tell the secrets of my prison house,
I could a tale unfold whose lightest word
Would harrow up thy soul, freeze thy young blood, Make thy two eyes, like stars, start from their spheres,
Thy knotted and combined locks to part,
And each particular hair to stand an end
Like quills upon the fretful porpentine.
But this eternal blazon must not be
To ears of flesh and blood. List, list, O, list! If thou didst ever thy dear father love-

Hamlet: O God!

Ghost: Revenge his foul and most unnatural murder.

Hamlet: Murder?

Ghost: Murder most foul, as in the best it is; But this most foul, strange, and unnatural

Hamlet: Haste me to know't, that I, with wings as swift As meditation or the thoughts of love, May sweep to my revenge.

Ghost: I find thee apt; And duller shouldst thou be than the fat weed
That rots itself in ease on Lethe wharf,
Wouldst thou not stir in this. Now, Hamlet, hear. 'Tis given out that, sleeping in my orchard, A serpent stung me. So the whole ear of Denmark
Is by a forged process of my death
Rankly abus'd. But know, thou noble youth, The serpent that did sting thy father's life Now wears his crown.

Hamlet: O my prophetic soul!
My uncle?

Ghost: Ay, that incestuous, that adulterate beast, With witchcraft of his wit, with traitorous gifts- O wicked wit and gifts, that have the power So to seduce!- won to his shameful lust
The will of my most seeming-virtuous queen. O Hamlet, what a falling-off was there, From me, whose love was of that dignity That it went hand in hand even with the vow I made to her in marriage, and to decline Upon a wretch whose natural gifts were poor To those of mine!
But virtue, as it never will be mov'd,
Though lewdness court it in a shape of heaven, So lust, though to a radiant angel link'd, Will sate itself in a celestial bed And prey on garbage.
But soft! methinks I scent the morning air. Brief let me be. Sleeping within my orchard, My custom always of the afternoon, Upon my secure hour thy uncle stole, With juice of cursed hebona in a vial, And in the porches of my ears did pour The leperous distilment; whose effect Holds such an enmity with blood of man That swift as quicksilverr it courses through The natural gates and alleys of the body, And with a sudden vigour it doth posset And curd, like eager droppings into milk, The thin and wholesome blood. So did it mine;
And a most instant tetter bark'd about,
Most lazar-like, with vile and loathsome crust All my smooth body. Thus was I, sleeping, by a brother's hand Of life, of crown, of queen, at once dispatch'd;
Cut off even in the blossoms of my sin,
Unhous'led, disappointed, unanel'd,
No reckoning made, but sent to my account With all my imperfections on my head.

Hamlet: O, horrible! O, horrible! most horrible!

Ghost: If thou hast nature in thee, bear it not. Let not the royal bed of Denmark be
A couch for luxury and damned incest.
But, howsoever thou pursuest this act,
Taint not thy mind, nor let thy soul contrive Against thy mother aught. Leave her to heaven,
And to those thorns that in her bosom lodge To prick and sting her. Fare thee well at once.
The glowworm shows the matin to be near And gins to pale his uneffectual fire. Adieu, adieu, adieu! Remember me. Exit.

Hamlet: O all you host of heaven! O earth! What else? And shall I couple hell? Hold, hold, my heart! And you, my sinews, grow not instant old,
But bear me stiffly up. Remember thee?
Ay, thou poor ghost, while memory holds a seat In this distracted globe. Remember thee? Yea, from the table of my memory I'll wipe away all trivial fond records, All saws of books, all forms, all pressures past That youth and observation copied there, And thy commandment all alone shall live

Within the book and volume of my brain, Unmix'd with baser matter. Yes, by heaven! O most pernicious woman!

O villain, villain, smiling, damned villain! My tables! Meet it is I set it down That one may smile, and smile, and be a villain; At least I am sure it may be so in Denmark. *Writing.*

So, uncle, there you are. Now to my word: It is 'Adieu, adieu! Remember me.' I have sworn't. . . . .

33. Which of the following is true at the beginning of the scene?

A. Hamlet knows that his father has been murdered.

B. Hamlet does not know the ghost is his father.

C. Hamlet does not know that his father is dead.

D. Hamlet is angry at his uncle the King.

34. Why is the Ghost doomed to a hellish underworld?

A. because he was murdered

B. because of the things he did when he was alive

C. because his murder must be avenged

D. because Hamlet does not believe him

35. What will save the Ghost from the horrors of his prison house?

A. The Ghost must pray.

B. Hamlet must listen to his father.

C. Hamlet must tell the world that his father was murdered.

D. The Ghost cannot be saved.

36. Why **most likely** does the Ghost refer to the murder as most foul?

A. because he was killed by a snake

B. because his wife has married his brother

C. because his brother killed him

D. because no one in Denmark knows he was murdered

37. What does the Ghost tell Hamlet about his mother?

A. that she was virtuous

B. that she had been a good wife

C. that she helped Claudius

D. that she had been adulterous

38. What does the Ghost make Hamlet promise?

A. That he will avenge his father's death but not kill his mother.

B. That he will kill Claudius and his mother.

C. That he will wait and let God avenge his father's death.

D. That he will do nothing until he sees the Ghost again.

39. Which of the following **best** describes Hamlet's father's death?

A. A snake was put in the garden to bite and poison him.

B. Claudius poured poison in his ear and he died quickly.

C. Claudius poisoned him and he had a slow painful death.

D. The Queen and Claudius came into the orchard and poisoned him.

40. Which of the following **best** summarizes Hamlet's promise in his last lines?

A. He will kill his uncle and his mother.

B. He will put all trivial matters aside and focus on avenging his father's death.

C. He will never forget the Ghost and will not rest until he has killed his father's murderer.

D. He prove to the world that Claudius is a murderer.

Practice Test 4

Composition

Read the following rough draft and answer the questions that follow.

The Beautiful Caribbean

(1) When most people picture the Caribbean they think of high rise hotels and beautiful beaches. (2) Tourism is certainly a big industry for this part of the world. (3) According to the World Resources Institute, a not for profit research group other activities are a serious problem.

(4) The Caribbean is a major oil-producing area and oil spills will caused wide-spread pollution problems. (5) The waters of the Caribbean are contaminated with tar. (6) An estimated 6.7 percent of the offshore oil production is lost through accidents and spills.

(7) Another major pollution problem is the result of poor sewage treatment facilities. (8) Most of the sewage is dumped untreated into the rivers or harbors or is piped to cesspools it seeps into the ground and causes serious ground water problems. (9) Many of the hotels have treatment plants but often they are overloaded and not maintained adequately.

(10) Sediment is another source of pollution. (11) The runoff from agriculture and mining clog the sea grass beds and coral reefs. (12) Bauxite that is mined and fertilizers such as DDT has been discovered in the oceans and in fish from the Gulf of Mexico and the Caribbean waters. (13) Even the beaches have suffered. (14) Sand is mined as a road building material. (15) Sand mining has taken its toll on the coastlines of many islands and has seriously compromised the marine ecosystems.

1. Which change should be made to sentence 2?

   A. rewrite to explain tourism

   B. eliminate the sentence

   C. combine the sentence with sentence 1

   D. rewrite to combine with sentence 3

2. Which of the following will correct sentence 3?

   A. add a comma after group

   B. remove the comma after Institute

   C. change problem to problems

   D. change activities to activity

3. Which of the following will correct sentence 4?

   A. change will caused to causes

   B. change will caused to have caused

   C. add a comma after Caribbean

   D. add a comma before and

4. Which of the following is a run-on sentence?

   A. (3)

   B. (7)

   C. (8)

   D. (14)

5. Which of the following will correct sentence 12?

   A. change water to Water

   B. change fertilizers to fertilizer's

   C. change has to have

   D. change oceans to ocean's

6. Which of the following would be the *best* rewrite for sentence 13?

   A. Even, the beaches have suffered.

   B. The beaches have suffered more than the land.

   C. Additionally, the beaches have suffered.

   D. The beautiful beaches have suffered as well.

Name _____   Date _____

Road Rage

Read the following rough draft and answer the questions that follow.

1) Picture this. 2) I am driving down the highway minding my own business. 3) As a matter of fact, I am being very observant of the traffic around me. 4) I am trying to be a courteous good driver. 5) Out of nowhere appears a large red SUV. 6) Before I could adjust my driving, this urbanassault vehicle is so close that I could not see its headlights. 7) What should I do? 8) If I had been given a few more seconds, I would have pulled into the slow lane. 9) That didn't happen because the red SUV passed me on the left and drove between my car and an eighteen-wheeler.

10) Now I'm no saint when it comes to highway driving. 11) I feel that it is my personal right to drive five to seven miles an hour over the speed limit. 12) If I'm in the passing lane, I'll follow the traffic pattern and drive 10 to 15 miles an hour over the limit. 13) My faults maybe many, but I do make a conscious effort not to interfere with the driving privileges of others, and I definitely make an exerted effort not to put my fellow road traveler's lives in jeopardy with reckless driving.

14) What needs to be done about road rage? 15) How can we help stop it? 16) It may seem funny to us when we see some "clown" showing his or her limited vocabulary by yelling at another driver. 17) We may feel the urge to return sign language when it is displayed to us on the highway. 18) However, we know that road rage really isn't funny. 19) Recently, the local news told the story of a young, 28 year old father who was beaten to death before his two children's eyes when he stopped his car to continue an escalating road rage incident.

20) Road rage is a serious problem that seems to be getting worse. Are the penalties for perpetrators serious enough? 21) If the highway patrol is not around should we take matters into our own hands? 22) Should all new drivers be required to take a course in how to handle road rage? 23) Should hostile drivers have their license suspended and given a hefty fine? 24) It is certainly a problem worthy of our concern.

All-in-One Workbook: Standardized Test Practice
© Pearson Education, Inc. All rights reserved.
369

7. Which of the following will correct sentence 5?

   A. appears to will appear

   B. appears to appeared

   C. appears to appearing

   D. appears to has appeared

8. Which of the following will correct sentence 6?

   A. this to ,an

   B. could to can

   C. is to was

   D. , this to this

9. Which of the following will correct sentence 10?

   A. no saint to not a saint

   B. comes to came

   C. driving to travel

   D. Now to Now,

10. Which of the following will correct sentence 12?

   A. lane, to lane

   B. 10 and 15 to ten and fifteen

   C. limit to limits

   D. drive to drove

11. Which of the following will correct sentence 13?

   A. many, to many

   B. others to others,

   C. effort to efforts

   D. traveler's to travelers

12. What most likely did the author mean when he referenced a "clown" in sentence 15?

   A. a slow driver

   B. the driver of the SUV

   C. a rude driver

   D. the young father

13. How does sentence 18 affect composition?

   A. It is not relevant and should be taken out.

   B. It emphases the seriousness of the problem.

   C. It changes the mood of the composition.

   D. It changes the position of the composition.

Reading For Success: Strategies for reading nonfiction

Read the following rough draft and answer the questions that follow.

(1) Nonfiction is prose that present and explains ideas or tells about real people, places, things, and events. (2) Your school books, magazines, newspapers, encyclopedias, and certain information on the internet are all examples of nonfiction. (3) So are biographies, autobiographies, and essays. (4) Although the writing is nonfiction that doesn't mean that you should accept everything that the writer tells you. (5) Instead, judge the facts for yourself and form your own opinions. (6) The following will help you read nonfiction effectively.

(7) Set a purpose for reading. (8) Before you begin, set a goal for reading a work of nonfiction. (9) You're goal may be to find facts, to analyze a writer's theory, to understand an opinion, or simply to be entertained. (10) Keep your purpose in mind, and look for details in your reading that support that purpose.

(11) Identify the author's main points. (12) Ask yourself what the author wants you to learn or think as a result of reading his nonfiction work. (13) These main points are the most important ideas in the piece.

14. Which of the following changes will correct sentence 1?

    A. that present to that presenting

    B. explains to explained

    C. that present to that presents

    D. explains to has explained

15. Which of the following is the ***best*** rewrite for sentence 3?

    A. So, are biographies, autobiographies, and essays.

    B. Biographies, auto-biographies, and essays are nonfiction as well.

    C. Biographies, auto- biographies and essays are nonfiction.

    D. So are many other kinds of writing.

16. Which of the following changes will correct sentence 5?

    A. opinions to opinions'

    B. Instead, to Instead

    C. yourself to yourself,

    D. own to his

17. Which of the following will correct sentence 9?

    A. may to will

    B. find to discover

    C. writer's to writers

    D. You're to Your

18. Which of the following is the ***best*** rewrite for sentence 12?

    A. Ask yourself what the author wants you to learn and think after reading his work.

    B. Ask yourself what the author wants you to learn or think as a result of reading his or her nonfiction work.

    C. Ask yourself, what the author wants you to learn or think as a result of reading the nonfiction work that he wrote.

    D. Ask your self, "What did I learn from reading this nonfiction?"

19. Why ***most likely*** did the author of this selection write the first sentence in the second and third paragraphs in bold?

    A. Because they are short sentences.

    B. Because this is an outline.

    C. Because they are topic sentences.

    D. Because they are the only important sentences.

Strategies For Success: Real-World Reading

Read this rough draft and answer the questions that follow.

(1)   Whether you are installing a new computer game or assembling a bicycle, you'll be most successful if you read the directions. (2) The owner's manual that comes with new products' includes directions and important information that will help you put together and use the product correctly.

Skim the Manual

(3) Get acquainted with the organization of the manual. (4) Review the table of contents to see what topics are covered in the manual what the product does and how the information is organized. (5) Read the introduction for a general idea of the product.

Check the Manual for Parts

(6) Before you completely unpack the create or box find the list of parts you should have for assembling the item. (7) Check off the parts one by one as you unpack them. (8) Sometimes special tools or connectors is necessary. (9) Make sure you have them before you proceed.

Read Specific Sections Careful

(10) Your preview will help you decide what parts of the manual you want to read. (11) You will probably read through most of the beginning sections of the manual but you can put off reading the supplementary material until a later time.

Read to Solve Problems

(12) Keep the manual for reference in case you have a problem with the product. (13) A troubleshooting section providing solutions to common problems is included in most manuals. (14) You can use the index to locate specific details that pertain to your problem.

20. Which of the following will correct
    sentence 1?

    A. Change bicycle, to bicycle

    B. Change you'll to you will

    C. Change game to game,

    D. Change most to more

21. Which of the following will correct
    sentence 2?

    A. Change directions to directions,

    B. Change will to shall

    C. Change products' to products

    D. Change that to which

22. Which of the following would be the **best**
    rewrite for sentence 5?

    A. Read the introduction for the best idea of
       the product.

    B. Read the general introduction to learn
       about the product.

    C. Read the entire manual to understand
       the product.

    D. Read the introduction for a general
       overview of the product.

23. Which of the following changes will
    correct sentence 6?

    A. Change create to create,

    B. Change box to box,

    C. Change parts to part

    D. Change should to will

24. Which of the following changes will
    correct sentence 9?

    A. Change them to those

    B. Change proceed to begin

    C. Change have to had

    D. Change Make to You make

25. Which change to the subheadings will make
    them correct?

    A. Manual to manual

    B. Parts to parts

    C. Careful to Carefully

    D. Problems to Problems'

26. Which of the following will correct
    sentence 11?

    A. Change sections to sections,

    B. Change manual to manual,

    C. Change supplementary to supplemental

    D. Change material to materials

27. Which of the following is the **best** rewrite for
    sentence 13?

    A. Providing solvtions to problems is what
       the manual is for.

    B. Trouble shooting sections are provided
       in all manuals.

    C. A troubleshooting section, providing
       solutions to common problems, is
       included in most manuals.

    D. Providing solutions to most commom
       problems is provided for in most
       manuals.

28. Which of the following is a run-on
    sentence?

    A. (2)

    B. (4)

    C. (11)

    D. (12)

Frederic Remington (1861–1909)

Read the following rough draft and answer the questions that follow.

1)   Remington is considered the best and most popular painter and sculptor of the old West. 2) He was born in New York and first traveled to the west in 1881. 3) He went to Montana to seek his fortune as a gold miner and then went to Kansas to try his hand as a rancher. 4) All these ventures failed.

5)   During these trips Remington made sketches of the landscapesand people. 6) He sold a few of those to popular magazines, and by 1885 he had decided to make art his profession.

7)   He quickly became successful. 8) By 1888 he was one of the nations most popular magazine illustrators. 9) His sketches of cowboys, soldiers, gunfighters, and Indian scenes were vastly popular with the people in the east. 10) Remington began creating paintings, in the 1890's he also turned his talents to sculpture.

11)   Remington's art rarely focused on generals or chiefs. 12) He preferred to feature average people that projected great strength of spirit and physical energy. 13) His West was full of conflict and rugged individualist, and a West that had escaped the structure of society and was quickly passing away into history.

14)   Remington saw the taming of the West as a tragic loss. 15) He built his art on his early illustrations. 16) A romantic view of the West that became more and more distant from reality.

29. What change should be made to correct sentence 2?

    A. New York to New York,

    B. west to West

    C. traveled to the west to traveled west

    D. was born to is born

30. What change should be made to correct sentence 6?

    A. those to them

    B. magazines, and to magazine and

    C. 1885 to 1885,

    D. had to has

31. Which of the following is a run-on sentence?

    A. During these trips Remington made sketches of the landscape and people.

    B. Remington began creating paintings, in the 1890's he also turned his talents to sculpture.

    C. Remington's art rarely focused on generals or chiefs.

    D. He preferred to feature average people that projected great strength of spirit and physical energy.

32. Which of the following is a sentence fragment?

    A. All these ventures failed.

    B. He quickly became successful.

    C. Remington saw the taming of the West as a tragic loss.

    D. A romantic view of the West that became more and more distant from reality.

33. What change should be made to sentence 12 to make it correct?

    A. that to who

    B. preferred to prefers

    C. spirit to spirit's

    D. He to Remington's

34. How could sentence 13 best be rewritten to improve clarity?

    A. His West that had conflict and rugged individualist; had escaped the structures of society and was quickly passing away.

    B. The West that had escaped the structures of society was passing away with the conflict and rugged individualist.

    C. His West was full of conflict and rugged individualist. Remington's West that had escaped the structures of society was quickly passing away.

    D. As the West passed away the rugged individualist tried to escape society's structures.

35. What change should be made to sentence 8 to make it correct?

    A. most popular to most, popular

    B. By 1888 to By, 1888

    C. nations to nation's

    D. illustrators to illustrator's

Writing Assessment Sample Prompts

Use the following two prompts to practice for writing assessment. which you will be required to take next year.

Writing Prompt 1

Read the following quotations about learning.

"Learning is not attained by chance, it must be sought for with ardor and attended to with diligence."
Abigail Adams (1744 – 1818)

"Learning without thought is labor lost; thought without learning is perilous."
Confucius (551 BC – 479 BC)

"That is what learning is. You suddenly understand something you've understood all your life, but in a new way."
Doris Lessing

"Learning is not compulsory... neither is survival."
W. Edwards Deming (1900 – 1993)

Write a brief essay on what learning means to you. You may use the ideas presented above, your own experiences, observations, and/or readings.

As you write, remember to:

- Focus on the meaning of learning.
- Consider the audience, purpose and context of your writing.
- Organize the ideas and details effectively.
- Include specific examples that clearly develop your writing.
- Edit you writing for standard grammar, spelling, and punctuation.

Name _____ Date _____

Writing Prompt 2

Read the following quotations about character.

"Character is like a tree and reputation like its shadow. The shadow is what we think of it; the tree is the real thing."
Abraham Lincoln (1809 – 1865), *Lincoln's Own Stories*

"People grow through experience if they meet life honestly and courageously. This is how character is built."
Eleanor Roosevelt (1884 – 1962), *My Day*

"Forming characters! Whose? Our own or others? Both. And in that momentous fact lies the peril and responsibility of our existence."
Elihu Burritt

"People seem not to see that their opinion of the world is also a confession of character."
Ralph Waldo Emerson

Write a letter to a friend on the meaning of character. You may use the ideas presented above, your own experiences, observations, and/or readings.

As you write, remember to:
- Focus on the meaning of character.
- Consider the audience, purpose and context of your writing.
- Organize the ideas and details effectively.
- Include specific examples that clearly develop your writing.
- Edit you writing for standard grammar, spelling, and punctuation.

PSAT PRACTICE TEST

CRITICAL READING
Section 1: Sentence Completion

Directions: *Each sentence below has one or two blanks, each blank indicating that something has been omitted. Beneath the sentence are five words or sets of words labeled A through E. Choose the word or set of words that, when inserted in the sentence, best fits the meaning of the sentence as a whole.*

Example:

Rosa was considered to be a ---- because as soon as she got money, she squandered it.

(A) miser

(B) spendthrift

(C) wretch

(D) tyrant

(E) plunger

1. At rehearsal, Ming felt ---- because she had not memorized her lines for the play while all the other performers had.

(A) abashed

(B) secular

(C) intuitive

(D) exhilarated

(E) feeble

2. The suspect was ---- because the investigator had more questions to ask.

(A) immersed

(B) detained

(C) impacted

(D) revoked

(E) impaired

3. The soldiers' ---- worsened after a British naval squadron ---- itself just off the coast of Massachusetts.

(A) plumage..imposed

(B) outgrowth..ordained

(C) partition..thwarted

(D) plight..situated

(E) plague..ransacked

4. The detectives distinguished the natural fibers from the ---- ones by using a special dyeing process.

(A) tawdry

(B) genuine

(C) synthetic

(D) wistful

(E) bereaved

5. Much of the criticism about the canal project ---- with the railroad promoters.

(A) quadrupled

(B) originated

(C) retracted

(D) segmented

(E) unraveled

All-in-One Workbook: Standardized Test Practice
378

6. Despite fierce opposition, the Republicans stood firm on their party's ---- that the institution of slavery should be eradicated.

   (A) expression

   (B) resumption

   (C) opprobrium

   (D) development

   (E) platform

7. After arguing heatedly for three hours, Bill and Sarah decided to ---- their relationship.

   (A) incapacitate

   (B) maroon

   (C) relinquish

   (D) sever

   (E) eclipse

8. Increased railroad construction ---- the market for food products and machinery.

   (A) stimulated

   (B) devastated

   (C) pillaged

   (D) recessed

   (E) extinguished

9. Throughout history, Aesop's fables have been ---- by teachers because of their ---- nature.

   (A) derived..formidable

   (B) patented..glamorous

   (C) revered..instructive

   (D) glorified..unimpressive

   (E) chastised..plausible

10. Salina's statements at the rally only served to further ---- her opponent, who was already upset.

    (A) coordinate

    (B) obliterate

    (C) antagonize

    (D) mystify

    (E) germinate

11. At the celebrity roast, performers' jokes were not viewed as ---- because they were delivered in a spirit of fun.

    (A) resilient

    (B) enviable

    (C) anecdotal

    (D) spurious

    (E) distasteful

12. The chief of the Cherokee Nation met with the governor to make a ---- in order to work together to preserve the land.

    (A) scholarship

    (B) covenant

    (C) liability

    (D) mechanism

    (E) projectile

13. Jallisa was being ---- when she taunted Bryan for being late to class even though she had been late earlier in the week.

    (A) impartial

    (B) mediocre

    (C) hypocritical

    (D) belligerent

    (E) adverse

Section 2: Reading Comprehension

Directions: *The two passages below are followed by questions based on their content. Answer the questions on the basis of what is <u>stated</u> or <u>implied</u> in the passages and in any introductory material that may be provided.*

QUESTIONS 14–19 ARE BASED ON THE FOLLOWING PASSAGE.

The following passage is an excerpt from Benjamin Franklin's The Autobiography.

I was put to the grammar-school at eight years of age, my father intending to devote me. . . . to the service of the Church. My early readiness in learning
(5) to read (which must have been very early, as I do not remember when I could not read), . . . encouraged him in this purpose of his. . . . But my father, in the mean time, from the view of the expense
(10) of a college education, which having so large a family he could not well afford . . . took me from the grammar-school, and sent me to a school for writing and arithmetic. . . . At ten years old I was
(15) taken home to assist my father in his business, which was that of a tallow-chandler and soapboiler. . . . Accordingly, I was employed in cutting wick for the candles, filling the dipping mold and the
(20) molds for cast candles, attending the shop, going o[n] errands etc.

I disliked the trade, and had a strong inclination for the sea, but my father de-clared against it. However, living near the
(25) water, I was much in and about it. . . .

From a child I was fond of reading, and all the little money that came into my hands was ever laid out in books. . . . This bookish inclination at length deter-
(30) mined my father to make me a printer, though he had already one son (James) of that profession. . . . I liked it much better than that of my father, but still had a hankering for the sea. To prevent
(35) the apprehended effect of such an incli-nation, my father was impatient to have me bound to my brother. I stood out some time, but at last was persuaded, and signed the indenture when I was yet but

(40) twelve years old. I was to serve as an apprentice till I was twenty-one years of age, only I was to be allowed journey-man's wages during the last year. . . .

Though a brother, he considered
(45) himself as my master, and me as his apprentice, . . . while I thought he demeaned me too much in some he required of me, who from a brother expected more indulgence. Our disputes
(50) were often brought before our father, and I fancy I was either generally in the right, or else a better pleader, because the judgment was generally in my favor. . . .

One of the pieces in our newspaper on
(55) some political point, which I have now forgotten, gave offense to the Assembly. He [James] was taken up, censured, and imprisoned for a month. . . .

During my brother's confinement, . . .
(60) I had the management of the paper. . . . [T]he paper went on accordingly, under my name for several months.

14. According to the passage, early in his life, Benjamin Franklin was most inclined to

(A) print newspapers

(B) perform mathematics

(C) read books

(D) make candles

(E) attend school

15. Judging from the passage, the young Franklin did not seem free to

(A) assist his family

(B) conduct scientific experiments

(C) express his ideas freely

(D) choose his own career path

(E) indulge his reading habit

16. The passage would best be described as a

(A) persuasive essay

(B) narrative

(C) how-to essay

(D) comparison/contrast essay

(E) fictional tale

17. The word *indenture* in line 39 means

(A) proclamation

(B) treaty

(C) acquisition

(D) waiver

(E) contract

18. When the author says, "I stood out some time" in lines 37–38, he means that he

(A) refused to go inside the family dwelling

(B) separated himself from his family

(C) moved to a friend's house for a while

(D) hesitated to commit

(E) refused to sit down for hours

19. Franklin found his working relationship with his brother unsatisfactory because

(A) Franklin expected to be his brother's equal

(B) Franklin wanted his brother to be more lenient

(C) his brother spent too much time reading

(D) Franklin wanted to be paid more for his work

(E) his brother made poor business decisions

A View of a Young African-American
An Excerpt from *Darkwater Voices From Within the Veil* by W. E. B. Du Bois

1)   I was born by a golden river and in the shadow of two great hills, five years after the Emancipation Proclamation. The house was quaint, with clapboards running up and down, neatly trimmed, and there were five rooms, a tiny porch, a rosy front yard, and unbelievably delicious strawberries in the rear.

2)   Mother was dark shining bronze, with a tiny ripple in her black hair, black-eyed, with a heavy, kind face. She gave one the impression of infinite patience, but a curious determination was concealed in her softness. The family were small farmers on Egremont Plain, between Great Barrington and Sheffield, Massachusetts. The bits of land were too small to support the great families born on them and we were always poor. I never remember being cold or hungry, but I do remember that shoes and coal, and sometimes flour, caused mother moments of anxious thought in winter, and a new suit was an event!

3)   Here mother and I lived until she died, in 1884, for father early began his restless wanderings. I last remember urgent letters for us to come to New Milford, where he had started a barber shop. Later he became a preacher. But mother no longer trusted his dreams, and he soon faded out of our lives into silence.

4)   Most of our townsfolk were, naturally, the well-to-do, shading downward, but seldom reaching poverty. As playmate of the children I saw the homes of nearly every one, except a few immigrant New Yorkers, of whom none of us approved. The homes I saw impressed me, but did not overwhelm me. Many were bigger than mine, with newer and shinier things, but they did not seem to differ in kind. I think I probably surprised my hosts more than they me, for I was easily at home and perfectly happy and they looked to me just like ordinary people, while my brown face and frizzled hair must have seemed strange to them.

5)   Very gradually,—I cannot now distinguish the steps, though here and there I remember a jump or a jolt—but very gradually I found myself assuming quite placidly that I was different from other children. At first I think I connected the difference with a manifest ability to get my lessons rather better than most and to recite with a certain happy, almost taunting, glibness, which brought frowns here and there. Then, slowly, I realized that some folks, a few, even several, actually considered my brown skin a misfortune; once or twice I became painfully aware that some human beings even thought it a crime. I was not for a moment daunted,—although, of course, there were some days of secret tears—rather I was spurred to tireless effort. If they beat me at anything, I was grimly determined to make them sweat for it! Once I remember challenging a great, hard farmer-boy to battle, when I knew he could whip me; and he did. But ever after, he was polite.

20. What is the point of view used in this passage?

A. third person in which the speaker reveals the actions and feelings of himself and the other characters

B. third person in which the speaker reveals only his actions and feelings

C. first person in which the speaker reveals the actions and feelings of himself and the other characters

D. first person in which the speaker reveals his actions and his feelings

E. first person in which the speaker reveals only his actions

21. According to the passage, which of the following statements best describes the speaker and his mother?

A. They did not have much money.

B. They did not buy new clothes very often.

C. Sometimes they did not have enough money for shoes, coal, or flour.

D. The speaker's mother was often worried about their finances.

E. all of the above

22. What does the speaker remember of his childhood?

A. missing his father

B. never being cold or hungry

C. playing with the children who were immigrants

D. winning every fight

E. helping his father in the barber shop

23. In paragraph 3, what does the speaker mean by this phrase "mother no longer trusted his dreams"?

A. Mother does not trust that the speaker will continue to do well in school .

B. Mother does not trust in dreams.

C. Father goes from one job to another, and Mother no longer believes that he will be successful.

D. Father becomes a preacher in a church that Mother does not like.

E. Mother does not trust that the speaker will win all of his fights.

24. Based on the context of the passage, which of the following does *not* describe Mother?

A. patient

B. worried

C. secretive

D. determined

E. kind

25. Which of the following statements is an accurate description of the speaker and his playmates?

A. The speaker and his mother were richer than most of his playmates and their families.

B. The speaker's home was bigger than the homes of most of his playmates.

C. The speaker and his playmates looked similar to each other in appearance.

D. The speaker was comfortable and happy in the homes of his playmates.

E. all of the above

26. Based on the context of paragraph 5, what does the word *daunted* mean?

A. angry

B. scared

C. discouraged

D. sad

E. fooled

Directions: *The three passages below are followed by questions based on their content. Answer the questions on the basis of what is* <u>stated</u> *or* <u>implied</u> *in the passages.*

The poetry of earth is never dead:
When all the birds are faint with the hot sun,
And hide in cooling trees, a voice will run
From hedge to hedge about the new-mown mead;
(5)   That is the Grasshopper's—he takes the lead
In summer luxury, —he has never done
With his delights; for when tired out with fun
He rests at ease beneath some pleasant weed.
The poetry of earth is ceasing never:
(10)   On a lone winter evening, when the frost
Has wrought a silence, from the stove there shrills
The Cricket's song, in warmth increasing ever,
And seems to one in drowsiness half lost,
The Grasshopper's among some grassy hills.

—"On the Grasshopper and the Cricket" by John Keats

27. What does the speaker mean by saying "The poetry of earth is never dead"?

(A) Nature is always alive with the music of its creatures.

(B) The earth will continue to exist long after its creatures are gone.

(C) Without the beauty of nature, the earth would cease to exist.

(D) Earth's seasons will never stop changing.

(E) Music and poetry make life worth living.

28. Which of the following statements is supported by the poem?

(A) The grasshopper sings a prettier song than the cricket.

(B) The cricket sings a prettier song than the grasshopper.

(C) The grasshopper sings in the summer, while the cricket sings in the winter.

(D) The cricket sings in the summer, while the grasshopper sings in the winter.

(E) The grasshopper and the cricket sing together throughout the year.

Della finished her cry and attended to her cheeks with the powder rag. She stood by the window and looked out dully at a gray cat walking a gray fence in a gray backyard. Tomorrow would be Christmas Day, and she had only $1.87 with which to buy Jim a present. She had been saving every penny she could for months, with this result. . . . Only $1.87 to buy a present for Jim. Her Jim. Many a happy hour she had spent planning for something nice for him. Something fine and rare and sterling—something just a little bit near to being worthy of the honor of being owned by Jim.

—from "The Gift of the Magi"
by O. Henry

29. This passage identifies the story's

(A) resolution

(B) climax

(C) stage directions

(D) falling action

(E) central conflict

30. From this passage you can infer that

(A) Della has lost her job.

(B) Jim and Della are frivolous with their money.

(C) Della is concerned only with material things.

(D) Della is thoughtful and loving.

(E) Jim hides his money from Della.

Dear Students:

I want to welcome you to the 8th Annual Southeast College Conference. . . .

You have reached a critical time in your life, a time filled with questions. Where do you want to go in life? How will you get there? Education is definitely the vehicle to your success in any career you choose. . . . It will empower you intellectually and enable you to grow into valuable, contributing citizens of your community. . . .

Please make today an opportunity of a lifetime. Ask questions, participate in the workshops, let your voice be heard and, most importantly, have fun. . . .

Senator Martha Escutia

31. What effect does the author hope to have on the students?

(A) She hopes that they will vote for her in the next election.

(B) She hopes that they will be inspired to join politics.

(C) She wants them to feel welcome at the conference.

(D) She hopes that they will agree to attend the conference.

(E) She wants them to memorize the conference schedule.

32. Which of the following words *best* describes the tone of this letter?

(A) friendly

(B) grave

(C) tense

(D) humorous

(E) impolite

All-in-One Workbook: Standardized Test Practice

WRITING

Directions: *The sentences below contain errors in grammar, usage, word choice, and idiom. Parts of each sentence are underlined and lettered. Decide which underlined part contains the error and mark its letter on your answer sheet. If the sentence is correct as it stands, mark (E) on your answer sheet. No sentence contains more than one error.*

33. The salad tastes <u>differently</u> with <u>the new</u>
    (A)   **(B)**
    dressing, which <u>contains</u> beets, garlic,
                     (C)
    <u>and pepper</u>. <u>No error</u>
    (D)   **(E)**

34. Phil and <u>her</u> admitted that <u>they were</u> the
              (A)   **(B)**
    ones <u>who broke</u> the window <u>last</u>
         (C)   **(D)**
    Saturday. <u>No error</u>
              (E)

35. Mrs. Solaf <u>will hire</u> a carpenter,
                (A)
    <u>either Williams</u> or <u>he</u>, to remodel <u>her</u>
    (B)   **(C)**   **(D)**
    kitchen. <u>No error</u>
             (E)

36. Politics <u>have</u> always intrigued me, so I
             (A)
    <u>decided</u> to <u>run</u> for president of the
    (B)   **(C)**
    <u>student council</u> this year. <u>No error</u>
    (D)   **(E)**

37. <u>How do</u> we know <u>whom</u> is coming to the
    (A)   **(B)**
    party if <u>we forgot</u> to ask for <u>an RSVP</u>?
             (C)   **(D)**
    <u>No error</u>
    (E)

38. <u>After the</u> break-in, I noticed that <u>only the</u>
    (A)   **(B)**
    suitcase and the radio <u>were</u> missing
                           (C)
    <u>from the</u> closet. <u>No error</u>
    (D)   **(E)**

39. It was <u>she</u> who sang <u>at the benefit</u>
           (A)   **(B)**
    concert last May <u>to raise money</u> for the
                     (C)
    <u>Red Cross</u>. <u>No error</u>
    (D)   **(E)**

40. <u>*Romeo and Juliet,*</u> one of William
    (A)
    Shakespeare's <u>most famous</u> works,
                  (B)
    <u>continue</u> to <u>charm audiences</u>. <u>No error</u>
    (C)   **(D)**   **(E)**

41. The doctor <u>who</u> I interviewed last May
               (A)
    <u>won</u> an award <u>for</u> <u>increasing patient</u>
    (B)   **(C)** **(D)**
    <u>satisfaction</u>. <u>No error</u>
    (B)   **(E)**

42. <u>Upon careful reflection,</u> a <u>thoughtful</u>
    (A)   **(B)**
    student <u>may decide</u> to forego the party in
            (C)
    favor of staying <u>home</u> to study. <u>No error</u>
                     (D)   **(E)**

43. As long as you <u>stay together,</u> you and <u>him</u>
               (A)   **(B)**

can spend <u>the entire</u> day at <u>Selson Beach.</u>
         (C)   **(D)**

<u>No error</u>
(E)

44. The <u>great</u> silver crescent <u>illuminated</u> the
        (A)   **(B)**

night sky as if <u>it was</u> a giant <u>floating</u>
             (C)   **(D)**

flashlight. <u>No error</u>
          (E)

45. The author <u>mentions</u> many <u>kind</u> of
          (A)   **(B)**

animals that <u>live</u> <u>along the Nile River</u> in
         (C)   **(D)**

Africa. <u>No error</u>
       (E)

46. Without a government <u>to provide</u> laws,
                (A)

individual citizens would <u>likely make</u>
                  (B)

their own rules, <u>causing a situation</u> that
              (C)

would likely <u>resemble</u> chaos. <u>No error</u>
        (D)   **(E)**

47. <u>To be</u> frank, a <u>good</u> play <u>needs to be</u>
    (A)   **(B)**   **(C)**

<u>rehearsed</u> for several days or <u>week</u> before
                     (D)

it can be performed. <u>No error</u>
              (E)

48. The oil spill could <u>have been</u> prevented
               (A)

<u>had</u> the workers on the rig <u>attempt</u> to
(B)   **(C)**

shut down the valves <u>more quickly.</u>
             (D)

<u>No error</u>
(E)

49. <u>As a sign</u> of good will, the manager <u>will</u>
    (A)   **(B)**

<u>address</u> the concerns that <u>were brought</u>
                     (C)

up in the company <u>survey.</u> <u>No error</u>
            (D)   **(E)**

50. <u>From the beginning,</u> the New England
        (A)

Federalists <u>opposed</u> the war because <u>he</u>
        (B)   **(C)**

felt President Madison <u>had been fooled</u> by
             (D)

Napoleon. <u>No error</u>
       (E)

51. The border collie <u>appeared strong</u> and
              (A)

confident <u>as</u> it <u>sprint toward</u>
     (B)   **(C)**

a sheep that <u>had veered</u> away from
           (D)

the herd. <u>No error</u>
      (E)

Directions: *The sentences below contain problems in grammar, sentence construction, word choice, and punctuation. Part or all of each sentence is underlined. Select the lettered answer that contains the best version of the underlined section. Answer (A) always repeats the original underlined section exactly. If the sentence is correct as it stands, select (A).*

52. **When it comes to sports, softball <u>is more easy mastered</u> than tennis.**

   (A) is more easy mastered

   (B) is more easily to master

   (C) is easier to master

   (D) can be easy mastered

   (E) is easier mastered

53. **Two members of the team, <u>she and I, assist</u> the coach in creating game plans.**

   (A) she and I, assist

   (B) they and I, assist

   (C) she and I assist

   (D) him and her, assists

   (E) she and I, assists

54. **It was Russ <u>and them who volunteered</u> to set up the tables and chairs for the party.**

   (A) and them who volunteered

   (B) who along with them, volunteered

   (C) and they who volunteered

   (D) and them, whom volunteered

   (E) whom volunteered with them

55. **Many students now use homework trackers because they help organize assignments, chart progress and <u>completion dates, and provide</u> a handy filing system for important papers.**

   (A) completion dates, and provide

   (B) completion, dates, to provide

   (C) completion dates to provide

   (D) completion dates and, provide

   (E) completion dates and providing

56. ***The Witch of Blackbird Pond*, <u>a Newbery Medal winner was written</u> by Elizabeth George Speare.**

   (A) a Newbery Medal winner was written

   (B) Newbery Medal winner written

   (C) a Newbery Medal winner written,

   (D) was the Newbery Medal winner written

   (E) a Newbery Medal winner, was written

57. **Eight weeks passed with little <u>improvement, so I completed</u> only three of the nine chapters.**

   (A) improvement, so I completed

   (B) improvement so I completed

   (C) improvement and I completed

   (D) that was to be improved yet I completed

   (E) improvement, so I had completed

58. <u>Having climbed a seemingly endless</u>
    **group of mountains, the crew felt
    a sense of satisfaction and
    accomplishment.**

    (A) Having climbed a seemingly endless

    (B) Seeming to climb endlessly

    (C) Endlessly climbed that large

    (D) Having climbed a seemingly ending

    (E) Having to climb an endless

59. **In two weeks, our football team
    <u>competed with a team</u> that has been
    undefeated for three straight seasons.**

    (A) competed with a team

    (B) competed against a team

    (C) competed with one team

    (D) will compete for a team

    (E) will compete against a team

60. **After entering the testing room,
    Hunter <u>quickly take his seat</u>.**

    (A) quickly take his seat

    (B) taking his seat quickly

    (C) quickly took his seat

    (D) quickly taked his seat

    (E) taking his seat quickly

61. **For my report on satellites, I gathered
    information from various sources
    including encyclopedias, periodicals,
    and <u>observations cited in reports
    by NASA</u>.**

    (A) and observations cited in reports
    by NASA.

    (B) and, what I found listed at NASA.

    (C) and, NASA's reported results from
    studies.

    (D) and several studies, of NASA
    documents.

    (E) and observation reports from NASA.

62. **Jamie Lee Curtis, a well-known
    <u>actress, she recently written</u> a
    children's book.**

    (A) actress, she recently written

    (B) actress recently wrote

    (C) actress recently has written

    (D) actress, recently wrote

    (E) actress when she writed,

63. <u>Students are becoming increasingly</u>
    **stressed because of increased
    homework, a greater number of
    extracurricular activities, and longer
    working hours.**

    (A) Students are becoming increasingly

    (B) Students became increasingly

    (C) Students' due to being increasingly

    (D) Students increasingly becoming

    (E) Increasing numbers of students
    will be

64. **In football, the issue whether to allow
    referees to use instant replay <u>has
    quite a controversy</u>.**

    (A) has quite a controversy.

    (B) becoming quite a controversy.

    (C) are becoming a controversy.

    (D) have become controversy.

    (E) has become quite a controversy.

65. **After carrying the 20-gallon fish tank
    75 yards from my neighbor's house,
    I <u>accidental dropped it</u> onto the
    doorstep.**

    (A) accidental dropped it

    (B) accidentally dropped it

    (C) on accident dropped it

    (D) dropped them accidentally

    (E) by accident dropped them

Directions: *Questions 66–69 are based on the following essay. The following passage is an early draft of an essay. Some parts of the passage need to be rewritten. Read the passage and select the best answers for the questions that follow. Some questions are about particular sentences or parts of sentences and ask you to improve sentence structure and word choice. Other questions refer to parts of the essay or the entire essay and ask you to consider organization and development. In making your decisions, follow the conventions of standard written English.*

(1) Today, many television viewers find themselves entertained when they're not even watching a program. (2) In fact, some people tune in to the Super Bowl with no intention of watching the game. (3) Just what is grabbing all the attention? (4) Well, they are the commercials.

(5) Commercials are big business. (6) Manufacturers spends millions of dollars to get their message to the target audience. (7) For instance, to sell a trendy clothing line, advertisers create commercials showing young people wearing hip clothes while dancing with attractive, smiling friends. (8) Automobile manufacturers even show their four-wheel-drive trucks at the tops of high cliffs, when it's obvious that the vehicles could only get there after being lifted by a helicopter. (9) All of this is done in the name of trying to get the sale.

(10) Just how far will they go? (11) They are willing to spend up to a million dollars for one 30-second spot of commercial time during the Super Bowl. (12) Though it seems like a lot of money for not a lot of time, that 30-second commercial can bring in millions of dollars in profit.

(13) If you want to see just how effective these commercials really are, take the time to notice how many people are wearing trendy clothes and driving rugged trucks. (14) Advertising seems worth the cost of expensive airtime.

66. Which is the *best* revision of Sentence 4?

(A) Commercials.

(B) It's the commercials, of course.

(C) They are, of course, the commercials.

(D) Well, the commercials is what it is.

(E) The commercials are what it is.

67. Which is the *best* revision of the underlined portion of Sentence 6?

(A) Manufacturers make millions of dollars

(B) Manufacturers spends a lot of money

(C) Spending millions of dollars

(D) Manufacturers spend millions of dollars

(E) Having to spend a lot of money

68. What would be the *best* way to begin Sentence 8?

(A) As yet another example,

(B) For an example,

(C) Some

(D) For instance, some

(E) To begin with, some

69. Which of the following *best* replaces the word *They* in Sentence 10?

(A) consumers

(B) advertisers

(C) commercials

(D) viewers

(E) young adults

Prompt 1

Directions: *Think carefully about the issue presented in the following passage and the assignment below.*

In "We Never Know How High We Are," Emily Dickinson speaks of the human fear of achieving greatness and importance. According to the speaker, we impose limitations on ourselves because life seems safer in a cage than outside.

Assignment: What is your view on the idea that it is safer for people to avoid challenges than it is for them to attempt to do great deeds? Plan and write an essay in which you develop your point of view on this issue. Support your position with reasoning and examples taken from your reading, studies, experience, or observations.

Prompt 2

Directions: *Think carefully about the issue presented in the following passages and the assignment below.*

1. Requiring students to wear school uniforms helps combat school violence and discrimination. When students dress the same, social and economic differences are less apparent, and students stop spending time judging others' clothing. This allows them to concentrate more on their schoolwork.

2. Dress codes are less restrictive than uniforms and cause less resentment among students. Students have a right to choose what to wear each day, as long as their clothing meets acceptable standards. When students wear what they feel is comfortable, they are more apt to do well in school.

Assignment: Do school uniforms help students achieve academic success, or are school dress codes more conducive to good grades and behaviors? Plan and write an essay in which you develop your point of view on this issue. Support your position with reasoning and examples taken from your reading, studies, experience, or observations.

Name _____ Date _____

Answer Sheet

Screening Test

1. Ⓐ Ⓑ Ⓒ Ⓓ
2. Ⓕ Ⓖ Ⓗ Ⓙ
3. Ⓐ Ⓑ Ⓒ Ⓓ
4. Ⓕ Ⓖ Ⓗ Ⓙ
5. Ⓐ Ⓑ Ⓒ Ⓓ
6. Ⓕ Ⓖ Ⓗ Ⓙ
7. Ⓐ Ⓑ Ⓒ Ⓓ
8. Ⓕ Ⓖ Ⓗ Ⓙ
9. Ⓐ Ⓑ Ⓒ Ⓓ
10. Ⓕ Ⓖ Ⓗ Ⓙ
11. Ⓐ Ⓑ Ⓒ Ⓓ
12. Ⓕ Ⓖ Ⓗ Ⓙ
13. Ⓐ Ⓑ Ⓒ Ⓓ
14. Ⓕ Ⓖ Ⓗ Ⓙ
15. Ⓐ Ⓑ Ⓒ Ⓓ
16. Ⓕ Ⓖ Ⓗ Ⓙ
17. Ⓐ Ⓑ Ⓒ Ⓓ
18. Ⓕ Ⓖ Ⓗ Ⓙ
19. Ⓐ Ⓑ Ⓒ Ⓓ
20. Ⓕ Ⓖ Ⓗ Ⓙ
21. Ⓐ Ⓑ Ⓒ Ⓓ
22. Ⓕ Ⓖ Ⓗ Ⓙ
23. Ⓐ Ⓑ Ⓒ Ⓓ

Practice Test 1

1. Ⓐ Ⓑ Ⓒ Ⓓ
2. Ⓐ Ⓑ Ⓒ Ⓓ
3. Ⓐ Ⓑ Ⓒ Ⓓ
4. Ⓐ Ⓑ Ⓒ Ⓓ
5. Ⓐ Ⓑ Ⓒ Ⓓ
6. Ⓐ Ⓑ Ⓒ Ⓓ
7. Ⓐ Ⓑ Ⓒ Ⓓ
8. Ⓐ Ⓑ Ⓒ Ⓓ
9. Ⓐ Ⓑ Ⓒ Ⓓ
10. Ⓐ Ⓑ Ⓒ Ⓓ
11. Ⓐ Ⓑ Ⓒ Ⓓ
12. Ⓐ Ⓑ Ⓒ Ⓓ
13. Ⓐ Ⓑ Ⓒ Ⓓ
14. Ⓐ Ⓑ Ⓒ Ⓓ
15. Ⓐ Ⓑ Ⓒ Ⓓ
16. Ⓐ Ⓑ Ⓒ Ⓓ
17. Ⓐ Ⓑ Ⓒ Ⓓ
18. Ⓐ Ⓑ Ⓒ Ⓓ
19. Ⓐ Ⓑ Ⓒ Ⓓ
20. Ⓐ Ⓑ Ⓒ Ⓓ
21. Ⓐ Ⓑ Ⓒ Ⓓ
22. Ⓐ Ⓑ Ⓒ Ⓓ
23. Ⓐ Ⓑ Ⓒ Ⓓ
24. Ⓐ Ⓑ Ⓒ Ⓓ
25. Ⓐ Ⓑ Ⓒ Ⓓ
26. Ⓐ Ⓑ Ⓒ Ⓓ
27. Ⓐ Ⓑ Ⓒ Ⓓ
28. Ⓐ Ⓑ Ⓒ Ⓓ
29. Ⓐ Ⓑ Ⓒ Ⓓ
30. Ⓐ Ⓑ Ⓒ Ⓓ

Answer Sheets

Practice Test 3

1. Ⓐ Ⓑ Ⓒ Ⓓ	11. Ⓐ Ⓑ Ⓒ Ⓓ	21. Ⓐ Ⓑ Ⓒ Ⓓ	31. Ⓐ Ⓑ Ⓒ Ⓓ
2. Ⓐ Ⓑ Ⓒ Ⓓ	12. Ⓐ Ⓑ Ⓒ Ⓓ	22. Ⓐ Ⓑ Ⓒ Ⓓ	32. Ⓐ Ⓑ Ⓒ Ⓓ
3. Ⓐ Ⓑ Ⓒ Ⓓ	13. Ⓐ Ⓑ Ⓒ Ⓓ	23. Ⓐ Ⓑ Ⓒ Ⓓ	33. Ⓐ Ⓑ Ⓒ Ⓓ
4. Ⓐ Ⓑ Ⓒ Ⓓ	14. Ⓐ Ⓑ Ⓒ Ⓓ	24. Ⓐ Ⓑ Ⓒ Ⓓ	34. Ⓐ Ⓑ Ⓒ Ⓓ
5. Ⓐ Ⓑ Ⓒ Ⓓ	15. Ⓐ Ⓑ Ⓒ Ⓓ	25. Ⓐ Ⓑ Ⓒ Ⓓ	35. Ⓐ Ⓑ Ⓒ Ⓓ
6. Ⓐ Ⓑ Ⓒ Ⓓ	16. Ⓐ Ⓑ Ⓒ Ⓓ	26. Ⓐ Ⓑ Ⓒ Ⓓ	36. Ⓐ Ⓑ Ⓒ Ⓓ
7. Ⓐ Ⓑ Ⓒ Ⓓ	17. Ⓐ Ⓑ Ⓒ Ⓓ	27. Ⓐ Ⓑ Ⓒ Ⓓ	37. Ⓐ Ⓑ Ⓒ Ⓓ
8. Ⓐ Ⓑ Ⓒ Ⓓ	18. Ⓐ Ⓑ Ⓒ Ⓓ	28. Ⓐ Ⓑ Ⓒ Ⓓ	38. Ⓐ Ⓑ Ⓒ Ⓓ
9. Ⓐ Ⓑ Ⓒ Ⓓ	19. Ⓐ Ⓑ Ⓒ Ⓓ	29. Ⓐ Ⓑ Ⓒ Ⓓ	39. Ⓐ Ⓑ Ⓒ Ⓓ
10. Ⓐ Ⓑ Ⓒ Ⓓ	20. Ⓐ Ⓑ Ⓒ Ⓓ	30. Ⓐ Ⓑ Ⓒ Ⓓ	40. Ⓐ Ⓑ Ⓒ Ⓓ

Practice Test 4

1. Ⓐ Ⓑ Ⓒ Ⓓ	13. Ⓐ Ⓑ Ⓒ Ⓓ	25. Ⓐ Ⓑ Ⓒ Ⓓ
2. Ⓐ Ⓑ Ⓒ Ⓓ	14. Ⓐ Ⓑ Ⓒ Ⓓ	26. Ⓐ Ⓑ Ⓒ Ⓓ
3. Ⓐ Ⓑ Ⓒ Ⓓ	15. Ⓐ Ⓑ Ⓒ Ⓓ	27. Ⓐ Ⓑ Ⓒ Ⓓ
4. Ⓐ Ⓑ Ⓒ Ⓓ	16. Ⓐ Ⓑ Ⓒ Ⓓ	28. Ⓐ Ⓑ Ⓒ Ⓓ
5. Ⓐ Ⓑ Ⓒ Ⓓ	17. Ⓐ Ⓑ Ⓒ Ⓓ	29. Ⓐ Ⓑ Ⓒ Ⓓ
6. Ⓐ Ⓑ Ⓒ Ⓓ	18. Ⓐ Ⓑ Ⓒ Ⓓ	30. Ⓐ Ⓑ Ⓒ Ⓓ
7. Ⓐ Ⓑ Ⓒ Ⓓ	19. Ⓐ Ⓑ Ⓒ Ⓓ	31. Ⓐ Ⓑ Ⓒ Ⓓ
8. Ⓐ Ⓑ Ⓒ Ⓓ	20. Ⓐ Ⓑ Ⓒ Ⓓ	32. Ⓐ Ⓑ Ⓒ Ⓓ
9. Ⓐ Ⓑ Ⓒ Ⓓ	21. Ⓐ Ⓑ Ⓒ Ⓓ	33. Ⓐ Ⓑ Ⓒ Ⓓ
10. Ⓐ Ⓑ Ⓒ Ⓓ	22. Ⓐ Ⓑ Ⓒ Ⓓ	34. Ⓐ Ⓑ Ⓒ Ⓓ
11. Ⓐ Ⓑ Ⓒ Ⓓ	23. Ⓐ Ⓑ Ⓒ Ⓓ	35. Ⓐ Ⓑ Ⓒ Ⓓ
12. Ⓐ Ⓑ Ⓒ Ⓓ	24. Ⓐ Ⓑ Ⓒ Ⓓ	

Answer Sheet for PSAT

1. Ⓐ Ⓑ Ⓒ Ⓓ Ⓔ	16. Ⓐ Ⓑ Ⓒ Ⓓ Ⓔ	31. Ⓐ Ⓑ Ⓒ Ⓓ Ⓔ	46. Ⓐ Ⓑ Ⓒ Ⓓ Ⓔ	61. Ⓐ Ⓑ Ⓒ Ⓓ Ⓔ
2. Ⓐ Ⓑ Ⓒ Ⓓ Ⓔ	17. Ⓐ Ⓑ Ⓒ Ⓓ Ⓔ	32. Ⓐ Ⓑ Ⓒ Ⓓ Ⓔ	47. Ⓐ Ⓑ Ⓒ Ⓓ Ⓔ	62. Ⓐ Ⓑ Ⓒ Ⓓ Ⓔ
3. Ⓐ Ⓑ Ⓒ Ⓓ Ⓔ	18. Ⓐ Ⓑ Ⓒ Ⓓ Ⓔ	33. Ⓐ Ⓑ Ⓒ Ⓓ Ⓔ	48. Ⓐ Ⓑ Ⓒ Ⓓ Ⓔ	63. Ⓐ Ⓑ Ⓒ Ⓓ Ⓔ
4. Ⓐ Ⓑ Ⓒ Ⓓ Ⓔ	19. Ⓐ Ⓑ Ⓒ Ⓓ Ⓔ	34. Ⓐ Ⓑ Ⓒ Ⓓ Ⓔ	49. Ⓐ Ⓑ Ⓒ Ⓓ Ⓔ	64. Ⓐ Ⓑ Ⓒ Ⓓ Ⓔ
5. Ⓐ Ⓑ Ⓒ Ⓓ Ⓔ	20. Ⓐ Ⓑ Ⓒ Ⓓ Ⓔ	35. Ⓐ Ⓑ Ⓒ Ⓓ Ⓔ	50. Ⓐ Ⓑ Ⓒ Ⓓ Ⓔ	65. Ⓐ Ⓑ Ⓒ Ⓓ Ⓔ
6. Ⓐ Ⓑ Ⓒ Ⓓ Ⓔ	21. Ⓐ Ⓑ Ⓒ Ⓓ Ⓔ	36. Ⓐ Ⓑ Ⓒ Ⓓ Ⓔ	51. Ⓐ Ⓑ Ⓒ Ⓓ Ⓔ	66. Ⓐ Ⓑ Ⓒ Ⓓ Ⓔ
7. Ⓐ Ⓑ Ⓒ Ⓓ Ⓔ	22. Ⓐ Ⓑ Ⓒ Ⓓ Ⓔ	37. Ⓐ Ⓑ Ⓒ Ⓓ Ⓔ	52. Ⓐ Ⓑ Ⓒ Ⓓ Ⓔ	67. Ⓐ Ⓑ Ⓒ Ⓓ Ⓔ
8. Ⓐ Ⓑ Ⓒ Ⓓ Ⓔ	23. Ⓐ Ⓑ Ⓒ Ⓓ Ⓔ	38. Ⓐ Ⓑ Ⓒ Ⓓ Ⓔ	53. Ⓐ Ⓑ Ⓒ Ⓓ Ⓔ	68. Ⓐ Ⓑ Ⓒ Ⓓ Ⓔ
9. Ⓐ Ⓑ Ⓒ Ⓓ Ⓔ	24. Ⓐ Ⓑ Ⓒ Ⓓ Ⓔ	39. Ⓐ Ⓑ Ⓒ Ⓓ Ⓔ	54. Ⓐ Ⓑ Ⓒ Ⓓ Ⓔ	69. Ⓐ Ⓑ Ⓒ Ⓓ Ⓔ
10. Ⓐ Ⓑ Ⓒ Ⓓ Ⓔ	25. Ⓐ Ⓑ Ⓒ Ⓓ Ⓔ	40. Ⓐ Ⓑ Ⓒ Ⓓ Ⓔ	55. Ⓐ Ⓑ Ⓒ Ⓓ Ⓔ	
11. Ⓐ Ⓑ Ⓒ Ⓓ Ⓔ	26. Ⓐ Ⓑ Ⓒ Ⓓ Ⓔ	41. Ⓐ Ⓑ Ⓒ Ⓓ Ⓔ	56. Ⓐ Ⓑ Ⓒ Ⓓ Ⓔ	
12. Ⓐ Ⓑ Ⓒ Ⓓ Ⓔ	27. Ⓐ Ⓑ Ⓒ Ⓓ Ⓔ	42. Ⓐ Ⓑ Ⓒ Ⓓ Ⓔ	57. Ⓐ Ⓑ Ⓒ Ⓓ Ⓔ	
13. Ⓐ Ⓑ Ⓒ Ⓓ Ⓔ	28. Ⓐ Ⓑ Ⓒ Ⓓ Ⓔ	43. Ⓐ Ⓑ Ⓒ Ⓓ Ⓔ	58. Ⓐ Ⓑ Ⓒ Ⓓ Ⓔ	
14. Ⓐ Ⓑ Ⓒ Ⓓ Ⓔ	29. Ⓐ Ⓑ Ⓒ Ⓓ Ⓔ	44. Ⓐ Ⓑ Ⓒ Ⓓ Ⓔ	59. Ⓐ Ⓑ Ⓒ Ⓓ Ⓔ	
15. Ⓐ Ⓑ Ⓒ Ⓓ Ⓔ	30. Ⓐ Ⓑ Ⓒ Ⓓ Ⓔ	45. Ⓐ Ⓑ Ⓒ Ⓓ Ⓔ	60. Ⓐ Ⓑ Ⓒ Ⓓ Ⓔ	

Answer Sheet

Short Answer/Essay

_____

_____

_____

_____

_____

_____

_____

_____

_____

_____

_____

_____

_____

_____

_____

_____

_____

_____

_____

_____

_____

_____

_____

_____

_____